Betty Garrett
and Other Songs

Betty Garrett and Other Songs

A Life on Stage and Screen

BETTY GARRETT
WITH RON RAPOPORT

MADISON BOOKS
Lanham • New York • Oxford

Published by Madison Books
4720 Boston Way
Lanham, Maryland 20706

12 Hid's Copse Road
Cumnor Hill, Oxford OX2 9JJ, England

Distributed by National Book Network

The hardback edition of this book was previously catalogued
by the Library of Congress as follows:

Garrett, Betty.
  Betty Garrett and other songs: a life on stage and screen /
Betty Garrett with Ron Rapoport.
    p.   cm.
  Includes bibliographical references and index.
    1. Garrett, Betty.   2. Actors—United States—Bibliography.
I. Title.
PN2287.G388A3   1997
792'.028'092—dc21   *97-24714*
                                              CIP

ISBN I-56833-098-7 (cloth : alk. paper)
ISBN I-56833-133-9 (pbk.: alk. paper)

∞ ™ *The paper used in this publication meets the minimum requirements of*
American National Standard for Information Sciences—Permanence of
Paper for Printed Library Materials. ANSI/NISO Z39.48–1992.
Manufactured in the United States of America.

For my mother, Octavia

My husband, Larry

My kids, Andrew, Garrett, and Karen

and Madison Claire

———————————

"If they run you out of town, be sure you're just ahead of them so it looks like a parade."

—Sally Stanford, famous San Francisco
madam and later mayor of Sausalito

"It ain't what happens to you, it's how you handle it."

—Anonymous

Contents

Contents

Coda

Acknowledgments

I would like to express my gratitude to a number of people who have been helpful in writing this book.

Robert E. Kimball, the eminent musical comedy historian, provided invaluable help with the musical references as did Edgar Bullington of the International Al Jolson Society, Jo Sullivan Loesser, Eric Blau, and Hilary Masters.

For their enthusiasm, encouragement, and help, thank you to Robin Adler, Deirdre Mullervy, Jon Sisk, and Glenn Popson at Madison Books. They made me feel as if I were actually doing something worthwhile. Thanks, too, to agents Mark Levin and Mike Hamilburg, who were instrumental in getting the book started and drawing up the contracts.

I am also grateful to Milo Mandel, my manager, and his wife, Isabel, for taking the time to plow through the manuscript and for offering their gentle suggestions and pats on the back.

Robert Culliver, my daughter-in-law's father, was the first to read the manuscript and made many good "non-show-biz" comments and suggestions.

To my son, Garrett Parks, I owe eternal thanks for his remarkable perception about the things that are important in this book and for his valuable suggestions. And to my younger son, Andrew Parks, Garrett's wife, Karen Culliver, and my granddaughter, Maddy Claire—thank you for bringing such joy into my life that it made me want to write this book.

Last but not least, monumental thanks to Ron Rapoport, my collaborator, who sat morning after morning and listened to my ramblings, then went home and tried to make sense of them. (And thanks to his wife, Joan, who had the tedious job of transcribing the tapes. I suggested hiring a secretary, but she would have none of it. She said she was having too much fun listening to me talk. Bless her!)

I am most grateful to Ron for how he kept my "voice," my way of expression, even when it was not so hot. He prodded me, kept me remembering and talking, then checked the dates and details. My memory, even of events from many years ago, turned out to be quite good, he tells me. What is nice is that we not only came up with a book but also with a warm, wonderful friendship I'm sure will last for the rest of our lives.

Betty Garrett
Studio City, California
August 1997

Grateful acknowledgment is made to the following for permission to reprint previously published material:

Allan Roberts Music Co.: "Humphrey Bogart Rhumba," by Allan Roberts and Lester Lee. Copyright © 1949 (Renewed) by Allan Roberts Music Co., administered by Music Sales Corporation and George Simon Music Co., administered by Len Freedman Music. International Copyright Secured. All Rights Reserved. Reprinted by Permission.

Beachaven Music Corp.: "Ok'l Baby Dok'l," by Sidney Miller and Inez James. Copyright © 1946 by Beachaven Music Corp. Reprinted by permission.

Blitzstein Music Co.: "Come Dance The Carmagnole," by Marc Blitzstein. Copyright © Blitzstein Music Co. Reprinted by permission.

Donaldson Publishing Co.: "It Made You Happy When You Made Me Cry," song by Walter Donaldson. © 1926; Copyright Renewal 1954 Donaldson Publishing Company. International Copyright Secured. All Rights Reserved. Used by permission.

Ellen C. Masters: Lines from "Hannah Armstrong" and "Lucinda Matlock" from *Spoon River Anthology* by Edgar Lee Masters. Originally published by the Macmillan Company. Permission by Ellen C. Masters.

Eric Blau: "You're Not Alone." An adaptation of Jacques Brel's "Jef" by Eric Blau from the musical "Jacques Brel Is Alive And Well And Living In Paris." Permission by Eric Blau.

Frank Music Corp.: "Baby, It's Cold Outside," by Frank Loesser. Copyright © 1948 by Frank Music Corp. Copyright © renewed 1976 by Frank Music Corp. Used by permission.

Herald Square Music, Inc.: "I'm Still Here," by Stephen Sondheim. Copyright © 1971 by Range Road Music Inc., Quartet Music Inc., Rilting Music, Inc. and Burthen Music Co., Inc. All rights administered by Herald Square Music, Inc. Used by permission. All Rights Reserved.

Irving Berlin Music Co.: Lyric excerpts of "What'll I Do?" by Irving Berlin. Copyright © 1924 by Irving Berlin. Copyright Renewed. International Copyright Secured. Used by permission. All Rights Reserved.

MCA Music Publishing: "Mary C. Brown And The Hollywood

Verse: You're Not Alone

> *I've been so many places in my life and time*
> *I've sung a lot of songs, I've made some bad rhyme*
> *I've acted out my life on stages*
> *With ten thousand people watching*
> *But we're alone now, and I'm singing my song to you.*

I didn't get that far. I didn't even get past the first line. It was a run-through of *Betty Garrett and Other Songs*, my one-person show that I had developed and performed at Theatre West, a theater group I had helped found in Los Angeles more than thirty-five years ago. My husband, Larry, had been there at every performance, standing at the back of the theater, glowing with pride, and I could always feel his presence.

Now I was scheduled to do my show at the Westwood Playhouse in a couple of weeks and Larry was gone. He had died the year before, on April 13, 1975, and I was trying to get through it at the theater, with my fellow actor-members sitting out front to give me support.

I sang the first line and it was as if someone grabbed me by the throat. I couldn't go on. My director, John Carter, jumped up on the stage, put his arms around me and said, "It's OK . . . take a minute and start again."

I did and got two lines out, but the tears came and I couldn't go on. I tried again . . . and again . . . and again, and finally I turned to my audience and said, "This is awful for you to sit through. . . . Please forgive me, but you might as well go home."

But they would have none of that. They shouted up to me, "No, no, keep going . . . we're with you . . . you can do it." I will be forever grateful to them for that loving support.

I started again and got through the first song and into the part about growing up in a music store where my mother played piano, and how my father taught me how to dance to "Ballin' the Jack"—joyous memories. I told a funny story about one of my first ventures in show business, when Cole Porter wrote me a song, and everyone laughed.

Then I went on to tell about making records with Jimmy Durante and Humphrey Bogart, and I clowned around with my beloved friend and accompanist Gerry Dolin to "Baby, It's Cold Outside," which won the Oscar for best song in 1949 when Red Skelton, Esther Williams, Ricardo Montalban, and I sang it in the movie *Neptune's Daughter*. I sang "South America, Take It Away," from *Call Me Mister*, the biggest Broadway hit I was ever in and told the story about Louis B. Mayer stamping on my toes and warning me not to get pregnant. I told about making movies with Frank Sinatra and Gene Kelly and Mickey Rooney at MGM. By then, *I* was laughing, too, and it was a blessed relief.

The hardest song to get through was Jacques Brel's "You're Not Alone." I remembered Larry watching me rehearse it one day in our living room. He sat there on the couch and tears filled his eyes.

No, Love, you're not alone
No matter how you feel
When shadows cut like knives
And none of this seems real
We wish away our lives
But somehow we survive . . .

But it was all right to cry with that song. Everyone seemed to know it was sung to Larry, for all the bad times he had with the blacklist, which had ended his career as a movie star in a single day. I got through that song and my fellow Theatre West members cried with me.

Then I went on to stories of playing at the Palladium in London and touring the provinces, all over England and Scotland, with wonderful British variety performers like Stan and Ann White, and "Vogelbein's Bears"—hilarious times.

Then the final song:

There isn't much that I have learned
In all my foolish years
Except that life keeps running in cycles
First there's laughter then there's tears.

And so there it was . . . my whole life in stories and song. But there is so much more!

First Chorus

The Music Store

My childhood was filled with music
For I was raised in a music store.
Where Momma played the piano
While I turned the pages of the score.

It's true about my growing up in a music store. My mother was manager of the sheet music department at Sherman Clay in Seattle. It was like a playground for a little girl and I would hang around every day after school and all day on Saturday waiting for her to get through work.

I would go up to the third floor and plink plink around on all the gorgeous grand pianos—Steinways and Becksteins and Mason-Hamlins and Baldwins—and then I would go down to the second floor where they kept the other musical instruments. I learned to play the ukelele there—it's still the only instrument I play in public.

Downstairs, Sherman Clay had all the latest phonograph records. I would take a whole stack of records and go into one of those little sound booths and listen to them all day. Then there was the sheet music, long racks of colorful sheets to songs like "Yes, We Have No Bananas," "Ain't She Sweet," "Willow, Weep for Me," and "Lullaby of the Leaves."

Some of the songs I loved best were strange ones for a little girl. They were sad songs and to this day I can't say what there was about them that appealed to me. I was not an unhappy child, but you would never have known it if you had heard me sing "Nobody Knows the Trouble I've Seen" or "The St. James Infirmary Blues" or a song that went

It made you happy when you made me cry.
It made you happy when we said good-bye.

3

By all the stars above you.
O gee, I'd hate to hate you like I love you.

And then there was the first popular song I ever learned to sing from beginning to end—Irving Berlin's "What'll I Do?" My mother and I were living in a boarding house run by two wonderful sisters, Mary and Midah Waller. Midah was a big bony woman who scrubbed the floors and did all the work while Mary sat and read her prayer book all day.

I remember once when I was only four or five years old, and all the other kids in the neighborhood were in school, sitting on the backyard swing just swinging and singing . . .

> *When I'm alone (swing forward)*
> *With on— (swing back)*
> *—ly dreams (forward)*
> *of you (back)*
> *That won't (forward)*
> *Come true (back)*
> *What'll I do? (jump out of the swing!)*

I don't remember feeling lonely. To me, it was just such a good song to sit and swing to. Many years later, when my sons were little, they had what was called a rider. It was like a teeter-totter but it went back and forth instead of up and down. I would put them on the rider and sing the same song to them, particularly when Larry and I were about to set out on the road with a show. I remember pushing those two little boys, back and forth, with their shining faces looking up at me, and singing . . .

> *What'll I do . . .*
> *When you . . .*
> *Are far . . .*
> *away . . .*
> *And I . . .*
> *am blue . . .*
> *What'll I do?*

After my parents were divorced, Mother and I often lived in what were called residential hotels. There was only one room, with the bathroom down the hall, but it was the cheapest way to live because we got two meals a day. Mother liked living in apartments better because there was more room and she could cook dinner, but after a while it would get too expensive and we would move back to a hotel. We seemed to do this about every six months.

Often, we would move back to the same hotel we had lived in before. The Clark Hotel and the Piedmont were my favorites for some reason and I remember coming back from my bath one night, crying and saying goodbye to each of the patterns in the rug because we were going to be moving the next day.

When my mother entertained in those days, I was put to bed on a cot in a little room that was kind of a dressing-room closet. Or, if we were in an apartment, I was in the "in-a-door" Murphy bed in the living room while the party went on in the kitchen. I used to love that.

I would lie in bed listening to the people laugh and talk and sometimes sing. My mother had a low melodious voice and she played the ukelele. When my mother demonstrated songs for customers at Sherman Clay, I loved to stand in the corner and listen. Of course, my mother wanted me to learn to play the piano but she made the mistake of asking a concert pianist she knew to teach me. He was a fine musician, but he was not a teacher at all. He was a very impatient man—the kind who would smack your hands if you made a mistake—and he terrified me.

In my one and only recital, I played "Für Elise," the Beethoven chestnut every beginning piano player learns, and when I got to the end of the first page I panicked so I plunked out a few closing notes, stood up, and took a bow. Then somebody in the audience blurted out loudly, "That's the shortest recital piece I ever heard."

That taught me a great lesson I have applied to acting: You must not panic! So even though a day or two after an opening night I usually break out in cold sores—which means my nerves are building up somewhere—I never get stage fright. Except when I have to play the piano.

But the piano was everything to my mother and one of the saddest things that happened later in her life was that she would not touch it any more.

5

"Mom, play something for me," I would say and I would name one of the songs she used to play at Sherman Clay.

"Oh . . . I can't play any more," she would say, sounding so depressed. "I just . . . you know . . ." and her voice would trail off.

One problem was she wore bifocals, but when you play the piano the lenses need to be reversed. You should be able to read the music through the reading part and look down at your hands through the distance part. I offered to get glasses that would do this for her but she said, "Oh . . . no . . . it wouldn't be any use. . . ."

What I should have done, of course, was just *get* them for her. Sometimes I think that is the story of my life. There are so many things I should have just *done*.

> *Now, daddy, how he loved dancin'*
> *And he'd come dancin' through the door.*
> *But daddy was a travelin' salesman*
> *One day we didn't see him anymore.*

My mother was engaged to another man when she met my father. She started working in the shoe store his father owned in St. Joseph, Missouri, and by the time Sam, the man she was engaged to, pressed her to set a date, she was so in love with my father that she called off the engagement. "Sam went out the back door," she used to tell me, "and your father came in the front door and proposed to me."

Daddy was a charming man, handsome with a bawdy sense of humor, which I am sure is where my scatological sense of humor comes from. I remember driving with him once and seeing a sign on a bus that said PUC, for Public Utilities Commission.

"Daddy, what does PUC mean?"

And without skipping a beat, he said, "Pee under the covers."

Daddy's name was Curtis, but his business associates called him "Pick" and when I asked my mother why, she said it was short for "Picklehead." He had a long, narrow face so "Picklehead" stuck, and then "Pick." But my father didn't mind. He was always laughing and teasing people, seeing what he could get away with. And because he was so good-natured and full of fun, he got away with plenty.

In those days, when a woman came in the store to buy shoes, the salesman would turn his head while she lifted her skirt slightly and unlaced her high-topped shoes. Then he would take them off and help her on with the new shoes, turning his head again while she laced them up. One day, my grandfather caught my father, who was then in his twenties, lacing a woman's boots right up to the top. My grandfather immediately took him out back of the store and gave him a good "whuppin'."

My mother's family were very strict Baptists and dancing was not allowed. But Daddy was a very good dancer so they would sneak out when her mother and father were asleep. "I think that's why I was so happy when *you* wanted to be a dancer," my mother once told me.

But my father was a trial to my mother from the very beginning. He became a traveling salesman after they were married, and he also became an alcoholic, which seems to be an occupational disease. An important part of the job was drinking with customers in some strange town and then going back to a hotel room that is filled with sample tables covered with shoes.

I never saw my father with a hair out of place or without a clean white shirt, a handkerchief in his pocket, and his suit pressed. He always looked so much like a dandy that only my mother and I could tell when he was drunk. Sometimes, he would just begin to cry. Big crocodile tears would roll down his face, his voice would get slurry, and he would look at me and say, "Tavie (short for Octavia), she's got my nose!" He was so worried that I was going to have a big nose.

During his binges, he would go three or four weeks without eating until he landed in the hospital. We would visit him there and we knew he was getting better when he began patting every woman he saw on the behind. He always got away with it because he was funny and boyish and people liked him so much. He would pat waitresses, me, his mother, any woman around. He once asked a nun in the hospital, "Are you happy in your work?" and he patted *her* on the behind. She just giggled.

When he came through Seattle on one of his trips, it was like a holiday. I loved having him around and I know my mother enjoyed it too. Up to a point.

Once she asked him for money to buy me an overcoat and he said, "Tavie, I'm dead broke. I can't. I'm sorry." The next day, he walked into Sherman Clay and said, "Tavie, come on outside. I've got something to show you." He had bought a brand new car. My mother stood on the curb and shouted, "Well, I hope you're satisfied, Mr. Rich Bitch!" and stomped back in the store.

Often, my father would call me and say, "Your mother's mad at me. Let's take her to dinner." But Mother could not stay mad at him long and she loved to tease him. For instance, my father could not carry a tune. I believe that anybody can be taught to sing and that people who think they can't are usually just scared. But my father really could not sing.

My mother and I used to make terrible fun of him when he would say, very seriously, "Listen, *listen* to me" and then try to sing his favorite song, "Cocktails for Two." He would sing "In some secluded rendezvous" and point his fingers up with the high notes and down with the low notes. But he did not hit the *right* notes and my mother and I would get hysterical while he got madder and madder.

Both my mother and father took me to the movies often and I particularly remember that my father was taken with a child star named Mitzi Green. She was only nine or ten, but she was very talented and did wonderful imitations of celebrities. My father was always saying to me, "Why can't *you* do that?" How excited and proud he would have been if he had lived to see me become a movie star— and to see me co-star in a Broadway show with Mitzi Green.

EVERY SUMMER when I was little, my father would pick me up in Seattle and take me on the train to the farm near St. Joseph, Missouri, where I was born on May 23, 1919. I would spend the summer there with my grandmother and his three cousins, Katherine, Hereford, and Vinton, and then he would bring me back.

I loved riding on the train and my mother would do a wonderful thing when I went on these trips. She would make a bunch of little packages and mark a time on them. "This you open after breakfast" and there would be a coloring book and crayons inside. "This you open after lunch" and there would be candy. "This you open before dinner" and there would be a book. Whenever I traveled, I had all these things to look forward to and keep myself busy.

At the end of one summer, my father did not come back to Seattle with me. Either he had to go out on the road selling or something else came up so he took me down to the railroad station and put me on the train for the three-day trip home. Then he called my mother and told her when I would be arriving. Well, of course, she wanted to kill him. "You put a four-year-old girl on the train *alone!*" she shouted.

But to my father, it was no big thing. He knew all the porters and waiters on the train and before we left he went around and greased the palms of every one of them. "My daughter is going to be traveling with you," he said. "Take care of her." They made up my berth and before we pulled out, my father tucked me in and introduced me to a friendly porter. Then he got off the train and stood outside the window and waved as we pulled out.

For the entire trip, the train was my playground. I wandered up and down the aisles, talking to everybody I saw and being treated like a queen. There was one woman who looked a little like Edna May Oliver—she had one of those big long horse faces—and when she said, "Hello, little girl," I turned to her and said, "You're ugly." I can't believe I was such a nasty little kid!

But instead of being offended, she said, "Come here." She took my hand, sat me down, and gave me some Jordan almonds, the kind with candy on the outside. I had never seen them before and they fascinated me. Then the woman told me very gently that you can't judge whether someone is beautiful by the way they look. When you are beautiful inside, she said, it begins to come out. I loved that lady and she made a lifelong impression on me.

When we finally arrived in Seattle, my mother was on the platform frantic with worry. But when I got off the train, one of the passengers, a handsome six-foot man, was holding me by the hand. He turned me over to my mother and said, "You don't have to worry about her, lady." It was one of the best trips I ever took.

HELLO DADDY

My father always brushed his tongue
When he brushed his teeth.
"There are as many germs on your tongue
As there are on your teeth," he would say.
"Oh, Daddy, don't be silly," I would say.
And my Mother would say,
"Curtis, you're drunk!"

He would blow into town
After a year or so on the road
And Mother would take me down
To see his sample rooms at his hotel,
And I would crawl down the long tunnels
Under the sample tables covered with white sheets
And thousands of shoes—all for the left foot.

And Daddy would dance around the room and laugh,
"How about Rippe's for dinner
And a movie at the Pantages after?"
"That's much too expensive, Curtis,"
Mother would say,
"You'd do better to buy your daughter
A pair of shoes—
She's practically walking on the pavement now!"

And Daddy would laugh and say,
"Weeny Betonka, what'll it be—
A new pair of shoes or the picture-show?"
And I would yell, "Oh, Daddy, the picture-show!"
And Mother would say, "Curtis, you're drunk!"

He never did buy me the shoes
And he wouldn't pay my tuition
For boarding school—
He said boarding schools made girls into snobs.
But he did buy me my first long formal
To wear to the Junior Prom.
One day, with a huge box in his arms,
He came into the store
Where I was waiting for my mother to finish work,
And he yelled from the doorway,
"Hey, Weeny Betonka, here's your goddam dress!"
And he threw the box across the store,
Over the heads of startled customers
And nearly knocked me down.

A couple of months after the Junior Prom,
In Missoula, Montana
He walked into a hospital—
Three weeks drunk, but not a sign of it—
Clean-shaven, suit pressed,
White handkerchief in his breast pocket—
He walked to the desk and said,
"If I die, please notify my daughter
At the Annie Wright Seminary
In Tacoma, Washington—
The finest girls school in the West!"
Then he walked into the hospital room,
Lay down on the bed
With all his clothes on
And died.

My mother went to bring his body back,
And she talked with the buyers
That he'd been drinking with the night before,
They spoke about how he had bragged about his wife
And daughter.
They had no idea that he and my mother
Had been divorced since I was two years old.
My mother didn't tell them.

I always brush my tongue
When I brush my teeth,
There are as many germs on your tongue, you know,
As there are on your teeth.

Hello Daddy,
I love you.

MY GRANDMOTHER'S FARM was on Route 1, just outside St. Joseph, and when I was very young it was my summer playground. There was always a new batch of kittens in the hayloft and I would lie there and watch them day after day until finally their eyes opened up.

There were two Airedales, Jerry and Dixie, that I adored. They were bigger than I was and I played with them in the tall grass of the orchard. My father's cousin Kattie said she could always tell where I was because she could see the tails of the dogs above the grass and she knew I was down there somewhere.

The farm was on thirty-two acres and two of my father's cousins took care of it. There was Heppie (short for Hereford), who was deaf but was a fine artist and worked as an engraver in downtown St. Joseph. There was Vinton, a manic depressive who acted very strangely but who did most of the real work on the farm. And there was Kattie, who ran the house and took care of my grandmother.

Vinton considered me a pest and would tell Kattie "Keep that kid quiet!" when I was sitting in a corner chattering away. But that didn't bother me and I kept following him around, especially when he milked the cows. He would give three squirts for the pail and one for the cat, which would make cat stand up on her hind legs and catch the milk in her mouth.

That was the most fascinating thing I ever saw and soon I was dying to milk the cow. I would get up close to watch and Vinton would say "Stay away from the cows! Get away!" and I would jump back. But I kept watching him and waiting for my chance.

One day when Vinton had driven into town, I went into the barn and found one of the smallest cows still in her stall instead of out in the pasture. I got a stool and a pail, went into the stall, sat down under the cow and got ready to milk her. Suddenly she moved over right on top of me. I was scared to death as her big pink bag of milk sat on my head with the teats sticking out in every direction like a wild pink hat.

I can't remember how long I sat there—it seemed like hours—until the cow decided to move again and I could run back to the house. My head was wet from sweat where the udder had been sitting on it and Kattie said, "My stars, child, you're perspiring. You must have a fever. You'd better get to bed." I never told her what had happened.

Kattie was in her twenties then, but there never seemed to be any question of her marrying. She was a tiny woman, barely five feet tall, and she did the canning and the cooking and all the housework. Looking back, I think her brothers were afraid of losing her. My mother always said she should have had her own family, but Heppie and Vinton made terrible fun of every beau she brought home so they never came back. One of the things I loved about her was that she could make bubbles on her tongue, blow them off, and watch them float to the ground. I've tried all my life to do that, but I never could.

With my grandmother, I am afraid, things were different. She was a mean, frustrated woman and the first person I ever hated. Part of this, I am sure, came from the fact that my mother said she was in many ways responsible for her problems with my father.

My grandmother had a number of children who had died and she had miscarried several times too. Maybe that accounted for her meanness. My father was her only child who had lived and she spoiled him terribly and threatened that if he ever moved away she would have a heart attack. When he and my mother were married, she said if they lived anywhere but in her house she would have a heart attack.

So my mother was stuck living with her mother-in-law. In the early days of their marriage, when my father was away a lot, my grandmother would run to the mailbox and if a letter was for my mother she would open it and read it. "That's from my husband," my mother would say. "Well, it's from *my* son," my grandmother would answer.

My battles with my grandmother were usually over nothing. Once, we fought like kindergarteners over a pencil and Kattie put us in different rooms. "Aunt Kate, I don't know which one of you is four years old!" she told her. Another time, my grandmother was lying on a couch and I took a running jump and landed on top of her. I think I wanted to kill her, just pound her to death. I'm sure I was just as much a trial to her as she was to me.

We were walking together in downtown St. Joseph one day when we passed one of those displays of false teeth that used to hang outside dentists' offices. I marched right up and said in a very loud voice, "Oh, Grandma, those are just like yours!" On another occasion, she took me to the home of a friend who had given me a piece of candy when we had visited once before. This time, I could not contain myself and said, "Where's my candy?" The woman gave me one, of course, but my grandmother was so mortified she took me home and locked me in a dark closet for an hour. But I got even with her. I spit on all her clothes.

The way she saved her hair in a big box in a closet also seemed disgusting to me. After brushing their long hair, the women of that era would comb the hair out of the brush and stuff it in a little decorated box with a hole in the top. It was just a way to dispose of it and ultimately throw it away.

Oh, perhaps they would sometimes save a lock as a memento—tie a ribbon around it to give to an admirer—but my grandmother saved it all. She said she was going to use it to stuff a nice big pillow and leave it to the family as an heirloom. She was sure we would want her old dirty hair.

The only time I can remember loving my grandmother was the night somebody drove by the farm and shot and killed Jerry, one of the Airedales I played with in the orchard. The other dog, Dixie, chased the car for miles and then came dragging back to the farm, defeated. I had never heard a gunshot before and I woke up and found my grandmother on the stairs.

"What was that?" I said. "It sounded like shingles fell off the roof." And she sat on the stairs with her arm around me and said, "No, someone hurt Jerry." Later, she told me Jerry died and that was just heartbreaking to me. It is the only tender moment I can remember ever having with my grandmother.

GRANDMOTHER'S CHAMBER POT

My grandmother used a chamber pot
Until the day she died.
Even after they built
A beautiful new bathroom on the second floor
Next to her room.
Her niece, who took care of her, said,
"Aunt Kate, if you're too lazy
To walk two steps down the hall,
You can just empty your own pot!"
And she did, until the day she died.

One morning when she was almost seventy
As she was walking down the hall
To empty her chamber pot,
The famous heart attack finally came.
And she died with the pot
And its contents
In her arms.

14

I bought a big white chamber pot
At an antique store the other day,
And I filled it full of Shasta Daisies
And set it in the middle of the dining-room table,
And I said softly,
"Hello, Grandmother—you old bat!"

WHEN I WAS eight years old, I suddenly acquired a stepfather. It was Sam, the man my mother had rejected in St. Joseph when she decided to marry my father instead. When she and Sam were engaged back then, they had talked about honeymooning at Lake Louise and Banff, which they both agreed seemed to be the most beautiful place in the world. And then, all this time later, she and I went to the movies and saw a newsreel feature about Lake Louise and Banff that made her think about Sam all over again.

He was in the meat-packing business in Canada by then and he must have stayed in touch because she wrote him a note about the newsreel. Though they had not seen each other in ten years, he wrote back immediately and asked her to marry him.

The next thing I knew we were on the train to Regina, Saskatchewan, by way of a town called Moose Jaw. Sam met us there and that is where he and my mother got married. After all the talk of Lake Louise and Banff, they were married in Moose Jaw, Saskatchewan. We should have realized it was an omen.

Sam lived in Regina and the first thing they did was put me in a Catholic school for a month while they went on their honeymoon. I was not Catholic and I was not Canadian and I didn't know any of the other girls so I felt very much the outsider. But I just loved the Catholic ceremony, the ritual and the drama.

My favorite time of the day was evening chapel. Three or four girls at a time would file into the chapel, dip their fingers in holy water, cross themselves, walk slowly to the altar, do a deep genuflection, and go to their seats. If you were late to chapel, you did this all by yourself and that was my great ambition—to get there late so I could solo.

And sure enough, one night my mother called long distance, which made me late to chapel and I got to do the whole thing by myself. I walked in. I dipped my fingers in the holy water. I crossed myself. I walked slowly to the altar and I did a deep, deep bow. When I came

15

up, I realized I had bowed with my back to the altar and my face to the congregation! I've always said that moment proved I was born to be on a stage.

At first, everything was fine. We lived in a very nice apartment, I was happy in school, and we certainly had a better life than we did in Seattle. But I soon discovered Regina is probably the coldest place in the world that has people living in it. The snow that was on the ground in November was still there in May with more snow on top of it. I developed terrible ear infections and fevers and was sick and miserable most of the time. And Sam turned out to be a very strange man.

He was big and rather handsome, a barrel-chested man who wasn't fat exactly but heavy. And he was very, very aloof. One day, my mother told me it was his birthday so I put together a package of the free samples kids used to send away for: shaving cream, after-shave lotion, little things like that. I wrapped them up and made a little card and put the package by his place at the table at lunchtime.

"What's this?" he said, and I said, "Open it, Daddy." (I had decided to call him Daddy.) He looked at the birthday card and all he said was, "My birthday was yesterday." Another time, he took me down to the slaughterhouse to watch the animals being killed, thinking a nine-year-old girl would enjoy such a thing. I found it sickening, of course.

The only moment of tenderness I can remember from him—and I remember it very vividly—was one night when I had a 104-degree temperature and one of my awful earaches and he carried me in his arms and walked the floor with me for hours.

After about a year in Regina, my mother came into my room in the middle of the night, dressed me, packed a suitcase, and hurriedly got us on a train to Seattle. She would not answer any of my questions about what had happened and it was several years before I overheard her talking to a friend. Her husband had been having an affair with his young male secretary.

My mother had suspected it after seeing them together and finally she made the secretary confess. The terrible part about it was the young man was not a willing partner at all, but was just afraid of losing his job.

Some time later—a little less than a year, I would say—I woke up one morning in Seattle and the room was full of presents. Sam had come through town on his way back from Paris and I guess he and my mother had sat and really talked for the first time. The scandal of his relationship with his secretary had been growing among his friends and business associates for some time so when he got the letter from my mother he thought she might set him on the right track, so to speak. He told her he was sorry.

"You're the only woman I have ever loved," he said. "I thought it would work out." That was the last we ever saw of him.

FADE OUT, FADE IN. Many years later, Larry and I were playing in summer stock in the Midwest and a couple came backstage and said, "We want to meet you because we know your father."

"My father? My father has been dead for years."

"No, no," the woman said, "we're neighbors of his down in Tennessee." And she pulled out a snapshot of a portly man standing next to a sweet, saintly looking little woman.

"He's married again, but he's so proud of you," the woman said. "He talks about you all the time, how your career is going, and so on."

I was stunned, of course, but one look at the picture and I could see it was Sam all right. He was wearing a hair net.

The more Larry listened to this, the angrier he became. As soon as we got back to the hotel, he called my mother and said, "Octavia, did you ever divorce your second husband?"

"No," she said.

"So he's a bigamist," he said. "You've got to sue him."

But all my mother said was "Oh, don't bother. He has had enough troubles." As far as she was concerned, it had all been so long ago and did not matter anymore.

WHEN WE RETURNED to Seattle from Canada, my mother went back to work at Sherman Clay and enrolled me in public school. Every day when I got back to the hotel, I called her at the store and said, "Mother-dear, I'm home." (Yes, I really did call her "Mother-dear.") The end of this arrangement came when I was hit by a car on my way home from school one day and did not call right away.

I was knocked out and the man who hit me took me to the hospital. I guess I started calling for my mother because when she got there, the doctor said, "Well, thank God, Mother-dear is here!"

I had also been having terrible stomach pains around that time. I would be hungry, start to eat dinner, have two bites, and then double over. My mother took me to a doctor, who seriously considered operating on me. In those days, children with chronic stomach aches were often diagnosed as having "enlarged colons" and it was almost a fad to have them undergo surgery.

My mother said there would be no operation, but she knew something was wrong and instinctively she realized it had to do with the way we were living. It just was not right for a nine-year-old girl to live in a hotel, keep irregular hours, and be alone so much of the time. So she asked around and discovered a boarding house for little girls across town. I would still go to public school, but during the week I would live in the house where there were other girls for me to play with and my mother would know I was well taken care of.

The boarding house was run by Deaconess Nosler of the Episcopal church, and Margaret Bateman, a nurse. Deaconess was a short bustling woman and Margaret was tall with a bony, beautiful Katharine Hepburn kind of face. For me, they were a throwback to Mary and Midah Waller, who ran the boarding house where Mother and I had lived years earlier. Deaconess did the housework while Margaret was the spiritual one. They called it the Mary and Martha Cottage, after Mary and Martha in the Bible.

Almost immediately after I moved into the boarding house, my stomach pains went away. If I did have an enlarged colon, and I seriously doubt it, the cure was nothing more complicated than regular hours and wholesome food. Within a year, we went back to the doctor who had wanted to operate and all he could say was, "Well, young lady, you've cured yourself." My stomach was fine and it never bothered me again.

The second benefit of living in the boarding house was discovering the joy of having an audience. I was the oldest of the thirteen girls living there so they became my captive audience.

I have no idea where some of my routines came from. I would improvise these long monologues—a Swedish woman on a bus, for instance: "Vat du yu mean, yu von't let me take my little doggie on de bus? I vill hit yu vid my umbrella!"

I had never seen a Swedish person in my life, on a bus or off. I must have heard someone with a Swedish accent someplace and the sounds must have amused me.

I also played my first role on a real stage at the Mary and Martha Cottage. I was Mary in the nativity scene during a Christmas pageant and the joke I have told ever since is that I played the Virgin Mary when I was nine years old and never got over it.

I still have pictures of ten or twelve of us dressed up as little angels singing carols and every time I see them they remind me of the program where the entire audience of parents and teachers was laughing and giggling as we sang. We were barefoot angels and I was told later that I was beating time to "Hark, the Herald Angels Sing" with my big toe.

For another program, I was given a poem to recite—"The Little Gray Lamb"—about a lamb that strays from the field and is brought back by the shepherd. As I began to recite I looked down at the front row and saw tears streaming down my mother's face.

I quit right in the middle of the poem and ran offstage, saying, "My mother's crying. Why is my mother crying?" They had to bring her backstage to tell me she was crying because she was so happy before I would go back and do the whole poem over again.

The delight I felt about performing even back then was an instinctive thing I never bothered to analyze. Years later, a songwriter named Bud Freeman put it into words when he told me he thought every child should take dramatic lessons the way they study the piano or the violin or dancing.

Self-expression, Bud said, is the most powerful instinct human beings have. It is above self-preservation because people have died in order to express themselves. It is above sex because people have become celibate in order to express their religious feelings. When you discover the way you can best express yourself, whether it is in music, art, performing, or domesticity, you are very lucky. People who cannot express themselves, Bud said, are the ones who become sick and neurotic.

I have always considered myself so fortunate that Margaret Bateman noticed the way I entertained the other little girls at Mary and Martha Cottage and mentioned it to my mother. "Has Betty ever seen Agna Enters or Ruth Draper?" she asked, referring to the popular dancer and mimologist of that era. "She should see them because of all these little plays and monologues and characters she is developing. It is something she would be interested in."

My mother had access to concert tickets through her job and at different times she took me to see Ruth Draper and Agna Enters. I think in the back of my mind I said to myself, "That's what I want to do some day."

E VERY SUMMER during this period, my mother would pack me off to visit her brother Norris Stone in Portland and I always looked forward to this.

Uncle Norris and Aunt Bess had six children. There was Elizabeth, the oldest; Norris Jr., whom we called Bo; Bob, on whom I had a big crush, and Billy. Looking back, I'm sure Billy had Tourette's syndrome, but all it meant then was that we made fun of him. There were also twin girls, Caroline and Helen, who were just a year younger than I was. I have pictures in which we look like triplets.

At the beginning of July, Uncle Norris would pile us all into his car and take us to a beach on the Oregon coast called Neskowin. There we would stay for the summer.

It was a completely unspoiled beach with big cabins and we took the same one every year. We ran around barefoot all day long, exploring the streams and tributaries that flowed down to the ocean. There was a big rock in the middle of the beach—it was called Proposal Rock—that sometimes was separated from the shore by the tide and sometimes you could walk over to. All in all, it was the most idyllic kind of life.

Uncle Norris, who was not rich by any means, used to order six quarts of milk every morning and there was always enough food to stock a grocery store. I was Cousin Betty from the outside and at the dinner table they would fight over who was going to sit next to me. And don't think I didn't love being this privileged person who was always the center of attention.

The only hitch was at night the twins wanted to share me and would push their beds together so I had to sleep on the crack. Being treated like this did one important thing for me as I grew up. It made me feel that, despite whatever upheavals there were in my life, I was someone special. I think everyone can use that feeling once in a while.

Aunt Bess died after the first summer and a year or so later Uncle

Norris met a wonderful woman who took over the family and spoiled them all rotten. Aunt Clara came from a family of nine kids so I guess she thought it was natural to make all the beds, do all the cooking, can peaches in the fall, and never ask for any help. She held that family together for years and she and I became so close that we stayed in touch and occasionally got together for the rest of her life.

Clara never lost her willingness to do just about anything for her family and she once told me how she and her four sisters took care of their mother—let's call her Ora; I never knew the name of Clara's mother or her sisters so I'll make up names—when she became infirm. Ora lived well into her nineties and instead of sending her to a nursing home the girls took turns keeping her for a month at a time.

Ora was staying at Clara's house when she discovered Liberace. She was practically bedridden by then, but she would get up every day, get fully dressed, put on her diamond earrings, and sit in front of the TV with a martini and watch Liberace. It was the highlight of her day.

As the month was coming to an end and it was time for Ora to move to her daughter Etta's house, Clara noticed she was getting very depressed. Clara quickly figured out that Ora was afraid she would not be able to watch Liberace. So she called Etta and said, "For God's sake, be sure to get Momma up every day at six o'clock and put her in front of the television set so she can watch Liberace."

The day came when Ora moved over to Etta's house and she was still very depressed. But that night at six o'clock Etta got her up, got her all dressed, put on her diamond earrings, sat her in front of the TV with her martini, and turned the set on.

"OK, Momma?" she said as Liberace came on.

"Oh . . . yes!" Ora said. "But how did he know where to *find* me?"

When I told that story to Liberace at a party once he laughed so hard I thought he was going to choke. Then he asked if he could use it in his act.

NORRIS JUNIOR, the one we called Bo, was as close to a brother as I have ever had and he grew to be quite alienated from his father. When he was in his thirties, he joined the merchant marine, went to sea, and started writing stories and sending them off to magazines. But he would give them Larry's and my address in Los Angeles because he did not want his father to know what he was up to.

The rejection slips and returned stories would pile up at our house until Bo came back from sea. Then one day, the *Saturday Evening Post* bought one of his Westerns. Bo had become a great authority on the lore of the Northwest and from then on he sold one marvelous story after another to the *Post, Colliers*, and other magazines.

Soon Bo was writing for the screen and he wrote one of the classic Westerns, *Ride the High Country*, starring Joel McCrea and Randolph Scott. That made Bo leave the merchant marine for good. He settled down to write movies and television shows for the rest of his life. We spent a lot of time together—he always came over to our house for the holidays—until he got cancer and went back to Neskowin. Bo played golf and stayed in a cabin on the beach where we had spent all those happy summers until he died.

WHEN IT CAME time for me to leave the Mary and Martha Cottage and go to high school, Deaconess Nosler did the most wonderful thing for me. I had written a little religious poem she had liked and she called the Episcopal bishop who ran the Annie Wright Seminary in Tacoma and recommended me for a scholarship.

The Annie Wright Seminary seemed like something out of a dream. It was a school where rich girls went—a beautiful place and far beyond our means without the scholarship. There were lovely buildings, spacious, rolling grounds, tennis courts, a swimming pool, and even a bowling alley.

We lived two to a room and wore uniforms so there was no difference between what the rich girls and the scholarship girls wore. And my biggest class might have had only thirteen students in it. I took four years of Latin and since there were only four girls in my class I *had* to learn Latin. And chemistry and French and English too.

Just before I went to the seminary, I had another one of my mysterious illnesses. I used to get swollen glands periodically and that summer I had been in the hospital for six weeks with a gland on the side of my neck the size of an ostrich egg. Right before school started, it just as mysteriously went away but the treatments weakened me to the point where I weighed about eighty-five pounds.

I also had dry, ugly-looking patches all over my face. Today, this is recognized as an allergy, but back then they thought it was some kind of fungus and prescribed ultraviolet treatments. They burned off a layer of skin once a week for six weeks thinking that would get down to the bottom of the fungus and kill it. It is a wonder I did not have skin cancer by the time I was fifteen and I think the spots that were left on my skin may have been due to those treatments.

On top of all this, my eyebrows grew together, I had absolutely straight hair, and there I was at this fancy school with all these rich girls with plucked eyebrows and permanents. They were all older than I was—exactly the opposite of the way things had been at the Mary and Martha Cottage—and I was viewed as this little runt. The other girls called me Bud, which stood for "Betty Under-Developed" because you could iron a shirt on my chest.

This sort of teasing went on all the time. Nobody was actually cruel to me, but I always seemed to be opening my mouth and putting my foot into it. I was used to just saying things, whatever came into my mind, instead of censoring myself the way a young lady is supposed to.

We rotated tables in the dining room every month and I remember sitting at the head table with the principal and saying, "I know why sailors have thirteen buttons on the flies of their pants." The reason was perfectly innocent—because of the thirteen original states—but it was treated as the most obscene thing anybody could have said at the dinner table.

I always seemed to be doing something like that so I became the class clown. And sometime during that school year, I got my first period and it was like telegraph wires were humming: "Betty's got the curse." What a year that was!

But despite all this, I don't remember being unhappy because I had a roommate who was worse off than I was. Tishelle—we called her Tish—was homesick and did nothing but cry all the time so she was considered the class pill instead of me. And after a while, I began to develop a few social graces. I learned table manners, how to get along with people, and how to give the façade of being a lady even when I did not feel like one.

I have come to believe boarding school, particularly for girls, is a wonderful thing at that age. We all said we would rather go to a school where there were boys, but I think there is a time in a girl's life when she needs to find out who she is without competing for boys and worrying about clothes.

In 1986, I went back to the seminary for our fiftieth anniversary and of the twenty-six girls in our class, eighteen showed up—all vibrant, interesting, active women. Much credit goes to the seminary for giving us a place where we could find our identity and our self-confidence and our vocations. Our motto was "On from strength to strength," which is a wonderful way of putting it.

> *Hail to thee our Alma Mater*
> *Seminary Fair*
> *May achievements crown thy labors*
> *Is our earnest prayer.*
> *Hearts turned toward our Alma Mater*
> *May our lives at length*
> *Prove thy daughters bear thy motto*
> *"On from strength to strength."*

Being at the seminary was surely one of the most important periods of my life. I went from being what we would call a street kid today to an educated and civilized adult. And my appearance underwent an amazing transformation too.

In my junior year, I was voted maid of honor in the May festival, which means the most popular girl in the class. I also became captain of the Gold Team (athletics at the school was divided into Blue and Gold teams) and graduated as salutatorian of the class. Tish, who had been such a pain when we were freshman, was the valedictorian, the brightest girl in the whole class and one of the most popular.

But I knew, and the people at the seminary knew, there was a part of me that would never become completely civilized. The principal once called me into her office and said, "You were seen shopping in Seattle without your hat." I said, "What?!" But it was true. I had spent the weekend at home and I had indeed gone shopping without wearing a hat. In those days a lady, especially an Annie Wright Seminary girl, simply did *not* go out without her hat *and* gloves!

There was no drama department at the seminary and that left things wide open for me. Whenever there was a special occasion or a celebration of any kind, I would put together a show where we would construct some scenery in the gym and stage little productions. I played the ukelele and got some of the other girls to sing songs and act in skits. Which always starred me, of course.

Near the end of our senior year, we did put on a real play, *Twelfth Night*, in which I played Maria. When it was over, the bishop, a very strait-laced, humorless man who was often at the school for special events, came up to my mother and said, "What are you going to do with your daughter?"

"What do you think I should do?" she asked.

"I think you had better put her on the stage," he said, in a tone that indicated otherwise I might become a gangster's moll. That was one of the recommendations that sent me off to my life's work. The other came from Martha Graham.

Martha was coming through town on a concert tour and my mother had a friend, Jean Baillargeon, who knew her and said she could arrange an introduction. I was supposed to actually dance for her, but there was no time so all we had was a short conversation.

I had taken classes during the summers at the University of Washington from Bonnie Bird and Gussie Kirschner, two women who had danced with Martha in New York, and they told her I was a hard worker who would probably develop into a good dancer.

I do not think Martha cared one way or the other, really. She just wanted to accommodate her friend. So on the basis of short conversations with three people she knew, and out of the kindness of her heart, she recommended me for a scholarship at the Neighborhood Playhouse in New York.

I had no idea then that this was a pattern that would repeat itself many times in the future. I had no idea how often I would be steered toward wonderful things by other people or simply fall into them by luck.

There was only one problem about leaving for New York, though. I was not sure I wanted to go. As exciting as the prospect was, and as ridiculous as it now seems, I would have stayed home if Bob Rodal had asked me to.

I met Bob, my first serious boyfriend, the summer I was sixteen. My mother and I and the Baillargeons rented a little cabin on Bainbridge Island in Puget Sound and the only way to get there was over the water to a ferry stop called Yeomalt. My mother would go back and forth to work every morning on a little ferry.

They held Saturday night dances on the island and when Bob asked me to dance it was the first time I had ever felt real physical vibrations. There were dances at the seminary, of course, but all you could do was meet a boy, dance with him—not cheek to cheek!—maybe write him a mushy letter and then only see him once or twice again. Dancing with Bob was quite a different thing.

Bob told me he was twenty-one but I found out years later he was really twenty-four and was afraid my mother would not let him go out with me if she knew the truth. I thought it was really something to be dating this older man and was sure that I was in love the way only a sixteen-year-old girl can be.

We dated all through the next year and wrote to each other, which is always a big deal when you are at school. To be able to show off letters from your boyfriend gave you real status. By the time Bob took me to the Senior Prom, I was absolutely certain I was in love and not at all sure I wanted to go to New York. All Bob had to say was "Don't go" and I wouldn't have. But he didn't say it and I didn't find out why for forty years.

In the 1970s, I took *Betty Garrett and Other Songs* to Seattle to do a benefit for the Annie Wright Seminary and I let Bob know I was coming. A friend who was there told me that during intermission Bob took out the dance program from the Senior Prom at the Annie Wright Seminary and showed it to the people at the table.

For some reason, Bob's wife, Marie, could not come to the show that night and Bob and I went back to the home of a friend where I was staying and sat in her kitchen until three in the morning. Finally, I just had to ask him.

"Why did you let me go to New York? Obviously we were both just crazy about each other and ready to get married."

"Because your mother scared the *shit* out of me."

"She *what?!*" I said, absolutely stunned.

"She sat me down and she said, 'Don't you ruin her chances to go to New York and use her talent as a dancer and actress. And don't you *dare* get her pregnant.' She really read me the riot act."

This was just astonishing to me because my mother was not like that at all. She was never a stage mother. But as Bob and I sat there talking, I said, "My God, was my mother wise. Can you imagine me marrying you and living on Bainbridge Island the rest of my life? I would have killed you or you would have killed me."

"You're so right," he said.

My mother had died without ever telling me any of this. I could only think what a smart lady she was to know what would have been the wrong thing for me to do and to figure out the right way to keep me from doing it.

That Wonderful Town

In the summer of 1936, my mother and I sailed to New York. She had found a boat that went from New Orleans to New York in four days and was determined to make our trip an adventure. So we took the train down the West Coast, across to New Orleans and, after two nights there, we boarded a boat called the *Dixie*. It was a rough trip, but I certainly didn't care. Especially when I found out there were entertainers on board and a master of ceremonies who staged shows in the evening.

The night before we docked in New York, John Tyres, who had a glorious baritone voice and went on to a professional career, sang along with some other entertainers. The passengers were encouraged to perform too, so I got up and in honor of our passage sang "Stormy Weather" as if I were the world's hottest blues singer. The next morning, we went past the Statue of Liberty into the harbor, which was a glorious way to see New York for the first time.

There was never any question that my mother would come to New York with me. She simply quit her job at Sherman Clay, packed up, and moved. Her friends told her she was crazy but she had faith that only good things could happen and it seemed the most natural thing in the world to both of us. We had been on our own together for so long that I would have been lost without her.

And for the ten years I lived in New York, I felt the same way. My mother was always so supportive of everything I did and yet she never demanded anything, complained, or made things difficult in any way. It was simply not in her nature to be a stage mother and we never had a problem, even when I stayed out till all hours on dates or at rehearsals. She enjoyed young people and when I was in a show she would sometimes cook scrambled eggs and bacon for the whole cast late at night. She loved doing it and everybody enjoyed having her around as much as I did.

For the rest of my mother's life, in fact, we were almost never apart except when I was on the road with a show. When I moved to Los Angeles after Larry and I got married and had kids, she had an apartment down the street and walked up to our house every day at noon. Later, when we bought the house where I still live today, she moved in with us. She sat by the phone, played solitaire, took our messages, and watched our sons when they were little. Garry and Andy are the only children I know who never had a babysitter.

When we got to New York, my mother supported me. Her experience at Sherman Clay quickly paid off and she went from one music store to another—Schirmer's, Harold Flammer, and Schroeder and Gunther.

Our living arrangements kept changing too. The first place we settled was in a dreary women's hotel on 57th Street. It was very dark and filled with old women who sat in the lobby all day, and after a couple of months, we had to get out of there. Mother said, "If I don't hear a man's voice soon, I'll go crazy."

Luckily, her friend Jean Baillargeon arrived in New York about that time and we shared an apartment with her on East 60th Street near Madison Avenue. It was a lovely place, which we certainly could not have afforded on our own, but then Jean went back to Seattle and we took an apartment in Tudor City on the East Side.

It was one big room with a Murphy bed, a studio couch, and one of those closet kitchens that you just open up to find an icebox, a hotplate, and a sink. We shared the place with Julia Randall, a dancer from Seattle who had come to be a member of the American Ballet, and another girl named Betty Rohan, who was also a student at the Neighborhood Playhouse.

The four of us were in one room and when you pulled down the bed and opened up the studio couch, everybody had to go to sleep because there was no place on the floor to walk. Rent was around $100 a month—the girls were being supported by their parents and we split it three ways—and my mother was making $35 a week so there was not much left over.

My mother cooked for us and I can't describe how many ways she found to cook Franco-American spaghetti on the hotplate. We had that and salad for one whole year at least. The next year, Julia went back to Seattle so Betty, my mother, and I moved into a smaller apartment in Tudor City. We all lived pretty cramped up for the two years I studied at the Neighborhood Playhouse.

I LOOK BACK on my days at the Neighborhood Playhouse and I marvel at them. From September to June, we went to class from nine to six every day in a big studio on 46th Street. And, oh, the classes we took.

Sanford Meisner, one of the greatest acting teachers in the country, taught drama. Martha Graham and her assistants, Anna Sokolow and Gertie Shurr, taught dance while Louis Horst, who was Martha's mentor and one of the great authorities on dance from the Elizabethan era on, gave courses in choreography that laid the foundations for the dance classes I taught years later.

Lehman Engel, one of Broadway's outstanding conductors, taught music. Edith Stebbins was an excellent speech teacher and Margaret Webster taught Shakespeare with great passion. Our voice teacher, Laura Elliott, had us practice by saying—and pretending it was true— "There's a great big oatmeal can stuck in my throat . . . and it's very round and very la-a-arge."

It was simply the best training in the world for a young actor, singer, or dancer. What these teachers emphasized above all was getting your tools ready—your body, your voice, your speech. These are lessons that have stayed with me all my life.

The fact that the Playhouse was run by two women made me feel right at home. Rita Wallach Morgenthau and Irene Lewisohn were constantly together and to me they seemed like Mary and Midah Wallace or the Deaconess and Margaret Bateman all over again. Rita was a little round lady who had a head tic that went from side to side and Irene was tall with a long Modigliani face who nodded her head up and down. They would occasionally stop in a classroom and when you looked up, one head would be going up and down while the other was turning left and right. It made you slightly dizzy.

And then there were the students. In my class, there was Danny Mann, who became the noted film director Daniel Mann, Nicky Conte, who became Richard Conte and had a long acting career in the movies, and Orin Jannings, who became a screen writer. Lorne Greene and Edmund O'Brien were in the class ahead of me and Gregory Peck studied at the Playhouse a few years later. Everybody was just so interested and committed, so determined to have careers in the theater, that the atmosphere was infectious.

When it comes to dedicated acting teachers, to those who taught for the sheer joy of it, there was never anybody like Sanford Meisner.

One of the first scenes I ever did for Sandy—I will never forget this—was from a play called *Dance Night*. It had a lot of good parts for young women and when I finished one of them in class, Sandy looked at me and said, "All right, now go out and come back and do it again. And this time do it *right!*"

I was almost in tears because I had no idea what he meant other than not liking what I had done. I went out in the hall where no one could see me and I did cry a little, then I came back in and did the scene again. "Well, that's more like it," Sandy said.

I went to lunch with Danny Mann after class and he said, "Do you know what Sandy said after you left the room? He said, 'Now that's talent.'" I sat there wondering why Sandy never told *me* that and it took me a while before I finally figured it out.

What Sandy stood for in acting above all was no nonsense. He would say, "Get down to who you are and work from there." He could see right through dishonesty and sometimes he could be vicious about it. He broke down all theatricality and insisted that we get acquainted with our tools and our selves and be able to use them.

The point he was making when he made me leave the room is that I had no specific motivational base to what I was doing. Coming back close to tears and determined "to show him!" gave that scene what it needed. Sandy could be mean but I came to realize he really liked me. I heard later he went to bat for me when it came to deciding who was to play the lead in our final play, *The Constant Nymph*, in which I played opposite Nicky Conte.

Years later, I ran into Sandy on the street in New York and he said, "I want to ask you a question. Do you use The Method in musical comedy?"

"Of course I do," I said. But Sandy sort of shook his head as if he could not quite believe it was possible to sing and dance and still go for the reality of the role.

Nearly sixty years after I took Sandy's classes at the Playhouse, he was still giving them despite the fact that over the years he had had more terrible things happen to him than any other man I have ever known. He was practically crippled when he was hit by a van and his hip was shattered. He was almost blind after two cataract operations and he lost his vocal chords to a laryngectomy so he sort of belched out his words, which made him hard to understand. Yet he kept teaching his classes with his friend Jimmy Carville interpreting for him.

I had a wonderful reunion with Sandy a few years before his death early in 1997. He was spending the summer at a house in Studio City and I took my sons, Garry and Andy, over to see him. Sandy had taught Larry in the Group Theater Studio in New York and here were these two boys who looked so much like him.

Sandy just held his arms out and said "Oh." It was so touching and Garry and Andy were so impressed to meet him. But that is the way it was with Sandy. I don't know anybody who worked with him who didn't think Sandy was the best.

WHILE STUDYING at the Playhouse, I was sure I would become a Serious Dramatic Actress. All the time I was there, I played only one comic role, Amanda in *Private Lives*, while the rest of the time I prepared only for heavy drama. Along with playing Tessa in *The Constant Nymph*, I was Julie in *Lilliom* and was also in *Awake and Sing* by Clifford Odets and *Time and the Conways* by J. B. Priestley. I was always dying of consumption or a broken heart.

The choreography I did for Martha Graham and Louis Horst was all very serious too, and so was the singing. Lehman Engel had us sing a theater piece by Kurt Weill called "Der Jasager" and a kind of Greek chorus that we sang while playing percussion instruments.

All this heavy drama made me a terrible snob about what my role in the theater should be. I remember sitting with my boyfriend of the time in a bar and talking down my nose about how I would *never* stoop to doing musical comedies. How could I know it would turn out to be the place where I had my greatest success and satisfaction? It's a joyous part of the theater and I guess it's where I really belong.

Being in New York, of course, meant not only studying the theater but going to it as well. It was an incredible era when you could see Ray Bolger one night, Tallulah Bankhead the next, and Gertrude Lawrence, Beatrice Lillie, Ralph Bellamy, or the Lunts the night after that. Once there were three productions of *Hamlet* on Broadway at the same time. You had your choice of John Gielgud, Maurice Evans, or Leslie Howard.

Balcony seats cost only $1.10 and this accounted for the fact that my mother and I never had an ironing board. Every time we got an extra two dollars and twenty cents, my mother would say, "Should we get an ironing board or should we go to the theater?" And I would always say, "Let's go to the theater." For years, we ironed our clothes on the floor.

THE SUMMER after I arrived in New York, I got a job as dance and drama counselor at Camp Barnard in Vermont for $65 for July and August. I had no business teaching either one. I had never tap-danced in my life so I just made up the steps. Some of the little rich kids I was teaching had been taking tap dancing since they were three years old and one day one of them said to me, "Miss Garrett, you know a lot of new steps we don't know."

I had expert help with my dancing lessons, though, in the person of an excellent accompanist named Elizabeth Wylie, who was nicknamed "Nudie" because, her mother joked, that is how she was born. Nudie would pound away at that piano and I was able to get all my little ballerinas to dance up a storm. Nudie and I are fast friends to this day.

During the summers, most actors in New York tried out for summer stock or the Borscht Circuit. I could never get a job in stock but the Borscht Circuit opened its arms. Many of the hotels and resorts in upstate New York and Pennsylvania ran extravagant entertainment programs for their guests. You couldn't make much money, but you got room and board and could honestly say you were polishing your skills and practicing your profession.

I spent my first summer on the Borscht Circuit at White Roe Lake in upstate New York. I got the job as part of a dance group through Alex Berg, a dancer I had worked with who later changed his name to Alex Bird. He also changed from straight to gay, which was fine with me except when he insisted on telling me every detail of his affairs!

Alex hired Betty Rohan too—my New York roommate who became "Peewee" because one of the other girls was Betty Weiss. That meant there were three Bettys. Betty Rohan was the shortest—hence "Peewee." The fourth member of the dance group was a tall, beautiful girl named Polly Smiley, who had been in our class at the Neighborhood

Playhouse. We were supposed to be paid $75 for the summer, but not long after we arrived we were told it would be $65, take it or leave it. It was too late to get another job, of course, so we had to take it.

The main house on White Roe Lake was an old rambling wooden building with a huge veranda where the comics "tumuled," as they used to say, with the guests. There were all kinds of organized games and sports, and a separate rec and dance hall with a stage where we did our shows, which featured established songs and production numbers. I remember doing "Love for Sale" with a long purple satin dress slit up to the hips.

The four girl dancers slept in one tiny room where there were two double beds. The room became even more cramped when Betty Weiss, who shared one of the beds with me, started dating a waiter named Solly who would show up in the middle of the night. I would huddle against the wall trying to ignore them, but the real problem came when Solly fell asleep. He had fits and he would suddenly scream and bite his tongue. Betty and I were constantly trying to revive him.

Many years later, when Larry and I were doing summer stock, we stopped at White Roe Lake. It was the off-season, but the same caretaker was still there after all those years and he took us on a tour. I found our old room and nothing had changed. It was the same tiny room, the same two double beds, and I swear they even had the same mattresses!

I fell in love that summer with the owner's son, Johnny Weiner, who was such a darling sweet young man that I did not hold against him the fact that his brother, the manager, had cut our salaries from $75 to $65. Johnny taught me to ride bareback on his beautiful horse Ranger and we had no trouble sneaking into any of the rooms when we wanted to be alone because he had the keys.

Johnny later became a teacher and we have stayed in touch all these years. After he retired, he started a library in the basement of a church in White Plains, New York. People donate books they no longer want and Johnny sells them for whatever anybody wants to pay. He takes nothing for himself and gives all the proceeds to the homeless. He also hires homeless people to work in the library—doing good in many directions at once.

Johnny married a lovely, brilliant woman and has children, grandchildren, and great-grandchildren. Except for a gray hair or two, he looks just the way he did when he was nineteen years old. Whenever we get together, I think to myself, "I had very good taste in boyfriends."

An important side effect of working at White Roe Lake was getting to know Danny Kaye. He had started there several years earlier and was a frequent guest. He would get up and hold an audience for hours without even breathing hard. He was doing his famous "Deenah" and his scat singing even then.

Danny saw me in several of our shows and I guess he decided I was talented, which was a great thrill for me because I thought *he* was the cat's pajamas. What's more, he put his actions where his mouth was. When we got back to town, he recommended me for a little satirical revue he was doing at the Keynote Varieties and later the Barbizon Plaza Theatre.

Two summers later, I ended up in the Poconos at Tamiment, which was the *crème de la crème* of the summer hotels and where we did an original musical revue every week—new songs, new dances, new sketches, new scenery.

And what a staff and cast we had! Jerome Robbins was one of the dancers. Carol Channing was a singer. Imogene Coca and Jules Munshin were the comedians. Reuben Ship wrote the sketches while Baldwin (Beau) Bergerson was the composer and Sylvia Marx wrote the lyrics.

The entire operation was run by Max Liebman, who later produced *Your Show of Shows* with Sid Caesar and Imogene Coca on television. When I saw that program with all the sketches, dances, and musical numbers, all I could think was, "That's just what we did every week at Tamiment."

Max was an incredible organizer and he was deadly serious about his schedule as I learned one morning when I came to rehearsal and found everybody sitting in a circle on the stage.

"You're thirty minutes late," he said.

I looked at my watch. "Rehearsal is at ten o'clock. It's only one minute after ten."

"There are thirty people here," Max said. "You are one minute late for each one of them. You are thirty minutes late." That is something I have never forgotten. It hasn't made me be on time, but I never forgot it!

This routine was very strenuous, but somehow I found the stamina to rehearse and perform and still dance all night in the ballroom and get involved with a waiter or a musician. Musicians were usually my downfall.

My roommate at Tamiment was Carol Channing and I simply fell in love with her. Here was this big wonderful blond lady who was absolutely gorgeous and ran around in very short shorts and bare feet. She had the men just panting and pawing the ground, but she was totally unaware of it.

Carol was terribly nearsighted and when she sat across from a man at a table in the dining room she would keep squinting and changing expressions provocatively. Later, she would come to me and say, "Behhhhtty, I don't know why the fellows all keep making passes at me." She was just trying to *see* them!

Max never quite knew how to use Carol in the shows at Tamiment. She was a unique talent and he could not quite figure out how to fit her in so she was always trying to please him by finding new numbers she could do.

Once she went up to one of the musicians and said, "Do you know a new blues number I could sing in the Saturday night variety show?"

The musician said, "Yeah, there's a new number out now called 'Blues 'n Tuchus.' Why don't you sing that?"

Now if you understand any Yiddish—and just about everybody at Tamiment did—you know that is a very obscene expression.

"Does it have lyrics?" Carol asked.

"Honey, if it doesn't have lyrics, I'll write them for you," the musician said.

A couple of hours later, Carol came back to our cabin and said, "Behhhhtty, I don't think Max likes me."

"Why?" I said.

"I told him I was going to sing 'Blues 'n Tuchus' at the Saturday night variety show and he just *stared* at me."

Musicians are *mean*! Funny, but mean!

Finally, in the middle of the summer, Max fired Carol. He simply didn't know what to do with her. She did wonderful numbers in which she imitated Ethel Waters and Tallulah Bankhead, but he didn't know how to use her in sketches or musicals so he finally let her go.

I was so upset when I got the news that I ran crying back to our room where Carol was reading *Science and Health* by Mary Baker Eddy.

"If they fire you, I'm leaving too," I told her.

But Carol just looked up and smiled and said, "That's all right, Behhhhtty. I don't mind." And she stood up and put her arms around me and patted me on the back. She was the one being fired but she was comforting me.

I would like to think that for the rest of his life Max Liebman would look in the mirror every morning, slap himself in the face, and say, "*I fired Carol Channing!*"

My job at Tamiment was what they called a soubrette, someone who always sang the sweet little boy–girl numbers, most of which were pretty drippy. But we all had to take part in some of the sketches and quite by accident this led me in a new and unexpected direction.

In one of the sketches, I was assigned the role of the offstage voice of an Irish landlady screaming at her husband. Jules Munshin and Imogene Coca played a couple who lived upstairs and every time they opened the window, they heard me screaming, in a thick Irish brogue, "Ah, ye coom home ivery Saturday night an' ye expect me ta have yr dinnir reddy . . ." and they would slam the window down and the voice would stop. The window itself was in a flat piece of scenery and I sat behind it as I delivered my lines.

The first day of rehearsal I kept getting the words mixed up—"Ah, ye coom home ivery Naturday Sight—no, Saturday Night. . . ."

I tried again and got it wrong again. And then again. I kept getting more and more frustrated as I sat on the floor and finally I said, "Ah, ye coom home ivery Saturday night an' ye nex me . . . Oh, *shit!*"

What had I done? There was absolute silence. I slowly rose to my knees and peeked through the window out into the audience.

There was Max Liebman rolling back and forth in the aisle in silent laughter. The idea that those words could come out of the mouth of this pudding-faced young girl singer seemed absolutely hysterical to him. It changed his whole attitude toward me. Max dug up a comedy song for me, put me in more sketches—including one about two crazy sisters that Imogene Coca and I did together—and generally gave me more to do in the show.

It's interesting that my career as a comedienne started with my saying "Oh, shit!"

The summer following Tamiment, I worked at a nearby camp called Unity House run by the International Ladies Garment Workers Union. There I met another influential person in my life, Robert Gordon. He was the director of the shows at Unity House and he gave me what I needed most—a good bawling out.

"You're not working hard enough on your singing and dancing," he told me. "You're just kind of sailing through life, leaving things to chance." At that particular time, this made a deep impression on me.

All in all, those summers were some of the best training I've ever had. I have often said I would love to go back and do a whole summer at Tamiment, go through all that rehearsing for those shows all over again.

But as wonderful as the summers were, it sometimes seemed that the best part was returning to New York. The first time I went to camp I was glad to leave because the city seemed so noisy, dirty, and unpleasant. But the moment I came back, I thought, "Wow! New York! This is my town!"

Later a lot of people told me they have had the same reaction. They think they hate New York, but give them a little time away and they suddenly realize how much they love it. After that first summer in the country, I felt like a New Yorker, and even though I go there only occasionally now, I still do.

Orson Welles, Martha Graham, and the Prettiest Piece in Greece

y first dramatic role on Broadway was as an understudy to an off-stage voice and I owed it all to Gussie Kirschner.

Gussie, who had been my dancing teacher during the summers in Seattle, had sailed to New York on the *Dixie* with us and she was the kind of person who would strike up a conversation with almost anyone she saw. She would go up to someone in the subway and say, "You have an interesting face. What do you do for a living?" Perfect strangers would soon be telling her their life stories.

Gussie went to Carnegie Hall one night where there was an attractive young man working as an usher. "Let me see your eyes," she said as he was concentrating on tearing tickets, and when he looked up in surprise she said, "Oh, you have wonderful eyes. You must *look* at people when you show them to their seats." The man was Dick Wilson and Gussie charmed him the way she did everyone else.

"What do you do when you're not an usher?" she asked him when they went for coffee after the show.

"I'm the stage manager for Orson Welles," he said.

"I have a young actress friend and I want you to get her a job with him," Gussie said, as if asking somebody she did not know to give a nineteen-year-old girl *he* did not know a job with Orson Welles was perfectly natural.

But the next thing I knew, I was walking down the aisle of the totally dark Mercury Theater and looking up at the stage where a tall, good-looking, baby-faced—and very thin—man was screaming at one woman up in the flies while another one was hitting him on the behind with a bolt of fabric.

"No, Jeannie, no, goddammit!" he was yelling at a woman I later

41

learned was Jean Rosenthal, one of the theater's great lighting directors. "Throw that other light over here!"

In the meantime, this little girl with long golden hair who looked like Alice in Wonderland was beating him with her bolt of material.

"Orson!" she pleaded, almost in tears, "Please! What color do you want? Just tell me. Stop a minute and tell me what you want!"

"Virginia, leave me alone!" he shouted at her. "Jeannie, move that light over there. . . . Virginia, I don't care about colors. I hate colors. I hate *that* color! Don't bother me with colors."

"But, Orson," she wailed, "you didn't like the other color. What color *do* you want?"

This went on for about fifteen minutes while I was standing in the dark theater, wondering what was going *on*. Finally, Dick told me that Virginia might look like a little girl, but she was Orson's wife. She was trying to decorate their apartment and wanted Orson to help her choose the curtains.

Dick finally got Orson's attention and said he wanted to hire me for one of the walk-on parts. "If it's OK with you, it's OK with me," Orson said, barely looking at me. That was my audition with Orson Welles.

Orson was coming off his great successes with *Dr. Faustus* and a modern-dress version of *Julius Caesar*. His energy and his imagination, and his genius at getting attention, had captivated Broadway and everybody was waiting to see if he could top himself. I think Orson was waiting to see, too, because he just went haywire with *Danton's Death*.

The first thing he did was tear up the entire stage. Then he built staircases that went down into the bowels of the theater. In the center of the basement, there was an elevator that rose at various times during the performance and at the back of the stage there was a huge cyclorama that extended from one side all the way across to the other and was made up entirely of masks.

The colors and the expressions on the masks would change depending on where the light was coming from. When the lights came from above, the angry faces symbolizing "the masses" would look down on Danton. When times were happy, the lights came up from below and the faces were smiling. The lights themselves were huge—somebody said they were big enough to use at Radio City Music Hall—and their effect on this incredible set was extraordinary.

There was one scene just after Danton had been guillotined where Vladimir Sokoloff, a wonderful old Russian actor who played Robespierre, rose in the elevator and stepped out into his chambers. He clasped his hands, gazed around and said, very theatrically in his marvelous accent, "Now . . . I am . . . a-*lone*." Suddenly all the masks lit up and frowned down on him. It was a wild effect.

In my one scene, I was supposed to be a maid and walk into Robespierre's chamber with a candle, but in one of the very first rehearsals my part was eliminated. It broke my heart, of course. My first real job in the theater and I got cut. But I was still part of the company that gathered in the basement and made crowd noises. So what if nobody would ever see me? I was still in an Orson Welles play on Broadway.

Danton's Death had a remarkable cast that included Joseph Cotten, Ruth Ford, Martin Gabel, Arlene Francis, Edgar Barrier, and Mary Wickes. Mary had one song, a bawdy number that she sang off stage:

> *Mister soldier, handsome soldier,*
> *Play me mild or play me rough—*
> *I just can't get enough.*

I was her understudy and I got to sing it one night when she had laryngitis, but except for that my contribution to the play was singing with the chorus and contributing to the noises and sound effects.

We all stood under the stage, doing a lot of what was supposed to be running in the streets and shouting "Off with his head!" "Down with Danton!" "Up with Robespierre!" "Vive la France!" And we sang "Come dance the Carmagnole and wait for the gun, wait for the gun!" That was Marc Blitzstein's version of a French Revolutionary song.

At one late-night rehearsal, Orson decided we needed the sound effects of noises over a village at night and he asked us for suggestions.

"How about a person snoring?" someone asked.

"Let me hear it," Orson said, and the actor snored, snorted, and exhaled with a long whistle.

Orson laughed and said, "Yeah, that's great."

Another actor barked like a dog.

"Fine, fine," Orson said. "You're a dog."

"A baby crying," I piped up and I let out with a pitiful high-pitched cry that could wake the dead. I was very proud of my sound effects so I was a little hurt when everybody laughed at me.

But Orson drew himself up indignantly. "Don't laugh," he said. "That sounds *exactly* like my baby daughter. Betty, you're a baby crying." It became my one solo in the show.

Then Joe Cotten suggested sex noises in the night and offered a few wonderful realistic sighs and moans—"oh . . . ah . . . yes . . . YES!"— that were *very* realistic. Orson loved it. The trouble was that after a week or two Joe got bored and his sex noises started to sound more like "hmmm . . . yeah . . . uh-huh . . . uh-oh! . . . yawn."

In the action scenes of the play, people would run up and down on a stairway leading from the basement to the stage and when there were intimate scenes the elevator would rise to the middle of the stage. There was one magnificent moment where Martin Gabel, who played Danton, is supposed to be in a bawdy house with his lady of the evening and as the elevator rises, they are in a passionate embrace.

That meant Martin and Arlene Francis, who played the lady of the evening, had to get onto a little platform in the basement so they would be ready to go up. The rest of us stood around in the dark waiting very quietly to make our noises and sing our songs.

After a while, it was clear that Martin and Arlene did not realize we were there and every evening they would get into position just a little earlier than the night before. It was not long before we saw that the love scene was not *acting* any more. We used to joke that the audience could see the steam rising before the elevator did. But it was not a case of "I love you, darling, but the show closed" because Martin and Arlene got married and went on to have a long and happy life together.

During rehearsals, Orson lived in the theater twenty-four hours a day—he napped on a couch in the aisle—and he ate there too, sending out next door to Longchamps for steak and so much pistachio ice cream I kept expecting him to turn green.

Sometimes the cast was expected to stay in the theater all night, too, just waiting for Orson to think of something. Often, he did not get to those of us under the stage until after midnight. I got used to coming home at six in the morning and my mother would get up, fix me something to eat, and go to work while I would go to bed. For this, we got $15 a week until Actors Equity found out and made Orson pay us $18!

Just to make things more complicated, I was doing what we call bicycling, running from Orson's rehearsals to Martha Graham's dance studio, and Orson made terrible fun of me.

"The Maa-aartha Gray-haaam dawnsuh has to leave rehearsals eaaaarrrly," he would intone as I tried to sneak out the door without being noticed.

One night, we were all marking time during rehearsals because Orson was off with some other members of the company doing a radio broadcast. Suddenly, sirens began shrieking in the street outside and Orson burst into the theater followed by policemen, reporters, and photographers.

The place was a madhouse and none of us knew what on earth was going on. Gradually, it came out that Orson had just done his famous "War of the Worlds" broadcast. I remember Orson standing in the lobby as the photographers were snapping picture after picture, throwing back his head, holding out his hands and saying "What . . . have I *done*?!" He knew very well what he had done. He had freaked out the whole world by making it think Martians had landed in New Jersey.

After all that energy and excitement, we were disappointed when *Danton's Death* was a failure. The reviews were not good and the show folded after only three weeks. *Danton's Death* turned out to be the Mercury Theater's last stage production.

IT'S A GOOD THING Martha Graham liked me or I would never have performed in her dance company.

As a girl back in Seattle, I had always thought of myself as a dancer above all, but by the time I had spent just a short time with Martha my visions of becoming a great dancer were gone. I have never stopped dancing, but the entire time I was with Martha I kept thinking, "This is just too *hard*!"

All the dancers in her company seemed to be made out of steel and they had years of dancing with Martha behind them. I would not say they were built differently from me, but with my long body and comparatively short legs I swear I had to work twice as hard as they did. I could not get my legs to go as high as they could and I could not do those hip-wrenching exercises on the floor. With my apple cheeks, innocent blue eyes, and no real training or technique, I'm sure I looked as if I had come right off the farm.

"Pudding-faced virgin" is one of the favorite things Anna Sokolow, Martha's tough assistant, used to call me, but midway through my second year, she paid me her greatest compliment. "You're a hard worker," Anna said.

I used to come home after dance class so sore my mother would get hysterical. My thighs were so stiff I was contorted into a position where you could see my knees coming through the door before the rest of me. And I was paralyzed with muscle soreness in the mornings to the point where I couldn't get out of bed. I would have to roll over and slide out on my hands and knees, then work my way up to a standing position.

Another thing that gave me pause was the realization that dancing takes every hour of the day. Even when you're not dancing, you're doing something related to it, like sewing your costume or working on your shoes. Julia, the ballet dancer who lived with us for a while, spent half the night in the bathroom so she would not keep us awake sewing ribbons on her toe shoes or darning the end of the shoes when they got worn down.

But even though I realized I would never be a great dancer, I loved Martha's classes and I loved Martha. She had the most amazing feet—they seemed permanently arched—and she walked with a wonderful dancer's stride. She wore wispy off-white costumes made of Japanese silk that floated around her as she glided among us, correcting this position or that. Then she would sit cross-legged on top of a table and weave images for us.

"The next time you see the opening of an MGM picture," she once told us, "I want you to look at the lion. Look at the way he turns his head. The lion is never so much a lion as he is when he turns his head." Then she would become the lion with a turn of her head.

Martha was tough with the women in her company. She would hit your legs if they were not turned exactly right or your back if it was not just the way she wanted it. She was completely different with the men, though.

Once we were doing an arm exercise and she went up to Nicky Conte, smacked him in the chest and said, "Get that chest up." Nicky winced and Martha got all concerned and said, "Oh, did I hurt you, Nicky?" and put her hand tenderly on his chest. We all cracked up because with a man she was a real flirt.

What made Martha keep me around, I think, is that I was a great bluffer. I could catch the spirit of a step even if I didn't have the technique. The only way I knew how to dance was with all my heart and Martha liked that.

So despite the fact that she knew I had no experience, she let me be a part of her company when it performed at Carnegie Hall and the Alvin Theater. *American Document* was one of the pieces I was in; *Primitive Mysteries* was another. There was one moment in that number where we all had to drop down into a crouching position and jump up into the air in one beat. I could get down all right, but I was always the last person to bob up, which made Martha furious.

There was one step, though, where I gained her approval. It was a ponylike dancing step and I loved doing it. "Betty Garrett is the worst dancer in this group," Martha would say as she watched me, "so how come she looks better than anybody else doing that step?"

Over a period of time, I got much more into acting, but despite my limitations I never gave up dancing. I still take tap-dancing classes once a week and until about a dozen years ago, I taught three dance lessons a week at a class for our Theatre West members.

In the acting workshop, I was always complaining that nobody knew how to move, no one was in control of their bodies. Finally, somebody challenged me: "OK, you teach a class." So I did and I always tried to remember the problems I'd had in Martha's classes. It made me feel good when people said, "This is a good class" because I felt I was getting things across to nondancers.

In a way, I suppose I will always think of myself as a dancer. Whenever I hear music, even a symphony, I find myself choreographing it, doing all the steps and twirls in my mind. Even when I cut vegetables, I go one-two-three, two-two-three, three-two-three unconsciously with the knife. Once you are a dancer, you just can't stop.

FOR THE NEXT four or five years, the seasons, the jobs, and the people just seemed to fly by one after the other. In 1940 I joined a semiprofessional group called the Flatbush Arts Theatre that did satirical and political revues in Brooklyn.

It was composed of doctors, accountants, writers, teachers, and even a butcher, as well as a few professionals. One of the members was a political organizer who was always trying to proselytize me. He was so determined that once when I was sick in the hospital, he came to visit and slipped some radical pamphlets under the covers.

The Flatbush Arts Theatre was run by Lou Cooper, a classical pianist, and his wife, Sylvia Siegler Cooper, who was one of the world's great dynamos. She was so pushy I once threw a Kleenex box at her when she came to our dressing room before a show and started bossing us around. But she was the one who kept everything together and made the group work.

We did benefits for everyone, from the Office Workers Union and the International Ladies Garment Workers Union to the *Daily Worker*. If these organizations paid us anything at all, it was usually only expenses. If there was anything left over, we might get five dollars, but we had to supply our own costumes and scenery. There were many times when I hauled fifty-pound suitcases across town on the subway.

Our material was very often politically oriented. I played the hooker in Marc Blitzstein's *The Cradle Will Rock*, which was the first time I had ever really sung on a New York stage. I also did "Beetsie, the Shorthand Speed Queen" in another Blitzstein opus. The music was difficult and I did not have a piano so I had to teach myself to sight read on the spot. I'm forever grateful for that skill.

The fact that Lou Cooper played piano for us made things even more difficult. He was a fine classical pianist, but the worst accompanist I have ever known. He would become so entranced with your performance he would forget to play or sometimes he would shift into another key without warning. That taught me one of the most important lessons a performer can learn: Just keep going! I knew where I was supposed to be and somehow Lou would manage to get back on track before the song was over.

After a while, the Flatbush Arts Theatre's shows became fairly well known and were regularly reviewed in the New York papers. In one of the shows, I did a number called "Jitterbug, Jitterbug, Fly Away" in which I wore a very short skirt that showed my behind when I jumped around.

Of course that was the picture they used in the papers. I was riding the subway one day when I looked across at a man reading *PM*, the great liberal newspaper, and there was my picture. I got out of my seat, went over, and crouched down in front of him to get a better look. "My God!" I said out loud, "That's me!" That was my first picture in a newspaper and it was thrilling. The man reading the paper thought I was crazy!

After a while, our shows began doing so well that we left Brooklyn, moved to Manhattan, and took another name. No more "Flatbush Arts Theatre." We were now the "American Youth Theatre," if you please. The shows were not much different, though. We still did revues with a lot of comedy, a lot of politics, and a lot of time off looking for work in between.

BETWEEN THE SUMMERS at White Roe Lake and Tamiment, I worked in the 1939–40 New York World's Fair in a big pageant called "Railroads on Parade." It took place in an outside auditorium in Queens where the stage was literally a block wide, and in the wings on each side was real railroad yard. Huge locomotives traveled across the stage on a track under their own steam while the audience sat in bleachers that held close to a thousand people. We did four one-hour shows every day.

As actors, singers, and dancers, we played in little scenes related to the history of the railroad and the particular locomotive on the stage at that time. One showed a gay-nineties wedding party, and the original Tom Thumb engine putt-putted on stage, stopped to let the bride and groom climb into a little car in the back, and then clattered off as everybody danced a Viennese waltz around the railroad tracks. At a different point in the show, another train, a more modern one, raced across the stage at sixty miles an hour!

Another scene featured a big yellow boxcar that had carried Abraham Lincoln's coffin across the country. We played farmers, townspeople, and ex-slaves who had come out to see the train and pay homage to Lincoln. We would go up and touch the boxcar and say good-bye to Lincoln as it moved slowly across the stage. They said the scene was based on a true incident after Lincoln's assassination. It was tremendously moving.

My second year at the Fair, they decided to show a contemporary passenger train. They took a big Pullman car and cut it in half so the audience could see a cross section of it. There were people having drinks in the club car, being waited on in the dining car, and so on. My part was to come into a little bedroom compartment with a porter. He would put my suitcase on the berth, I would tip him and he would leave.

Then I took my hat off and put it up on a shelf as the train slowly began to move across the stage. Next, I took my jacket off and hung it up. Then, very dreamily, I took off my skirt and, with the train moving all the time, I slowly began to roll down my stockings. Then I undid my blouse and took it off and just as I was reaching around to start unfastening my brassiere, the train would go off. As a friend of mine once remarked, "So did half the men in the audience!"

Because the Fair only played from April through September, in the fall and winter I had time to be in the Keynote Varieties and Barbizon Plaza revues Danny Kaye had recommended me for. They paid no money but they were good showcases and excellent training.

Once, a boy–girl number I was doing in the Barbizon Plaza Revue was not working out and had to be cut and I remember sitting in the back of the theater heartbroken and crying. All of a sudden, I looked up and there was Danny, who was the star of the show, handing me his handkerchief. He sat down beside me and put his arm around me.

"You all think I'm so wonderful," he said, which was the truth. He was an amazingly talented man and the cast just adored him. "You laugh at my jokes. You think everything I do is marvelous. Well, I can't get an audition on Broadway! And when I *do* get one, they don't think I'm very funny. I can't get a job that pays! I may be a big frog in a little pond here, but I get turned down a *lot*." That was such a comfort to me and a dear thing for him to do. I kept that handkerchief for a long time.

Some years later, when Larry and I were doing one of our vaudeville shows out on the road, Danny happened to be in town and came to the theater. All of a sudden, in the middle of the act, he just ran out onto the stage, picked me up, and carried me off. He was a very big star by then and the audience went wild. It made the day for all of us.

One of the other great favors Danny did for me was to recommend me to his manager and lawyer, Lou Mandel, who became my lifetime manager, business partner, and surrogate father. Danny had a terrible falling out with Lou, though, and after that Danny and I lost touch.

Whenever we ran into each other afterwards, there was always a great reunion with hugs and laughs and promises to get together, but we had no real contact any more, much to my regret.

DESPITE ALL MY RUNNING back and forth between jobs wherever I could find them and summer camps in the Borscht Circuit, my mother and I were always a little desperate for money and one Christmas I worked at Saks 34th Street. Then, in the winter of 1939, between the "Railroads on Parade" seasons, I became a chorus girl.

It started when a funny little man named George Libby lost one of the girls for a chorus line he was sending to Boston the next day and somebody recommended me.

Chorus work was considered kind of cheesy in those days, especially in night clubs. You were supposed to sit and have drinks with the customers and my mother was very suspicious. What kind of place is this—she wanted to know. What would I have to *do*? But George Libby told her it was honest work so she decided she would just have to trust in him. She stayed in New York and I went to the Latin Quarter in Boston.

The owner was Lou Walters—the father of Barbara Walters—and he arranged a room for me in the Charlotte Cushman Club for Theatrical Young Women. One look at it and I never wanted to leave.

Two roommates and I shared a big beautiful room for which we each paid four dollars a week. For another thirty-five cents every morning we got our breakfast. And I mean *breakfast*. At night when I came in, there would be a card on a table by the entry way and I would write "Please wake me at nine o'clock. Scrambled eggs, bacon, orange juice, coffee, and toast."

And at nine o'clock, there would be a knock on the door, and Henri, the house man, would come in and say, "Mees Ga*rrett*, your break*fast* ees ready." And he would put a tray on the bed with a rose in a vase, the newspaper, my mail, and my beautiful breakfast. I only made $25 a week, but living like this I could send $15 back to my mother!

And did we ever earn our money! We did three shows a night—a dinner show, a midnight show and one at 2 A.M.—and every other week we would start at ten in the morning rehearsing a new show. That meant we were working from 10 A.M. to 2 A.M.

I decided I'd better not tell George Libby or Lou Walters I had never been a tap dancer. I had taken only a few lessons and here I was in a line of real chorus girls. I was awed at the way they tapped their feet off at rehearsals and I would stand behind them as inconspicuously as possible and do what I had done in Martha Graham's company—fake like crazy. Then we would come home and I would get them to teach me the steps.

My two roommates, Inky and Pauline, were very good dancers and extremely patient with me so by the time the show was ready I could do most of the steps passably. I missed a lot of taps but you could not tell because everybody else was tapping so loudly.

There was one thing I could do with the best of them, though, and that was shake my behind. George Libby would always put me at the end of the line so I would be the last girl shaking her behind as we came off the stage. It was my greatest triumph as a chorus girl.

Even though we were putting in new shows all the time, there were certain set things in all of them. The opening number always had a military theme and the next one was always ethnic, depending on who was the star that week. One time, we had a singer from Holland so we came out almost stark naked except for Dutch caps and wooden shoes.

Another time, the headline singer was French, so naturally we did the Can-Can. Out we came in our big skirts and did the high kicks and the splits. At the end, we reached down, lifted our skirts up, showed our panties, and danced in a big circle.

The first night we did the Can-Can, I was dancing past the bandstand at the back of the stage when one of the musicians pointed at me and pantomimed, "You forgot your pants!" I was in a panic until I got back to the dressing room and discovered I had *not* forgotten my pants at all. I told you musicians are *mean*!

There was always a "black light" number. That's a special light that only picks up things in the dark that have been painted with phosphorescent paint. All the other lights would be turned off, we would wear gloves or hats or shoes that had been painted so they glowed in the dark, and we would do these crazy movements that made it look as if detached hands, feet, eyeballs, and teeth were floating in midair. There was one girl in the line who had to keep her mouth closed because she had caps on her teeth and real teeth glow in the dark but caps don't. She was the only girl in the line who wasn't smiling.

Looking back, I'm sure we must have been the weirdest chorus line there ever was. Two of the girls were six feet tall, one was under five feet, and all of the rest of us were in-between. This meant that when we did the big showgirl numbers, George Libby had a problem because we certainly could not wear costumes that made us look alike. George solved this by subscribing to the Flo Ziegfeld philosophy: You pick the best feature of each girl and put her in a costume that emphasizes it.

One girl had an absolutely exquisite face, with big eyes and dimples and a gorgeous smile. George put her in an old-fashioned outfit with a high neck, a big picture hat, and a parasol that she would parade around in. The girl with the great boobs would have practically nothing on them but would be wearing a big fluffy skirt. And the girl with legs up to her armpits would be bundled up on top so her gorgeous legs would show.

Then they came to me. I could not compete with the girl with the beautiful face, I had short, chunky legs, and you could still iron a shirt on my chest. But they decided I had a very attractive belly button.

So I would wear a big blouse with ruffles and a huge hat and a lot of feathers covering my legs. But from the bottom of my bust down almost to my pubic hair I would be completely naked, sometimes with a little sapphire or ruby in my belly button. I would teeter around on six-inch heels so I would be as close to the height of the six-foot girls as I could get.

At the end of the showgirl number one night, I was standing in my favorite pose when I heard a big laugh. I looked down and there was a drunk who had crawled onto the stage and was pulling the feathers off my costume, saying "She loves me . . . she loves me not."

One of the things the girls in the line introduced me to was an old showgirl tradition for passing the time. We spent long periods just waiting in the dressing room, because the comic would be on stage for twenty-five minutes and the headline singer had her own long act.

We could not sit down in our costumes because they would get wrinkled and the sequins were scratchy, and most of the time it was just too hot to put anything else on. So we spent a lot of time just sitting there stark naked—six or eight of us in a tiny room—and looking at ourselves in the mirror.

After a while, someone would pick up an eyebrow pencil and start drawing on herself. You would draw a little pig around one breast.

53

Eyes, ears. (The snout is already there.) And then maybe you would draw a pussycat around the other breast. Eyes, ears, and whiskers. Moving down you would draw a whistling sailor, the belly button being his mouth (mine usually had a ruby in it). If you kept going lower, you'd get to Monty Wooley!

I told Betty Bruce, a dancer who was a dear friend, about this a couple of years later when we were in *Something for the Boys*, with Ethel Merman. Betty became hysterical with laughter and said, "You've got to show Ethel. You've got to show her this," and she dragged me down to Ethel's dressing room where I showed her my pig drawing.

"My God!" Ethel said, "if I did that it would be a cow!"

After I had been at the Latin Quarter for a while, Lou Walters came in one day and said to George Libby, "Get those old ladies out of there. They look like a bunch of hookers, all of them. Except you can keep that little girl at the end of the line who shakes her can." And everybody got fired except me.

Even George Libby was eventually fired. He was replaced by Buster Keim, whose daughter Betty married Warren Berlinger, who played my son in *Who's Happy Now* at the Mark Taper Forum in Los Angeles more than thirty years later. It's an itty-bitty world.

AFTER A WINTER at the Latin Quarter, I went back for my second season at the World's Fair in 1940. When it ended, I tried out for my first featured role on Broadway and I got it. Just like that, they said, "You're hired." I was terribly excited, of course. A little *too* excited, I'm afraid.

The show was *All in Fun* and the producer was Leonard Sillman who did *New Faces* and other revues. I was cast as Helen of Troy in a big production number about the Trojan war. I was to sing:

I'm the prettiest piece in Greece.
And no one can deny it.
I cause a riot, wherever I go.
With my violet eyes, my ruby lips,
My figure a dream of tailors.
And my face that launched a thousand ships
And twenty-thousand sailors.

For four days, I rehearsed and rehearsed the song. After a while, something strange began to dawn on me. As I walked back and forth, I would hear somebody else doing my number in another rehearsal room.

In those days, producers were allowed to hire several people for the same part and they had five days to decide which one to keep. If you were kept for five days, you were automatically on salary but if they let you go earlier you did not get a cent. I had no inkling of this and on the fifth day Leonard Sillman, whom I will never forget or forgive, called four of us out on the stage and had us sing the same song one after the other. Then he fired three of us.

I shudder with embarrassment when I remember my reaction. I cried and pleaded and said, "Why? Why are you firing me? Please, let me stay." I thought I had a job, I didn't understand what was happening and the only thing I could think of doing was to beg.

It was humiliating, but I had my revenge. *All in Fun* was a huge flop. And I learned an important lesson. Rejection is a part of show business and I never again crawled in front of anybody or cried about losing a job.

MY NAIVETE about show business was not cured overnight, as I soon found out when I auditioned with a band leader named Mark Warnow. I got the job and the next thing I knew a man came up to me and said, "Now, dear, you'll need someone to handle your contract."

I did not know anything about him—he had just been hanging around—but I said OK. I was so innocent I signed a contract giving him fifty percent of my earnings. Forever! Luckily, that was just about the time when I bumped into Lou Mandel again.

Lou, as I mentioned, was Danny Kaye's manager and I had met him, his wife, and four-year-old son, Milo, during my summer at Tamiment. He came to all the big Saturday night shows and Danny had recommended that he watch my work. By the time I got back to New York we had become great friends. I told Lou about the contract and the terms I had agreed to and he hit the ceiling.

He went straight to the man who had conned me and said, "The contract you have made this girl sign is absolutely illegal. If you don't release her immediately I will take you straight to court." That was the end of that, thank goodness, and I never saw the man again. And Lou became my manager for the rest of his life.

He handled my career, and later Larry's, for almost fifty years. Lou was more than our lawyer. He was our business partner, our friend, and during the dark days that lay ahead, our savior. When Lou died, his son stepped in and took over where his father had left off. Milo Mandel had become one of the top theatrical lawyers in Hollywood by then and today *he* is my lawyer and my friend.

NOT LONG AFTER the *All in Fun* fiasco, I put together a nightclub act. The Village Vanguard was a hot club for young performers then and I was on the bill with Eddie Haywood, the jazz piano player, and his trio, and Richard Dyer-Bennett, the folk singer.

I did a number called "I Beg Your Pardon, Miss Arden" in which I wore glasses and a funny hat and complained about how cosmetics did not work for me, and another one called "A Pretty Girl Milking Her Cow." I also sang a straight simple version of "Cockles and Mussels."

Looking back, I know my act was not really very good, but I got nice reviews and it seemed to go over well with the audience. One night, Leonard Sillman, the producer of *All in Fun*, came backstage and told me he thought I was very good. I was proud of myself for not spitting in his eye.

I started doing some political material at the Vanguard. One of my friends wrote a song that was considered quite radical called "The Four Rivers" in which the Mississippi, the Yangtze, the Thames, and the Don represented the four main powers of the world. The idea was that these rivers could all run together some day. Pretty subversive, eh?

But to sing something like this in a nightclub *was* rather radical and it got some attention in the press. Later, I was sure this song is what got me on the lists of suspected fellow travelers for the first time. I love the term "fellow travelers."

I was in some overtly political shows in the early 1940s too, some with the American Youth Theatre and some with other groups. One was a review called *Meet the People*. It was a big success in New York and I went out with the road company, which included Henny Youngman, Jack Albertson, Joey Faye, and Curt Conway.

In one number, I played Miss Hollywood, a Sleeping Beauty who is awakened by Prince Charming (played by Frank Maxwell) to social injustice, racial discrimination, and the plight of the Okies in the Oklahoma Dustbowl. One number went "A union label has the magical power to make you look more beautiful."

Politics and change were all around us then—it was particularly strong in the theater—and I was becoming very much aware of political issues. Most of the songs I sang in these shows were just entertainment, but there was usually one that was politically oriented. One that I sang in an American Youth Theatre show was a pro-union number called "Don't Sing Solo."

The more involved in the politics of the day I became, the more it seemed to me that the Communists, Socialists, and other radical groups were the only ones who were really *doing* anything about discrimination, better housing, Spanish Civil War orphans, and so on. These were the things that spoke very deeply to my innate sense of justice, and anybody who was actually doing anything about it appealed to me.

There was no reason not to become involved unless you were just uninterested and that is why it seemed natural to want to do something. So I joined the Communist Party. I was not interested in party affairs at all, especially when at the one meeting I attended everyone was over fifty and all they talked about was how to deliver the *Daily Worker*. "What am I doing here?" I thought.

But I did enjoy performing at fund-raisers for progressive causes. I was totally committed and that is one of the things that got me in trouble later on. When the vigilantes started compiling lists of suspect organizations and causes, I had performed for just about all of them. I went to so many they started calling me "The Benefits Girl" and until I left New York for Hollywood, you could always find me marching in the streets at demonstrations for one cause or another with Pete Seeger, Burl Ives, Josh White, Leadbelly, Zero Mostel, and others.

I had never been exposed to anything like these causes at home and I was reminded of how isolated and backward we had been when I took my mother to an event at the Village Vanguard one night and Canada Lee, the great black actor, came over and asked me to dance. When I got back to the table, my mother said, "If your father were alive, he would have horsewhipped you."

This was probably true. My father once read in the paper that an

Annie Wright Seminary girl had married a sailor and he just flew into a rage. "If you ever marry a Jew, a nigger, or a sailor, I'll kill you," he said.

What amazed me about that reaction, then and now, is that he was not that way at all. He had been around black people back home in Missouri and he had Jewish friends. But they, of course, were "special," the great cliché of prejudiced people. That is the way he was raised.

To my mother's credit, she became very liberal-minded by the end of her life. We had a black maid who told her she did not want to work for a woman because she was Jewish and my mother just chewed her out. "It's terrible for you to say that," she said. "You of all people should know what prejudice is like." God bless my momma!

WHEN I AUDITIONED for the road company of *Meet the People*, Shelley Winters tried out at the same time. I got the job and she didn't, but Shelley pestered the stage manager to let her stay around anyway and learn the routines. And wouldn't you know it, the night before we went to Detroit one of the girls went to the hospital with appendicitis and who else knew the show but Shelley?! So we ended up rooming together.

At one point in our lives, Shelley and I had gone with the same guy, although not at the same time. One day in Detroit, I went to the theater and she was standing outside the stage door with an envelope in her hand. She was obviously very agitated.

"What's the matter, Shelley?" I said.

"Here," she said. "I found this on your dresser and I saw it was from Teddy so I thought it was for me so I took it. When I got to the theater, I saw it was for you so I read it."

"What?!"

"I read it," she repeated.

All I could do was laugh. "Oh, Shelley, I really don't care."

Later, she wrote to Teddy, "You really should be careful about what you say in your letters to Betty because she leaves them around."

But it was impossible to stay mad at Shelley for long. You just had to get used to the fact that everything she ever felt or thought or wanted just came rushing out. And besides, she has given me a lot of great stories to tell about her for all these years.

In 1942, The American Youth Theatre did a show called *Of V We Sing* that got a lot of attention in the press. It was not so much because of the jokes, although they were funny, or the songs, although they were clever. What really made the newspapers sit up and take notice was the fact that Lee Barrie, Adele Jerome, and I took our clothes off in a number called "You've Got to Appease with a Striptease." We sang:

> *You just loosen the League of Nations,*
> *And you drop international law.*
> *First you slip off a strip of Sudeten,*
> *Then you reach for a section of France . . .*
> *One by one you discard each treaty*
> *While the diplomats sit on their rumps.*
> *'Cause you've got to appease*
> *With a strip tease . . .*
> *And you've got to give them the bumps.*

By the time we were finished singing, we were down to slips and panties that had "Munich" or "America First" and a swastika on our behinds. All in the name of art and patriotism, of course. The headlines in the papers were "Stripping for the Axis."

We realized things were getting a little out of hand when the *Police Gazette* called and asked if they could take pictures of us doing this song. The *Police Gazette* was what passed for a risqué national publication in those more innocent days but we did not mind. Publicity was publicity.

The only problem was that Shelley Winters, who was not in the number, heard about the photo shoot, called the *Police Gazette*, and changed the time. By the time Adele, Lee, and I showed up, the pictures had already been taken and Shelley was the one who ended up in the *Police Gazette*.

The American Youth Theatre did another show called *Let Freedom Sing* that was taken over and financed by Joe Pevney and his wife, Mitzi Green, the former child movie star my father had admired so much. The show was not working in rehearsal so they brought in Robert Gordon, my dear director friend from Unity House. He pulled things together and brought in Harold Rome who dug a wonderful political number called "Sittin' on Your Status Quo" out of his trunk. Bob also brought in the comic Phil Leeds and we did a number dressed as kids with lollipops in our hands and another one satirizing war rationing in which we sang, "Your sister is a HOAR-der."

The show opened at the Court Theatre in New York and just got killed although my numbers were favorably reviewed. I will never forget Mitzi Green's graciousness about that. She gave a pep talk to the company, made sure we enjoyed ourselves during the short run, and has been my model of "grace under fire" ever since.

But even though *Let Freedom Sing* was a flop, I was lucky to have been in it because it led to my first on-Broadway show.

Don't Worry, Darling, Some Day You're Going to Be a Big Star!

C ole Porter was the most polite man I ever met, but he could not hide the fact that he was not at all happy to see me. He was not happy because I had made him come up to Boston on a Sunday morning late in 1942 and he was not happy because I, this Little Miss Nobody, was making him write a new song just for me.

The rest of his new show—*Something for the Boys*, starring Ethel Merman—had gone beautifully in tryouts and both Mr. Porter and Mike Todd, the producer, were sure it was going to be a big hit on Broadway. But not every song Cole Porter ever wrote was a good one and I think he wrote a bad one just for me. "So Long, San Antonio" may have been one of his worst.

The song opened the second act of the show and I played a war bride whose husband is stationed at an air field in San Antonio while she has to go home to Alabama. I sat on my suitcase in the railroad station and sang this sad, dreary song:

> *So long, San Antonio.*
> *Too bad we had to part.*
> *Please tell Private*
> *"Well-you-know"*
> *To take good care of my heart.*

Private "Well-you-know" was Cole Porter's dumb little joke about military security. The song opened the second act of this big happy musical and dragged it to a complete halt. On opening night in Bos-

61

ton, I knew I had laid a huge turkey egg right in the middle of the stage. There was no question they were going to have to cut it.

Mike Todd threw a big party at the Ritz Hotel to celebrate the opening, but I was so embarrassed I wouldn't go. Instead, I went down to the railroad station with Lou Mandel, who had come up from New York to see the show and was going back.

"Lou! They're going to fire me."

But Lou said, "Don't worry, darling. You've got a run-of-the-play contract. They can't fire you."

"They can't?"

"Not only that, they're not going to leave that dreary song in the show. They're going to have to write you a new song." And then, just like Warner Baxter in *42nd Street*, Lou said, "Don't worry, darling, some day you're going to be a Big Star!"

Lou had negotiated an unusual contract. In fact, he had manipulated a whole set of unusual circumstances.

Let Freedom Sing had been about to close a few months earlier when Lou arranged for us to tour on a circuit that took Broadway shows to Brooklyn and New Jersey. That gave it two more weeks of life, which was just enough time for Lou to drag Mike Todd over to see it.

Mike liked "Sittin' on Your Status Quo" and he liked me. He was producing a new Cole Porter musical, he told Lou, and I could be Ethel Merman's understudy. But Lou wanted more.

"I don't want Betty just sitting around in the wings for a year and maybe never getting on stage at all," he said. "She's got to have her own part with her own song, she's got to have a run-of-the-play contract, and she's got to be paid $250 a week."

These were unheard-of demands for an unknown, but Mike Todd was a gambler and he went for it. Without consulting the writer, the director, or the composer—without asking Cole Porter if he *wanted* me to sing a song in his show—he agreed to Lou's demands.

So there I was on a snowy Sunday morning at the Ritz Hotel in Mr. Porter's fabulous suite, which was filled with fresh flowers. No matter where he went, Mr. Porter always had fresh flowers. With him was his pianist, Lew Kesler, who hated me on sight!

"Well, dear, I understand we have to write you a new number," Mr. Porter said. "I thought San Antonio was a lovely song but maybe it just wasn't for *you*." (That sent a dagger right through my heart.)

Then he said, "Tell me, dear, what kind of songs *do* you like to sing?" And I said the two things guaranteed to make Cole Porter throw up: "Hillbilly songs and boogie-woogie."

I'll never forget the expressions on their faces. Lew Kesler just audibly went "Bleah!" But Mr. Porter, being the kind man he was, simply asked, "Let me hear you sing a hillbilly song."

So I turned to Kesler and said, "Just give me a little um-pa, um-pa in F." He played an introduction and, with all the gestures, I sang:

> *Where have ya been, Billy boy, Billy boy? Where have ya been,*
> *charmin' Billy?*
> *I have been to see my wife,*
> *She's the darlin' of my life.*
> *But she's a young thing*
> *What cannot leave her mother.*

I sang the whole song—cherry pie and all—and finished with a kick and a big "Yeah!"

After a long silence, Mr. Porter said, "All right, let me hear you sing a boogie-woogie song." So at ten o'clock on a Sunday morning in the Ritz Hotel in Boston, I sang, in my best impression of the Andrews Sisters:

> *In Harlem there's a little place where everyone goes,*
> *To see the way the washerwoman washes her clothes.*
> *If you like Boogie Woogie rhythm she's got a beat,*
> *Let the boogie woogie washerwoman give you a treat!*
>
> *Rub-diddle-ub-dub, That's just the way she rubs.*
> *Rub-diddle-ub-dub, She wears out all her tubs.*
> *She rubs and rubs her knuckles right on down to the nubs.*

And I finished with another kick and a "Yeah!"

The two of them looked dumbstruck. Finally, Mr. Porter said, "Thank you very much" and I went back to my room in the Touraine, a theatrical hotel in Boston, and cried some more.

But at five o'clock that evening, a manila envelope was delivered to my room and inside was a brand new Cole Porter song. I took it to rehearsal the next day and Jack Cole, the choreographer, and I arranged some simple steps to go with it. We put it in the show that night. The song was "I'm in Love with a Soldier Boy" and it went:

I'm in love with a solder boy
So in love with a soldier boy,
I'm in love with an Army man.
And can he send me?
Yes, he certainly can.

The last two lines of each verse were sung in a fast boogie-woogie rhythm. Cole Porter had put the two songs I had sung for him together! He had come up with a combination of hillbilly *and* boogie woogie.

Every moment that he's away
I just hang on the phone all day
And at last when I get his buzz
Say does it rock me?
Yes, it certainly does.

It was not the greatest song Cole Porter ever wrote, but there was something very charming about the way it worked in the show. In fact, it stopped *Something for the Boys* that night and it stopped the show every night for a year. Ethel Merman had an entrance that walked right into my applause and God bless her, if she didn't make me come out and take another bow.

When I told people about this later, they would say, "Oh, no, not Ethel." But to me she was just as generous as she could be. As for Cole Porter, he called and said, "Darling, you were wonderful." And Lou Kesler and I later became great friends. Isn't it nice to hear a show business story that ends happily?

AFTER *Something for the Boys* got to Broadway, Bill Johnson, the leading man, did a lovely thing for me. Bill was an excellent singer and as he saw me just belting out my one song night after night, he became very concerned. For all the dancing and acting classes I had taken, I had never had any training as a singer and Bill was afraid I might be doing some permanent damage to my voice.

"I'm giving you a Christmas present," he said. "Six months of lessons with my singing teacher." She was Madame Lazzari, a big wonderful Italian woman who got me through a bad time because I was starting to develop almost chronic laryngitis. She taught me how to sing properly, the laryngitis went away, and I have been grateful to Bill ever since.

One day at five o'clock, I was taking my lesson from Madame Lazzari when the stage manager called. "Ethel has laryngitis," he said. "You're going on tonight."

"What?!" I screamed, and I ran over to the theater. As soon as I got there, I started trying on Ethel's costumes, which was a problem because she and I were built completely differently. She was big-busted with no hips at all while I have no bust but do have hips. So they adjusted the costumes as fast as they could, I rehearsed with the orchestra, and then went back to Ethel's dressing room, which she had insisted I use. I was trembling with nerves and excitement when Ethel called.

"How ya doin', kid?" she croaked through a terrible case of laryngitis.

"Oh, Ethel. I'm so nervous."

And she said—and I think Ethel originated this line—"Listen, kid, if they could do it better than you, *they'd* be on the stage and *you'd* be in the audience."

Thank God I didn't learn until later that the theater management had wanted to close the show that evening.

Something for the Boys was a hit on Broadway and it had a Cole Porter score, but what the audiences came to see was Ethel Merman. As soon as they discovered she was not going on, the people who ran the theater said, the audience would want their money back. But Mike Todd, always the gambler, would not listen.

"Let's give the kid a chance," he said. "She's been rehearsing all year and she's going on. If she bombs, we'll close tomorrow." Then he sat down and wrote a classic speech for Bill Johnson to read in front of the curtain.

"Ladies and gentlemen," Bill said, "I'm sorry to tell you that Miss Merman will not be performing tonight. She's ill."

Of course, the whole audience just groaned. But Bill held up his hands for silence and said, "*But!* . . . we have with us a young lady who knows the part and we think she's wonderful in it. So I hope that those of you in front of the curtains will join us behind the curtains in wishing Miss Betty Garrett all the luck in the world. Who knows? Tonight, a *star* may be born."

Well, who was going to leave the theater after that? Nobody. I played the part for a week and hardly anybody turned in their tickets. And all because Mike Todd was a man who loved to take chances and had such a generosity of spirit about giving other people a chance too.

THE WEEK I went on for Ethel in *Something for the Boys*, Lou Mandel saw his chance. He knew Vinton Freedley had a new musical in the works and, just as he had dragged Mike Todd to New Jersey to see me the year before, he made sure Vinton Freedley saw me too.

Vinton was known as the high society producer on Broadway as opposed to Mike, who was a "street guy." Through the years, he had produced several Gershwin and Porter musicals and he always showed up on opening night in a tuxedo, white scarf, and high silk hat with all his Social Register friends in tow.

The show he was producing this time was *Jackpot* with Jerry Lester as the lead comic and I auditioned more for him than for Vinton because Jerry wanted to see whom he would be working with. I sang my famous rendition of "Billy Boy," Jerry broke up, and I got the job.

Jackpot was really a strange show. Vinton had produced a show called *Dancing in the Streets* that had starred Mary Martin and had closed on the road. He tried to save the score but Vernon Duke and Howard Dietz ended up simply writing similar songs instead.

Nanette Fabray and Allan Jones were the romantic leads and Jerry Lester, Benny Baker, Mary Wickes, and I (we called ourselves the Four Bananas) had a lot of numbers together. I played a top sergeant in the army—now *there's* casting for you—and Jerry sang a song to me called, "I'm in Love with My Top Sergeant." I came back with, "I'm in Love with My Buck Private," which always struck me as one of the most unattractive lyrics I have ever sung.

Everybody in the show got along famously and it reached the point where we could hardly bear to be apart so the Four Bananas all made up in the same dressing room. Nanette and Allan had the star dressing rooms on the first floor off the stage and we felt sorry for them because we were having so much fun upstairs.

On the road, *Jackpot* was a huge hit. We went on an extensive pre-Broadway tour—New Haven, Hartford, Boston, Washington, Baltimore, Philadelphia—and got rave reviews. The only bad notice came from a reviewer who called it the silliest show he had ever seen. But that was just one man and we took it as a compliment. We were certain we were going to be a smash when we got to New York.

Opening night on Broadway was one of Vinton Freedley's high society affairs, all tuxedos and evening dresses and noses so high in the air nobody could see a thing. And here we were in this goofy slapstick show at which they *did not laugh at all!*

It was at that moment I learned there is nothing more devastating for an actor than a complete lack of audience response. When you are used to laughs and they do not come, there is simply nothing you can do. I have heard athletes say that if they make a mistake they have to forget it and go on, just keep playing. But an actor can't forget it. You are up there feeding on the laughter and the involvement of the audience, and if it doesn't come, your timing goes off and you can't get it back.

Our opening night reviews responded to the audience and were just terrible, although after the high society first-nighters went home, we started getting the big laughs we had received on the road. But the reviewers just wouldn't let us up. They not only hated us on opening night, they kept on hating us.

They wrote Sunday pieces about how awful *Jackpot* was, and when they wrote reviews of other shows, they kept coming back to the big turkey playing down the street. Vinton Freedley was determined to keep the show open, though, and somehow we managed to run a couple of months before we finally had to give up. *Jackpot* was not the greatest show in the world, but it was the most fun.

WHEN *JACKPOT* CLOSED, Lou Mandel found me another nightclub job, this time uptown, a step up from the Village Vanguard in more ways than one. La Martinique was *the* nightclub in New York then—Danny Kaye had just performed there with great success—and though my act had not improved much, the reviewers were kind and the audiences were good.

What I was really hoping for then was another Broadway show but in the meantime Lou got me bookings at the Clover Club in Los Angeles and the Camellia House at the Drake Hotel in Chicago while he looked around.

Before I left New York, though, I discovered that Lou had more than nightclubs on his mind. Sam Goldwyn had just cast Danny Kaye in his first movie, *Up In Arms*, and they were looking for an actress to play opposite him. Danny was still Lou's client then and Lou wanted to get the role for me.

Lou and Sam Goldwyn were two of a kind. They had a lot of dealings with each other and they both knew how to battle and bargain. Sam would make certain demands and Lou had a way of saying, "I can't do that. If the shoe were on the other foot, would you want me to do that to you?" Sam understood that.

Lou took me up to see Mr. Goldwyn in his suite at the Ambassador Hotel on Park Avenue and the first thing he said was "Why do you all *do* that to yourselves?"

"Do what?"

"Pile up your hair like that. Do you have a hairbrush?"

My hair looked like just about every other woman's in the '40s, down in the back and built up into an exaggerated beehive in front.

I handed Mr. Goldwyn my hair brush and the next thing I knew he was sticking his fingers in, pulling all the pins out, and brushing it straight down. "There, now you look like a woman should look."

The part in the movie eventually went to Connie Dowling and I don't think my hair had anything to do with it. Connie's hair was lovely in the picture, though, all down and natural so it moved when she shook her head. I always wondered if Sam Goldwyn did her hair, too.

THE CLOVER CLUB was a Los Angeles gambling establishment they were trying to convert into a legitimate nightclub. It was very elegant, but a couple of weeks after my two-week engagement it closed for good. I hope it was not my fault.

On one of my first nights there, an old friend, Sam Locke, came by and said he had an idea that might interest me. Sam had written some sketches for the Flatbush Arts Theatre and the Barbizon Revue and was now involved with the Actor's Lab in Hollywood. This was the first of the small theater groups in Los Angeles to do new plays and innovative productions of the classics. It had a superior ensemble company that included performers such as Morris Carnovsky, Lee J. Cobb, and Ruth Nelson.

At this time, they were producing evenings of short theatrical pieces. One was an evening of comedy, Sam said, and they wanted to include a musical comedy number. "I've got a very funny Hollywood sketch," Sam told them, "and the girl who did it in New York is in town. I bet she'd do it for you." He meant me.

The sketch was one Sam had written for the Flatbush Arts Theatre. I played a starlet who is having her footprints preserved in cement outside Grauman's Chinese Theatre while she is talking to an interviewer.

I am this sweet, naive child with a drippy Southern accent who says, "I want to thank all my lovely producers and directors and writers, etc., etc., etc."

I go on so long that when I try to take my feet out of the cement, I discover I'm stuck. Instantly, I turn into this screaming virago with a Brooklyn accent yelling at the top of my lungs as all the ushers and bystanders try to pull me out. It was as if Marilyn Monroe turned into Barbra Streisand. Finally, they just pick me up and carry me shrieking offstage with the cement block still on my feet. I told Sam doing the sketch at the Actor's Lab sounded like fun.

A few days later, we went over to the theater to rehearse and after a while I noticed that a terribly good-looking guy was constantly sticking his head out from the wings. "Need anything?" he would say. "Everything all right?"

Finally, I just had to ask, "Who is that cute fellow who keeps popping in here all the time?"

"Oh, that's Larry Parks," somebody said, "He's the producer of this show."

So I was introduced to Larry and he asked me out. It was just supposed to be coffee at Brittingham's, a big cafeteria and bar near the Columbia Studios that was a gathering place for movie people, but Larry ordered champagne cocktails instead. That should have been a clue. Then he drove up to the top of Mulholland Drive where we looked down on the city.

"You're the girl I'm going to marry," he said.

"Sure I am," I said, not taking him seriously at all.

I was leaving for my club date in Chicago in two weeks, and Larry and I spent most of the intervening time together. We went to the beach and he told me later that was so he could see my legs. "If you had skinny legs, I couldn't have married you," he said. "But you have dancer's legs and I love those."

I had no trouble with Larry on that score, though. I thought he was simply gorgeous. He was a weight-lifter with a wonderful physique and when we walked down the beach together everybody always looked at him, not me.

As for the rest of him, Frank Sinatra once said, "I hate your husband."

Genuinely startled, I asked why.

"Because he has a noble head. My head looks like a walnut."

Looking back, I will never understand how Larry made up his mind about me so quickly because he was the kind of man who would do research to buy a toothbrush. It would take six months to buy a car, for instance, because he would visit every dealer in town and study *Consumer Reports* to make sure he got the best car at the best price. Once he told me he had a big crush on Barbara Stanwyck and that I reminded him of her. That is the only reason I can think of for his quick decision.

The more we talked during those two weeks—and in all our phone calls and letters in the weeks that followed—the more we realized that we agreed about almost everything. We had the same attitude about show business and our ambitions in it. Our religious background was the same, although neither one of us was particularly devout. Our political views were the same and our deep feelings for our families, too.

Once, Larry wrote, "Do you like onions? If you don't like onions, I can't marry you." I told him I liked onions just fine.

Another time, he said, "I have a confession to make. I once joined the Communist Party."

"Oh, good," I said. "So did I." It was not long before we realized we were just made for each other.

I had always been a pretty wild girl when I was in New York. I used to get engaged about every six months, it seemed, because I figured if you are in love you are supposed to get married. But thank God, something would click at the last moment and I would say, "No, I don't want to settle down," or "No, I don't want to spend the rest of my life with this person."

And, of course, I was dumped a couple of times myself. Once, I tried to make a list of all my boyfriends and I lost track. It is nothing I am terribly proud of. It just happens to be true.

Shortly after I met Larry, I was sitting in a coffee shop with Bob Russell, a song-writer friend, and Frank Tarloff, who had married Lee Barrie from my American Youth Theatre and "Stripping for the Axis" days. Frank later won an Academy Award for writing *Father Goose*.

"When are you going to stop flitting around and settle down?" Frank said. "Now that young fellow you introduced me to the other day," Bob added, "he's a nice guy and he seems to be crazy about you. What about him?"

He was talking about Larry and I said, "Well, that's a possibility." And as I said it, I realized it *was* a possibility.

The most important thing, I think, is that Larry and I were both at a stage in our lives where we were *ready* to get married. I was twenty-five, he was thirty, and we were just ready. That is what makes marriages work, I think.

If I still had any doubts, they were swept away when I met Larry's mother. She was living in Joliet, Illinois, where he was born and when I left Los Angeles for my club date in Chicago, Larry asked me to go see her. "Just promise me one thing," he said. "Watch your language."

I agreed it was a reasonable request. So on my day off from the Camellia House, I took the train out to Joliet and fell absolutely in love with Leona Parks—Larry called her Nenny. We hit it off instantly and soon she was dragging out Larry's baby pictures—one showed Larry dressed as a little farmer boy.

"Wouldn't it be wonderful if Larry and I could have a little boy like that?" I thought. One of the greatest joys of my life is that we ended up with two little boys like that.

Larry and I kept writing and he came to visit his mother and me in Chicago. Then we had to go our separate ways because he was starting production at Columbia on *Counter-Attack* with Paul Muni and I was going into rehearsals for a new Olsen and Johnson revue on Broadway called *Laffing Room Only*.

I went back to New York excited about the show but also feeling a little blue about being away from Larry too. By September, I was down to 119 pounds—I had weighed 125 for years—and one day my mother said to me, "I don't know what's the matter with you. I think maybe you'd better get married."

This was a shock because my mother had *never* said anything like that before. She had never really approved of any man I ever went out with, in fact. It was the only possessive thing about her. She would say, "I don't like that boy," and that was that.

But she had met Larry when she visited me in Chicago and he had impressed her the way he impressed everybody he met. I think that was the final straw.

Before *Laffing Room Only* started rehearsals, I called Larry and said, "I'm coming out. Do you want to get married?"

"When? What date?" We settled on September 8, 1944. We had known each other four months.

L A R R Y   W A S   the dirtiest-looking bridegroom you ever saw. He had a three-day growth of beard for his part in *Counter-Attack*, and because he was shooting until 7 P.M., we got married at nine o'clock at night. We had not had time to send out invitations and Larry's friends used to say he just went down the street and whenever he recognized anybody he said, "Come to my wedding."

Lloyd Bridges was his best man, but I had not met him or his wife, Dottie, until they arrived to take me to the church. Lloyd—everybody calls him Bud—and Larry had worked together at Columbia where they had become best friends.

Bud and Dottie lived out in the San Fernando Valley then and Larry gave him a lot of his gas coupons so he could get back and forth to the studio. After their son Beau was born, Larry gave him his meat coupons, too, because he felt they needed them more than he did.

Larry spent a lot of time at the Bridges house and Dottie, who was so impressed with the way he fed and played with Beau, became determined to find him a wife. It always frustrated her that he was never interested in any of the girls she picked out for him.

"I want a girl who's in the business," he would tell her. "I don't want someone who wants to talk about washing machines when I come home after work. And she's got to be talented and she's got to want to have children and she's. . . . " He had a lot of things on his list besides dancer's legs.

"You'll never find her," Dottie said, but she told me later that when we were riding to the church that night she said to herself, "Well, son of a gun, Larry found her." And Dottie and I formed a friendship on the spot that has lasted more than fifty years.

Since I had no father to give me away, I called Marc Platt, an old friend from my dance classes in Seattle. Marc danced in *Tonight and Every Night* with Rita Hayworth and several years later he and Larry took turns dancing with Rita in *Down To Earth*.

It took us a little while to get the wedding started. My cousin Caroline, one of Uncle Norris's twins, had come down from Portland to be maid of honor, but she did not have a nice dress so she had to go out and buy one on Hollywood Boulevard. It turned out to be too long so I had to hem it for her and that made me late for my own wedding.

The ceremony was at the Gardner Street Church on Hollywood Boulevard and since there was no vestibule Larry, Bud, and Mark Platt stood outside on the sidewalk and waited. Later, Larry said that as buses kept going by he seriously contemplated getting on one and going to Hawaii. Luckily, I was only ten or fifteen minutes late.

Larry and I had a one-month honeymoon on the beach in Malibu and then we lived apart for two years. I know it sounds like a terrible way to begin a marriage, but somehow it worked. In a way, in fact, it was almost ideal. We never fought, we were incredibly busy with our careers, and when we did get together it was like a honeymoon all over again. Sometimes, Columbia would send Larry to New York on a publicity tour—which was great because it was all paid for—or I would get a short vacation and go out to California.

Lou Mandel, who was Larry's manager by then as well as mine, was partly responsible for this arrangement. He did not want me to come to Hollywood and wait around for someone in the studios to hire me. Lou knew it did not matter who you were on Broadway if they did not know you in Los Angeles, and he was afraid I would settle into a domestic life and that would be the end of my career. And as much as I hated to leave Larry, I just could not imagine not working so there was never really a conflict.

This set a pattern we followed for many years. Several times, a job in New York or in a road company would come up and I would say, "I don't want to go. I'd rather stay home."

"You must do this," Larry would say. "It's a wonderful part for you."

And I never said to him, "Don't take that job. I want you here at home." From the very beginning, we both recognized the importance of each other's career and we never lost that feeling.

LAFFING ROOM ONLY was the nuttiest show I ever appeared in. In fact, I think it is the nuttiest show I ever heard of. There were more seltzer bottles, more shotgun blasts, more rabbits, more midgets falling out of boxes, more men wearing women's underwear than you could possibly imagine. The fact that I managed to get through four songs every night with all the crazy things going on still amazes me. I think the American theater really lost something when vaudeville died.

Olsen and Johnson were the stars of the show, but the comedian I really loved was Frank Libuse. He got his start as the original terrible headwaiter in Billy Rose's nightclub who insults people, hits them on the head with the menu, and puts them all in the wrong places.

In *Laffing Room Only*, he played a variation on this theme, the head usher. He told people they were there on the wrong night, showed them to the wrong seat, tore up their tickets, led them tripping over three aisles of people to get to their seats, pretended a woman had goosed him, and on and on. He was simply outrageous.

Once people finally did get to their seats, of course, they would turn around and wait for Frank to do the same thing to the next group of customers. The poor people who showed up last did not know what was going on while everybody in the theater was laughing at them as this bumbling usher was embarrassing them to tears. And for a grand finale before the curtain went up, Frank would crawl over the musicians into the orchestra pit and lead the overture.

In the show itself, Frank played the piano accompanying Margot Brandner, a statuesque, red-haired soprano. As she sang, Frank would do things in back of her such as fall off the piano stool. At the very end of the act, Margot would hit a high note and fly straight up into the wings. She had been on a harness all the time.

I had a number called "Stop That Dancing" and another one called "Boston Harbor," where we all wore Revolutionary War costumes and were supposed to be at the Boston Tea Party. The last line of the song was "You can get that way on tea." I was so naive I could not understand why people laughed at it. It was a long time before I learned tea was another word for marijuana.

I also did a striptease as a running gag throughout the show. I would come out in a gorgeous blue sequined cape, pull a brassiere or stockings or a garter belt out from under it and throw them to the audience. Then, at the very end, I would open the cape and be standing there in long underwear. Oh, for my days at the Neighborhood Playhouse when I insisted I would never be anything but a Serious Dramatic Actress.

The critics were not thrilled by *Laffing Room Only*, but the audiences adored it. We played the Winter Garden Theater a year and then had long engagements in Detroit and Chicago.

THE WINTER GARDEN THEATER was at 53rd and Broadway and my dressing room was in a great spot. It hung right over the street and on matinee days I could look down and watch all the action up and down Broadway.

One day, I saw the cop on the beat, who was also the guard for our theater, grab two eleven-year-old boys literally by the ears and drag them inside. He brought them up to my dressing room and said, "I caught these two young men trying to sneak into the theater. They *say* they're friends of yours."

One of the kids had big black shoe-button eyes, long eyelashes, and curly black hair, and the other one was a wiry little blond kid. They looked up at me with such pleading eyes that I just could not turn them over to the cop. "Yeah, they're friends of mine." The cop did not believe me for a minute, but he left them with me.

They were very thankful and I said, "Listen, if you guys want to see the show, let me know and I'll go down during the overture and open the side door and you can sneak in."

Their names were Howie Sobol and Marty Nedboy and they came to the show that Saturday and every Saturday after that. Sometimes they brought their whole neighborhood with them. They would bring me flowers—from a day-old florist's shop, I think—which by the time they had made it down from the Bronx on the subway were all wilted.

I often took them home after the matinee where my mother gave them pineapple juice and cookies—they were very impressed because they had never had pineapple juice—and they told me how much they wanted to get into show business. Howie's father was a burlesque comic and it was his big ambition to be a nightclub comedian, which was a step up.

He was always saying, "How do I get into show business, Betty? Tell me what to do." There wasn't much I could tell him, of course, except to keep trying.

Fade out, fade in: More than thirty years later, I was pushing my shopping cart in Gelson's market and a pudgy man with balding temples came up to me and said, "Betty Garrett? I don't know if you remember me. My name is Marty Nedboy."

Of course, I just fell on him and said, "Marty! My God! How *are* you? How is Howie? Did he ever get to be a nightclub comic?"

"Yeah," Marty said, "a pretty good one, too. But then he became a writer and now he's a director here in Hollywood."

I was doing *Betty Garrett and Other Songs* at the Westwood Playhouse then and I invited them to come. I could not resist telling the audience this story and when I finished, I said, "I think Marty and Howie are in the audience tonight. Are you there?"

And these two grown men, like the eleven-year-old kids they used to be, stood up and waved their hands. "Here we are, Betty! . . . And we paid for our tickets!"

Two weeks later, I joined the cast of *Laverne and Shirley* where Howie Sobol, by then known as Howie Storm, was my first director.

THERE WAS NEVER any doubt I would be in the cast of *Call Me Mister*. The director was my dear old mentor Bob Gordon from Unity House and *Let Freedom Sing*. The songs were by Harold Rome, who had written numbers for that show. And the musical director was Lehman Engel, who had been my music teacher at the Neighborhood Playhouse.

It was the spring of 1946 and the show was a revue celebrating the end of the war. "Call me mister" was what servicemen said when they took off their uniforms for good, and one of the qualifications for the men in the cast was that they had to have been in the service themselves.

The show was brilliantly conceived and put together, but one of the reasons it ran two years on Broadway was that it captured the mood of a country that was so relieved the war was over and was ready to get back to civilian life. For years afterwards, people would come up to me and say, "I saw that show right after I got out of the army and I can't tell you how much it meant to me."

The opening number was set in a railroad car where a group of soldiers was sitting and Larry Winters, who had a glorious baritone voice, started singing, "This train is a goin'-home train, this train. . . ."

One by one, all the other soldiers joined in like a gospel chorus. Soon everybody was singing, the words were overlapping as in a round, and the song was getting louder and more stirring every second. The effect was simply electric. You could feel the audience going, "Wow!" as it got into the spirit of soldiers going home, the war being over, the jubilation of the moment.

By the time the show segued into the next number, which was Jules Munshin leading a chorus of "Sound Off!", we could do no wrong. The audience was going wild. The show was five minutes old and already it was a hit. We did not need the reviews the next day to tell us—although they were all raves—we could feel the acceptance and the excitement in the air. It was the greatest opening night I have ever been a part of and as I thought back to the opening night of *Jackpot*, I had to laugh at the difference.

The songs I sang in *Call Me Mister* were written for me and they fit like a glove. One was called "Little Surplus Me" in which I played a waitress at the PX who wonders what is going to happen to her now that the war is over:

> *Once this lunchroom was crowded the whole day long—*
> *Full of laughing and wisecracks and song.*
> *Now here I stay, wasting away,*
> *Among the ham and eggs and cereal.*
> *Look at Me! And Whaddya see?*
> *Another piece of surplus war materiel!*
>
> *I'm just like a munitions dump-spot*
> *Loaded with old TNT,*

No one has room—no one goes boom for
Little surplus me.

See—
What are you gonna do with
Lonely deserted,
Unreconverted,
Little surplus me.

In another song, "Yuletide Park Avenue," I played an eighty-year-old dowager giving thanks to all the department stores in New York she has shopped at over the years:

Bergdorf-Goodman, Bonwit Teller, Henri Bendel, too,
All our thanks to you—heartfelt thanks to you.
Wanamaker, Lord and Taylor, also Best and Co. Ho ho ho ho.
Thank you, thank you so much, thank you, thank you so.

Arnold Auerbach wrote a funny sketch in which I played the mother of a man just back from the army (played by Glenn Turnbull) who had been told her son was now used to a lot of discipline. So I wore a helmet, carried a pistol, and screamed at him like a top sergeant. Shades of *Jackpot!*

I was having a ball rehearsing all this wonderful material and then one day it got even better. "We've got to give Betty another solo number," Bob Gordon told Harold Rome. "The songs she's singing now are very cute, but she's got to have something to stop the show."

In *Meet the People*, there was a song called "In Chichicastenango" and I had performed it many times at Unity House. There was something terribly funny about me, the least Spanish person you can imagine, singing this mad Spanish song. Bob mentioned it to Harold, who said, "I have a kind of Spanish song in my trunk, but it's not very good." He took it out for another look and it turned out to be very good indeed. It was terrific, in fact.

I sang "South America, Take It Away," as a worn-out hostess in a canteen where everybody is doing the latest Latin dances, while all I want to do is sit down and rest my aching back. I wore a fabulous blue dress with strings of beads that swayed with every movement I made and a big banner that said HOSTESS across my chest. Four guys in Army uniforms kept sweeping me out onto the floor to dance the samba, the conga, or the rumba while I kept complaining about it:

Take back your samba Ay! your rumba Ay!
Your conga Ay! yay, yay!
I can't keep shaking Ay! my rumble Ay!
Any longer Ay! yay, yay!
Now maybe Latins Ay! in their middles Ay!
Are built stronger, Ay! yay, yay!
But all this makin' with the quakin'
And this shakin' of the bacon
Leaves me achin'!
Olé!

First you shake it and you put it here.
Then you shake it and you put it there.
That's enough. That's enough. Take it back.
My spine's out of whack.
There's a great big crack
In the back of my sacroiliac.

"South America, Take It Away" became *the* big hit of *Call Me Mister.* It stopped the show every night and before long everybody in New York was talking about it, writing about it, and acting as if it were the funniest thing they had ever seen. To this day, I blush when I remember the reviews—and what Walter Winchell, Ed Sullivan, Earl Wilson, and the *New Yorker* magazine wrote about me—and that number was the major reason.

Imagine getting the Sunday *New York Times* and finding yourself dancing in a Hirschfeld drawing. Or picking up the *Herald-Tribune* and reading this from Nathaniel Benchley: "Would anybody like a poke in the nose? Very well, buster, all you have to say is you didn't like Betty Garrett in 'Call Me Mister.' Aha, I thought so."

I ended up winning the Donaldson Award—the forerunner of the Tony—for best performance in a musical. The other winners that year were Marlon Brando, Ray Bolger, Judy Holliday, Louis Calhern, Barbara Bel Geddes, and Paul Douglas. Not bad company.

I played in *Call Me Mister* for a year and toward the end, I was starting to get a little dingy. The rhyme scheme in the song was based on "samba, rumba, conga," but they came up in a different order in every verse so the next line would rhyme.

One night, I walked out on the stage and drew a complete blank. I could not remember a thing. I started singing, "Take back your father, Ay! your mother, Ay! your toothbrush, Ay! yay, yay!" and all the time Lehman Engel was standing in the orchestra pit shouting, "Samba! Rumba! Conga!"

Finally, he got me back on track, I finished the song and left the stage certain I was going to be bawled out or teased unmercifully. But nobody said a word. Either they did not know the difference or they thought it was part of the song.

> *I got a wriggle and a diddle*
> *And a jiggle like a fiddle*
> *In my middle. Olé!*
>
> *I think it's time to call a truce.*
> *I'm tellin' youse I'm shakin' loose.*
> *My poor caboose.*
>
> *All this goin' and this comin'*
> *To this fancy Latin drummin;*
> *Numbs my plumbin'.*
>
> *South America! Take it away. Olé!*

The cast recording of *Call Me Mister* was a big hit, too, but my version of "South America, Take It Away" was never heard on the radio. Somebody had decided that the line "There's a great big crack in the back of my sacroiliac" was dirty!

So the Andrews Sisters quickly recorded a version in which they sang, "There's a strange click-clack in the back of my sacroiliac." That became very popular on the air and in the record stores. I made peanuts on my recording!

But being a star in one of the biggest shows on Broadway—only *Annie Get Your Gun*, which opened a month later, was as big a hit—was what counted and it all seemed like a dream somehow. The dream only got better with the exciting news from Hollywood that there were soon going to be *two* stars in the family. Larry was going to get his chance.

You Ain't Seen Nothin' Yet

Not long after Larry came to Hollywood, he got a job as an extra playing a Roman guard in a biblical movie with camels in it. He was paid $11 a day and the camels got $25!

Later, Larry got a job playing opposite Arthur Shields, who was testing for a part in *Here Comes Mr. Jordan*. Shields didn't get the part but Harry Cohn liked the looks of the young kid who was just helping out and signed him to a seven-year contract for $75 a week. That started a period during which Larry might have made more B movies for Columbia than any other man alive.

His first picture was *Mystery Ship*, in which the lead was Paul Kelly, who had once served a sentence for manslaughter and was notorious for his short fuse. During the shooting, Larry dropped a piece of machinery on Kelly's foot and stood there paralyzed with fear, anticipating the famous temper. But Kelly just smiled and said, "It's all right, kid. I won't kill you."

Among the forty-one movies he made were *Harmon of Michigan*, with Tom Harmon, the star football player; *The Boogie Man Will Get You* with Boris Karloff and Peter Lorre; *Blondie Goes to College*, with Arthur Lake and Penny Singleton; and *Reveille with Beverly* with Ann Miller and Nat King Cole. There is a picture in Larry's collection of Nat at the piano that is signed "To Parky (one of Larry's nicknames). I'll always give you five—Nat Cole."

I have stills of Larry as an Indian boy playing opposite Yvonne De Carlo in James Fenimore Cooper's *The Deerslayer*, which had a huge cast that included horses, elaborate costumes and sets, the works. They made the entire movie, from beginning to end, in seven days!

Mystery Ship was the first movie in which Larry had a line to say and that's what it was, too. One line. It was a very important one, though, because a lot of special effects depended on it.

The movie took place down in the hold of a battleship where suddenly there was a big explosion and a flash of light and then a flood of water that rushed in and inundated everybody. Right in the middle of all this, Larry had to run in and shout, "Sir! We've been attacked by a submarine."

Larry rehearsed the line over and over.

"*Sir!* We've been attacked by a submarine."

"We've been *attacked* by a submarine."

"We've been attacked by a *sub*marine."

Finally, everything was ready. The set was absolutely quiet—no visitors allowed. The director looked around one last time and said, "Camera rolling . . . *action!*"

There was an explosion and a flash of light, and the wall of water broke through and engulfed all the actors as Larry came running in and delivered his line. But then the director yelled "*Cut!*"

Larry, who was standing there dripping wet in the middle of everything, looked over at the director, who was sitting there with his head in his hands.

He finally looked up at Larry and said, "We've been *subbed* by an *attack* marine?"

They had to do the whole thing over again.

In 1944, Larry began to get some roles in movies with bigger budgets (so-called A pictures). He got nice notices for his performance in *Counter-Attack* with Paul Muni and later starred opposite Evelyn Keyes in a Western called *Renegades*. Then Harry Cohn decided to do a film about Al Jolson.

In Hollywood, *The Jolson Story* was known as Cohn's Folly. Sidney Skolsky, a newspaper columnist, had peddled his idea for a movie biography of Jolson all over town and when Columbia finally bought it, everybody laughed and said who wants to see a movie about that old has-been? But Skolsky had idolized Jolson as an entertainer and finally convinced Harry Cohn.

At first, Jolson wanted to play himself. He even made a test, which I later saw. It was pretty awful. Jolson must have seen he was too old, too, but then he decided he wanted a big star to play the part. He had seen Jimmy Cagney play George M. Cohan and felt he deserved no less. And Harry Cohn was so nervous about the chance he was taking that he auditioned just about every actor in town.

Larry, who was on the Columbia lot the entire time, was the first person tested and finally, after almost a year, they came back to him. They put him in blackface, had him sing "Toot Toot Tootsie," and tested him again.

"That's it," said Cohn, and he gave Larry his first big starring role.

Jolson dubbed all the songs, but he was still unhappy that an important actor was not playing him and the filming got off to a slow start.

One problem was that the script was just a mess and Cohn assigned Sidney Buchman, a brilliant writer-producer at Columbia (*The Awful Truth*, and *Here Comes Mr. Jordan*) to fix it. Every day after shooting, Buchman, Larry, and Evelyn Keyes, who played Jolson's wife, would meet in the back room at Schwab's drugstore where Buchman would write the next day's scenes and Larry and Evelyn would rehearse. Buchman never got any credit for the script, nor did he want any. I think he did have a bit of a romance with Evelyn, though.

Things picked up after the studio bosses screened some of the first rushes.

"Wow! This is going to be a great picture!" Harry Cohn and the other Columbia executives thought. In all their planning for the movie and agonizing over it, there was one thing they had not counted on that was making it work brilliantly. It was Larry.

Once they saw the power of the combination of his acting and Jolson's singing, they knew they really had something and got behind *The Jolson Story* in a big way. They set up rehearsal space on a huge sound stage, assigned their best technicians, and pulled out all the stops. And Larry, who realized what was happening, was able to make some demands, too.

He insisted that he be given time to prepare each song to perfection. He may not have been a big star, but he was an experienced actor and he knew when to say "Don't rush me. Leave me alone until I learn this number."

I always thought Jolson's voice was better in *The Jolson Story* and *Jolson Sings Again* than when he was younger. The keys were set lower so his voice was richer and more powerful and came across beautifully on the sound track. And Larry, who brought an incredible energy to the role, was a fresh new face who had not been stereotyped in any previous starring roles, and that added to the whole effect. The amazing thing was that Larry had never seen Jolson perform.

To this day, people think Larry was mimicking Jolson, that he had copied his gestures from his movies, but that is not what happened. Warner Bros., Jolson's old studio, had passed on making the movie when it was first shopped around, but when Jack Warner learned his bitter rival Harry Cohn was making it he tried to get Jolson to bring it to him instead. Jolson stayed with Columbia, and Warner was so mad he would not let the studio borrow any of Jolson's movies.

Columbia even offered to have Larry go over and sit in the Warner Bros. studio and watch, but they would not give an inch. There was nothing anybody could do. The only performance Larry ever saw was in one movie, in which Jolson was part of an all-star cast and sang one number, "California, Here I Come," in blackface.

Jolson himself was not much help, either. He and Larry had one session together and it was clear he still was not happy that an unknown actor was playing him.

"Let me see what you're doing, kid," he said and Larry demonstrated one number. "No, no, you're moving around too much," Jolson said. "I'll show you how to do it."

He then proceeded to do everything but hang from the chandeliers! Jolson began pestering everybody so much they had to let him know he was not really welcome on the set. Finally, he got the message and went to Florida.

In the end, Larry played the part based on just the sound and the energy of Jolson's voice. Audrene Bryer, a choreographer who was also too young to have seen Jolson perform, set the movements, which Larry practiced in front of a full-length mirror in a rehearsal hall. And Truck Krone, a sound man and great jazz enthusiast, ran the playback machine when Larry practiced synchronizing his actions to the songs.

It's a wonder Larry did not go deaf making that movie. I came to Hollywood for a little while before *Call Me Mister* started rehearsals and when I went on the sound stage while Larry was working, the music was so loud I couldn't stand it. Larry stood next to speakers that I swear were twelve or fifteen feet square and while he was synchronizing the songs the sound just pounded on his body. He could hear Jolson breathe, he said. He could feel him begin to articulate each word. He even got laryngitis because he was singing as loud as Jolson so it would all look real.

Truck Krone would sit with his finger on the controls of the playback machine and turn up the volume so the music just blasted through the set. Larry would be singing "California, here I come . . ." and, in the musical intervals, Truck would make the orchestra go, "WAAHH, WAAHH," and give Larry what amounted to a kick in the pants. The music just pelted him with Jolson's energy and the essence of the man's performance penetrated his system. To me, it was proof of what a good actor Larry was.

People who knew Jolson have told me, "My God, Larry got him down movement for movement," which was ridiculous. When you see old Jolson movies, you recognize that Larry did not move like him at all, but he did capture his energy and vibrations—and ego. The synchronization of the songs was so phenomenal that one critic joked they seemed to be shooting down Larry's throat so that even his tonsils were synchronized. But what made it all work so well was that Larry did not do an impersonation of the man, he *became* him in a way no mere imitator could have.

The Jolson Story was a tremendous hit—it was Columbia's first real musical blockbuster—and the studio publicity machine worked overtime promoting the fact that I was in one of the biggest shows on Broadway at the same time Larry had become an overnight sensation in Hollywood.

My favorite memory from that time is climbing on a ladder at Radio City Music Hall and changing the marquee letter by letter from "The Jolson Story with Larry Parks" to "Larry Parks in The Jolson Story."

The effect of *The Jolson Story* went beyond that of just a movie. It revived Jolson's career in the last years of his life by giving him a radio show and allowing him to make new records. It even got to the point where young girls started screaming and falling down everywhere he went, the way they did for Larry. And Jolson adjusted to the part Larry had played in bringing him back into the limelight. They did one of Jolson's radio shows together and the interplay between them was charming.

I think the movie also softened Ruby Keeler's attitude toward Jolson. Their marriage had been a stormy one and Ruby was still so bitter that she insisted her name be kept out of the movie. She wanted absolutely no association with Jolson at all, she said. So Evelyn Keyes played a fictional Broadway star named "Julie Benson" in the movie, even though everyone knew it was really Ruby.

In later life, though, Ruby began to recall her good times with Jolson. I made several appearances with her and she talked about him without bitterness. She liked being remembered along with him, in fact, and told some sweet stories about their work and life together.

"I just didn't want my family disturbed with all the publicity," she said. Ruby was quite crippled by then—she could not walk without a cane—but she was still a bit of a ham. And by God, she could still dance. At the drop of a hat, she would get up and tap her little heart out while holding on to somebody for support.

SHORTLY BEFORE they began shooting *The Jolson Story*, Larry discovered his mother had cancer. Nenny had come out to California for our wedding and had not been feeling well so he sent her to a doctor who gave them the bad news. She never went back to Joliet, but just moved into the little house in Hollywood Larry had bought.

All during the filming, Nenny got sicker and sicker—I think she was operated on three times—and Larry would come home from the studio and try to take care of her as best he could. They were both going through so much hell and were so desperate that at one point they even brought in some quack with a machine that was supposed to cure cancer.

I finally moved to California shortly before Nenny died and until that moment I did not know just how much agony she was in. She was almost completely bedridden by then and taking enough painkillers, the doctors said, to kill a horse. But even they did not help much. Despite the medication, she was still quite alert. She would try to get up for dinner every night, but she would end up just sitting with us for a little while, sipping water.

One day, she called me into her room and said, "Get a pencil and paper. I want to give you some instructions. It will upset Larry too much if I try to talk to him about them." And then she gave me complete directions on how she wanted her funeral, who she wanted to conduct the service, and where she wanted to be buried: "In Forest Lawn, near a tree." And she gave me the full recipe for her watermelon pickles. "Larry loves them," she said.

Nenny's last days were the most agonizing I have ever seen anybody go through. Larry would not put her in the hospital so she stayed in bed at home, unable to lie still, tossing from side to side in pain. It got to the point where painkillers did not work at all so when she finally died it was a blessing.

Larry and I always believed she had hung on until I got to California to make sure her son was in a stable marriage. She just never understood this silly business of a husband and wife living three thousand miles apart.

When I saw what agony Nenny was in, it amazed me that Larry could make a movie that was so important to him and required such concentration at the same time he was trying to cope with her. It made me a little angry, in fact, that he had not let me know exactly what he was going through. He just would not let his emotions out if he thought it would distress me. This was not the last time that he would keep things from me, that he would refuse to tell me what he was thinking in times of trouble. And it was not the last time this attitude would frustrate me.

Nenny's condition was not a secret on the set of *The Jolson Story*, and when it was finished, Harry Cohn did a lovely thing. Before the movie was released, he brought Nenny by ambulance to a screening room where he set up a gurney in the aisle. I think she may have been the first person outside the studio to see the movie and that it may have done more good for her than all the medicine in the world. Cohn had the reputation as one of the meanest men in Hollywood, but that day he was one of the nicest.

LARRY NEVER REALLY knew how to feel about Harry Cohn. He was awfully hard to like sometimes, but he certainly knew how to make movies. He hired people with great talent, like Frank Capra and Sidney Buchman, and then he got out of the way and let them do their work. Creative people liked working at Columbia for that reason and despite all his flaws Larry admired him, too.

Cohn was also fond of Larry, but there was often an angle to his kindness. He dreamed up a publicity stunt where Jolson was supposedly so delighted with *The Jolson Story* that he gave Larry a car. It was actually Harry Cohn who asked Larry, "What can we do for you, kid?" and Larry jokingly answered, "You can buy me an MG." Cohn decided that pretending to have Jolson give it to him would get a lot of press and he was right.

Sometimes, Cohn would make other kinds of goodwill gestures.

When I was still in New York, he would call Larry and say, "Hey, kid, what are you doing tonight? You want me to send a girl over, someone real beautiful?"

"God, I could have had anything," Larry used to say. "Or anybody."

There were occasions when Cohn's largesse went even further than that. "You ought to have a nice big house, not that little one you live in," he would tell Larry. Or, "You're driving around that old Ford. That's not a car for a movie star." And he would offer to lend Larry money. Keeping his actors constantly in debt to the studios was a good way to keep them in line.

We were driving somewhere with Glenn Ford once and he told us, "I owe my whole life to Harry Cohn because of the money he has loaned me. It's good for me to get myself in hock because otherwise I'd be lazy. My philosophy is that if you overspend you have to keep working."

We thought that was really strange and luckily Lou Mandel did, too. He encouraged us to live modestly and not overspend just because we had good incomes, and Larry drove his MG for years. Finally, when our finances got a little better, we bought twin convertible Fords and often we would go places separately because he would be driving over from the studio and I would be coming from home. Afterwards, we would drive home side by side shouting back and forth from car to car.

ONE NIGHT during the run of *Call Me Mister*, Lou Mandel brought a heavyset, well-dressed man with white hair backstage after the show.

"Betty, I'd like you to meet Louis B. Mayer," he said.

It was all I could do to keep from laughing. What a sly dog Lou is, I thought. Always thinking ahead, always auditioning me for my next job while I was still working at the one I had. He had done it with Mike Todd, he had done it with Vinton Freedley, and now he was doing it with Louis B. Mayer.

Lou felt there was nothing more that I could accomplish on Broadway and he also knew that after two years of living apart it was time for Larry and me to be together. I was anxious to go to Los Angeles, of course—Nenny's illness made it particularly urgent—but I also knew the time was right professionally. I had spent five years getting started in New York and five years working steadily in one Broadway show after another, so moving to Hollywood made perfect sense.

"You were very good in the show, darling," Mr. Mayer said. "We must talk." It all seemed very vague to me, just a few hints, but it was not vague to Lou. The next thing I knew he had negotiated a one-year contract with MGM that paid $1,500 a week, which was not bad in those days and was $500 more than I was making in *Call Me Mister*.

This was just one more example of things falling into place for me with a minimum amount of effort on my part. Lou or Larry or even my mother always seemed to arrange things. One of them would say "You must do this" and I would say OK. It was never my driving ambition or brilliant planning that got me what I wanted. It was the people around me.

I can't count how many times my career seemed to be over and I never really felt any angst about it. I would think, "Oh, well, that's the end of that" and then, pow! all of a sudden I would have a ten-year career on the two biggest shows in television, or I would be back on Broadway in a musical at the age of seventy. I always felt there was some kind of good luck following me around and—with apologies to Tennessee Williams—I have always depended on the kindness of friends and family.

The publicity for *The Jolson Story* was at its peak around this time, and Larry and I were burning up the phone lines about finally being together when my contract with the show was up. The fact that MGM was noted for its musical comedies made the prospect of going to Hollywood attractive from a professional point of view, too. It was all so exciting. And then I got a call from Harry Cohn.

He was in New York, he said. Would I come over to his hotel for dinner? Well, of course I would and that is when I found out what a fox he was. We had dinner in his suite with a butler waiting on us—the full treatment—and we talked about Larry, the success of *The Jolson Story* and Hollywood in general.

Just to make conversation, I said, "I heard from Larry the other night. He was at a party at Evelyn Keyes's house."

"Oh," Cohn said. He raised his eyebrows and paused for a second. "He was at *her* house? Hmm."

"You old bastard," I thought. "You offer to send girls over to Larry and now you're implying something is going on between him and Evelyn Keyes."

I was not worried in the slightest because I knew what kind of man Larry was, although I have to admit that years later, when I read the autobiography Evelyn wrote, I thought, "If she says she slept with Larry, I'll die." I was relieved when she said he was always the perfect gentleman.

But I played innocent with Harry Cohn and pretended I didn't know what he was talking about.

"Oh, yes," I said, "Larry said it was a wonderful big party and he had a great time."

"Well, you know," Cohn said, "it's not good for a husband and wife to be apart. Why don't we make a few tests with you and see how you photograph and maybe you can be under contract at Columbia, too? We'll give you little parts to start with and you'll work your way up. It would be nice to be with your husband, wouldn't it?"

"Oh, yes. It would be very nice."

I never told him I had already signed a fabulous contract with MGM.

I ARRIVED AT MGM in January 1947 and the first thing I realized is that nobody knew who I was. Most of the producers and the top studio people on the lot didn't get to New York much, didn't read the New York papers, and couldn't have cared less about the stars of Broadway shows. It was another world to them and made me realize for the first time what a gulf there was between Hollywood and *anything* on the outside.

For months, I just wandered around the lot not knowing what to do. Even the famous MGM commissary, which was the studio gathering place, seemed a little forbidding. There was a writers' table, a producers' table, and a directors' table, and I didn't really belong at any of them. And when a picture was shooting, everybody from the cast sat at one table and anyone else was out of place. More than once, I looked in and then timidly backed out and went to the coffee shop and ate alone.

One day, I stuck my head in the door and I could hear someone shouting from across the room, "You're very talented!" It was Oscar

Levant, one of the few people who kept up to date on Broadway shows.

Another day, Ava Gardner beckoned me over to her table. "I'm so glad you're on this lot," she said. "You're the only one who dresses as sloppily as I do." I have loved Oscar Levant and Ava Gardner ever since.

Another problem was that when I arrived at MGM it was the home of so many truly beautiful women. Along with Ava, there was Lana Turner, Elizabeth Taylor, Esther Williams, and Hedy Lamarr. And then I came along, this kind of kooky lady with a big nose. I look at pictures of myself from that era now and think, "Hey, I wasn't so bad," but compared to them I was a dog.

Every once in a while somebody would give me a script and I would take it home and read it and say, "Why did they think of me for this part?" One was a war story with Clark Gable called *Homecoming* and Lana Turner ended up playing the part. I could have done it, I suppose, but what would have been the point? Obviously, nobody at the studio had any idea what I did.

The time I spent waiting around was not wasted, though, because I started working with Lillian Burns, an MGM acting coach. Lillian was married to George Sidney, the director, and was a very dynamic woman who was a perfect coach for the movies. She would act out a whole part with you moment by moment. Lana Turner, who worked constantly with Lillian, just swore by her and no wonder. I would see Lana's pictures and recognize Lillian's expressions in every scene.

Lillian helped me a great deal, too. "We have to make a test so everybody in the studio can see what you can do," she said. Here I was already under contract, but Lillian arranged an elaborate screen test that we shot in full technicolor with prerecorded sound over a two-day period.

I did a scene from *Born Yesterday* with Barry Nelson, a song from *Annie Get Your Gun* with John Raitt, and a solo dramatic scene from *Bury the Dead.* The test ended with me sitting in bed reading while the actor playing my husband, whose face you can't see, is sleeping. I put down my book and sing "I Don't Know Why I Love You Like I Do" and when I finish my husband turns over and gives me a kiss.

Lillian thought it would be fun to have Larry play my husband so she called Columbia and asked if he could come over and do it.

"Sure," Harry Cohn said, "if you'll loan me Gene Kelly for my next picture."

"But it's just a *test*," Lillian said. "Nobody off the lot will ever see it." Cohn would not budge, though, so I did the scene with Cameron Mitchell.

As the months went by, I became more and more frustrated about not being in a movie and a little concerned about what would happen when my contract was up.

And then I got my big break. Some actresses are discovered at drugstores. Some are discovered on magazine covers. Some are discovered in bit parts. I was discovered at Louis B. Mayer's birthday party.

Mr. Mayer's birthday was celebrated on the Fourth of July and it was a real holiday on the MGM lot. His long-time secretary, a marvelous little old lady named Ida Koverman, always put together a huge party in the commissary that everyone on the lot was *commanded* to attend. Even the biggest stars, who normally wouldn't think of going to something like this, were expected to be there.

The entertainment was usually provided by some of the top actors at the studio, but this year Ida decided to use the new contract players who had arrived during the past year. Ida asked me to be a part of it so I worked up a few numbers with my friend Sy Miller, a fine studio musician and composer who was my accompanist at the time.

The only problem with Ida's plan was that all the new actors at the studio that year except me were children. The mistress of ceremonies was a little British girl named Katharine Beaumont who had done Sleeping Beauty for Disney and had a veddy, veddy cultured voice. She was about twelve years old but she sounded like Beatrice Lillie as she stood up with her little piece of paper and said, "I should like to introduce my veddy good friend, Frankie Day."

Frankie Day turned out to be a nine-year-old girl dressed in a sequined costume with black satin shorts, bow tie, and silk hat and carrying a cane. She came out singing a hot little number that went "Here comes Bigtime Frankie Day," while doing a tap dance. Every time I see a child doing something like that, I want to strangle the parents.

The second performer was a girl named Laura Campbell, who was fourteen years old, quite plump, and looked like Queen Elizabeth as a little girl. She sang an operatic aria in a pure little soprano voice, and as I glanced around I could see people like Spencer Tracy, Joan Crawford, Clark Gable, and Greer Garson looking as if they would rather be anywhere else in the world.

Then Katharine Beaumont stood up and said, "I should like to introduce my veddy good friend, Betty Garrett." I had never seen this child before in my life, of course.

For some reason or other, I had decked myself out in a white crepe dress with a huge red poppy on the skirt with a green stem winding up around over my shoulder. I had a big black hat with a red poppy on it, long black gloves, and high-heeled ankle-strap shoes. I had never dressed like that in my life and I looked like a junior Hedda Hopper.

I looked around at the audience and it was one of those magical moments when you just happen to say what is on everybody's mind. "I think I'm a little old for this program," I said and they all fell apart. I'm not sure I have ever had a bigger laugh, on or off stage. I particularly remember seeing Frank Sinatra nearly falling off his chair.

Well, after that, I could do no wrong. Everything I said, they laughed at. Every song I sang, they applauded. Jimmy Durante came on after me and did his routine where he ends up breaking a piano into a thousand pieces, which made everybody laugh even more. Mr. Mayer's birthday party was a big success that year and the next day I was called into four or five producers' offices and walked around the lot with at least that many scripts under my arm.

BIG CITY had one of the most ridiculous plots imaginable. Even by Hollywood standards, it was preposterous. A baby is found abandoned on the doorstep of a New York brownstone where a Jewish rabbi, a Protestant minister, and an Irish cop live on different floors. They all fall in love with the child and a judge rules they will take care of her together until one of them gets married and then he will get full custody.

Everything is fine for a while, but then the policeman falls for a nightclub singer—she is really a stripper but you could not say that in the movies then—who also loves the little girl. The dancer takes her to Coney Island, where she shows her how to paint her nails and use lipstick, teaches her the bump and grind, and lets her get sick on hamburgers and cotton candy.

Everybody starts to worry that the policeman might marry this disgraceful woman and they end up in court where the dancer has a tearful scene in which she says, "I may be from the wrong side of the tracks but I know how to love a child."

The child becomes so upset she runs away, which makes everybody realize how selfish they have been. It all ends up happily with the entire cast of the movie standing around the piano singing "God Bless America." Just your good old basic MGM plot.

Big City was actually so dumb that it was wonderful and the best thing about it was the cast. Joseph Pasternak, the producer, had a thing about casting actors in parts completely opposite from what you would expect. So Danny Thomas played the rabbi. Lotte Lehman, the famous opera singer who played his mother, sang an Irish folk song to her supposedly Jewish son, who was really a Lebanese comic.

Robert Preston played the minister, George Murphy was the cop, Margaret O'Brien was the little girl, Edward Arnold was the judge and I, in my first movie role, played Shoo Shoo Grady, the nightclub performer. I sang one of the world's truly silly songs in the picture, "Ok'l Baby Dok'l."

> *Ok'l Baby Dok'l, Ike'll like'll love'll you*
> *If you'll Ok'l Baby Dok'l love'll me.*
>
> *Ok'l Baby Dok'l, Ike'll like'll hug'll you*
> *If you'll Ok'l Baby Dok'l hug'll me.*

Later in the movie, Margaret O'Brien sang it, too, and I had to laugh when I saw she had hammed it up more than I did. I also sang "Don't Blame Me" with the Page Cavanaugh Trio. It's a lovely song but I can't hear it to this day without laughing. It was my first experience with prerecording, which is singing the music first and synchronizing your mouth and actions to the sound later.

In order for the singer to know when to come in during the actual filming, they put a little mechanical noise one beat before every phrase and sometimes even in the middle of a phrase if there is a pause. As soon as you hear it, you know when to start mouthing the words. Larry told me that at Columbia the noise was a little "pop" so when he was doing *The Jolson Story*, he would hear "pop-pop, though April showers, pop-pop, may come your way. . . ."

At MGM, though, they had to do things bigger and better than anybody else. The first time I brought home "Don't Blame Me," I put it on the record player and fell on the floor laughing. Instead of a little "pop," MGM's sound cue was a loud "PPTTHH, PPTTHH." It sounded like something Spike Jones had dreamed up, a fart before every phrase.

"PPTTHH, PPTTHH, Don't blame me, PPTTHH, PPTTHH, for falling in love with you, PPTTHH, PPTTHH." I simply could not sing the song with a straight face, which was pretty embarrassing when we were on the set. It took all the discipline I had ever learned on Broadway to finally get through it.

Larry and I had never really had a proper honeymoon so after the filming was completed, we went skiing at Mount Hood in Oregon. If you were under contract, you were not allowed to make a move without letting the studio know where you were so I gave them the number of the ski lodge and we drove up the coast.

We had no sooner arrived than the studio called. I had to come back right away for some looping, which meant they had to replace something on the sound track that had not been recorded properly.

"But I just got here. Do I have to do it right now?"

"Yes, you do."

So I drove from Mount Hood to Portland, flew to Los Angeles, and took a cab to MGM. The sound man gave me a pair of earphones so I could hear the part that needed to be redone while I was watching the action on the screen.

Something had gone wrong during the final scene when we were all singing "God Bless America" and it had happened just as the camera panned across me while I was singing "From the mountains. . . ." So I watched it once or twice and then, in time to what I was doing on the screen, I sang, "From the mountains. . . ."

"Good," the sound man said, "that's fine."

"Is that all?" I said. "Couldn't you have gotten anybody else to do it?"

"We tried, but there is nobody in this studio who sounds like you."

I got back in the cab, went to the airport, flew back to Portland, picked up the car, and arrived back at Mount Hood at three in the morning. Larry woke up as I stumbled through the door and said, "What was that all about?"

I thought a second and then I sang out, "From the mountains. . . ."

BIG CITY had still not been released when my MGM option was up and I was nervous about what would happen. Were they going to keep me? Were they going to let me go? It was all quite agonizing. And then, the day before the year was over, Ida Koverman summoned me to Louis B. Mayer's office.

Mr. Mayer was sitting behind a *huge* desk and in front of that desk there was a little chair for me. A very slippery little chair, I soon discovered.

Mr. Mayer had a reputation for being a crier. He could make big crocodile tears pour down his face as well as any actor. And what a performance he put on for me that day. He cried, he yelled, he whispered, he pounded his desk, and said things like, "I *told* Helen Hayes to go back to New York because she was no good for pictures."

"Uh-oh, they're not going to pick up my option," I thought.

"I *knew* when Katharine Hepburn wore that red dress to that political rally, people would think she was a Communist!" he said.

"Uh-oh, he's heard something about my politics," I thought.

"I *told* Mickey Rooney not to marry Ava Gardner—he'd ruin her."

I didn't know what to think about that one. And all the time he was crying real tears. Then he got around to me.

"I saw you in that Broadway show," Mr. Mayer said, meaning the night Lou Mandel had brought him to see *Call Me Mister*. "You were pretty good, but I didn't know how you'd come across in the movies. But when I saw you in that love scene with George Murphy [in *Big City*] . . . well. . . ."

He got up and walked around the desk and stood right next to me, his huge belly hanging over me. "When I saw you in that love scene with George Murphy, I knew every red-blooded man in the audience would want you for his girl."

"It's not enough to have it in your head!" he yelled, and he poked me in the head. "You've got to have it in your heart!" and he poked me in the heart.

Then he came around behind me and put his hands on my shoulders and shouted, "To have a career today is a great *weight* on your shoulders!" On the word "weight," he pushed me down so hard I slid right off the chair. He didn't even notice.

Then Mr. Mayer walked over to the door and I thought, "Oh,

good, it's time to go!" But then he got around to what I guess was the point of the conversation.

"It's all very well, my dear, to have a husband and a family, but it's even more wonderful for a woman to have a career. It keeps her independent! Besides, when you get pregnant it upsets the shooting schedule!"

"Oh, yes, Mr. Mayer. Oh, no, Mr. Mayer." I found myself promising never to have any children!

"Good, good," he said. "I can see you're a girl with her *head* in the clouds (poke, poke) but you've got your *feet* on the ground." And he *stamped on my toes!*

"Aaaaah, thank you, Mr. Mayer. Goodbye, Mr. Mayer." I hobbled out of his office.

I limped past the receptionist who said, "Congratulations, Miss Garrett."

"What for?"

"Your option has been picked up."

And that's how I found out!

AFTER THAT FIRST YEAR at the studio, things changed overnight. I went from having nothing to do at all to making one movie after another.

Within just a few years, I played opposite Mickey Rooney in *Words and Music,* Frank Sinatra in both *Take Me Out to the Ballgame* and *On the Town,* and Red Skelton in *Neptune's Daughter.* I was in movies with Judy Garland, Gene Kelly, Esther Williams, and Jules Munshin, my old pal from Tamiment and *Call Me Mister.* And I played pretty much the same part in all of them. I was either the kooky sister of the leading lady, the man-crazy best friend, or the tough gal with the heart of gold.

It simply was not part of the movie formula then for the leading lady to be a comedienne. I had always loved Carole Lombard and Jean Arthur when I was growing up because they were glamorous and still funny, but nobody was making screwball comedies anymore and musicals followed a very strict form.

When we were doing *Take Me Out to the Ballgame,* I asked Stanley Donen, who was the choreographer, why I wasn't picked to play the leading lady. She was the owner of a baseball team and the kind of feisty character I could play. Stanley just looked at me as though I were crazy. In those days, the leading lady simply had to be "glamorous" and I just was not thought of that way. It was not until Judy Holliday came along that they broke the mold and realized a leading lady could be funny, too.

Looking back now, though, I realize that I was lucky to play the parts I did because they were more interesting and funny than typical movie heroines. I would see a lot of old musicals and think, "God, I'm glad I didn't have to play *that* dumb part. That would have been so boring."

Not to put too much social import into it, but the characters I played were really modern women. They had jobs, they went after what they wanted—including men—and they were just more fun. A reporter interviewed me for a magazine article around that time and her first question was, "How does it feel to be the ugly duckling in all your movies."

"I don't think I'm *ugly*," I said, but I guess I didn't think of myself as being all that attractive, either.

MICKEY ROONEY is the only person I have ever worked with who absolutely wore me out. His energy was simply overpowering.

When we were making *Words and Music*, we would finish a scene and he would say, "Want to hear me play the trumpet?" and he would drag me to his dressing room and play the trumpet. Then he would say, "I just wrote a wonderful song," and he would sit down at the piano and play. "You want to dance?" he would say and he would pick me up and dance me around the room. He was hyper and completely crazy.

One day, I finally said to him, "Mickey, I have to lie down. Leave me alone."

But what a genius he was to work with. He had a photographic memory and would walk on the set in the morning, pick up the script and say, "Is this what we're doing today?" He would look down at the script, turn the page, look again, and turn the next page. Once through the script and he would never look at it again. He would have it memorized.

As for *Words and Music*, it was one of those big-budget, all-star MGM musicals in which dozens of singers appeared. Lena Horne,

Judy Garland, Gene Kelly, Perry Como, just about everyone on the lot was in it. The movie was really just an excuse to put together a lot of glorious Rodgers and Hart songs, but it also masqueraded as a biography and the plot was simply a crock.

Mickey played Larry Hart and I played his girlfriend, which was a laugh because Hart's homosexuality was the worst kept secret in show business. I used to tell people I was playing Doc Bender, Hart's long-time paramour.

I had actually met Larry Hart in New York a couple of times in a restaurant called Ralph's on 45th Street. Ralph was very kind to actors and would lend them money or even let them sleep upstairs above the restaurant in an emergency. He did not mind if you sat all evening over a cup of coffee.

Sometimes you would be sitting there late at night and this little person would walk by and stand there with his chin practically on your table and just listen to your conversation. That was Larry Hart. He was really not much taller than the table and he would look from one person to another and smile while you talked.

If you said, "Larry, come sit down, join us," he would say, "No, no, I'm just listening." And he'd stand there, smiling. Then he would walk over to another table and listen in on someone else's conversation. Once, when I was sitting with Jackie Leonard, the outrageous irreverent comic, Larry came up and rested his chin on the table. "Who ordered John the Baptist?" Jackie said.

In *Words and Music*, they gave me one of my favorite Rodgers and Hart songs to sing, which was not as well known as it is today. The only place I had ever heard it, in fact, was at a jazz club on 52nd Street where Mabel Mercer sang:

> *Behold the way our fine-feathered friend*
> *His virtue doth parade.*
> *Thou knowest not, my dim-witted friend,*
> *The picture thou hast made.*
> *Thy vacant brow and thy touseled hair*
> *Conceal thy good intent.*
> *Thou noble, upright, truthful, sincere*
> *And slightly dopey gent.*

101

The legend is that Larry Hart wrote "My Funny Valentine" to himself. When he wrote

> *Is your figure less than Greek;*
> *Is your mouth a little weak,*
> *When you open it to speak,*
> *Are you smart?*

he was really making painful little jokes about himself. It was not only a lovely song, but it was so appropriate to the situation in the movie, which was where Mickey Rooney and I first meet.

But when the studio muckety-mucks saw the rushes in the screening room, they said, "What's that song? Is that a Rodgers and Hart song? That's a dumb song." And they cut it out of the picture. They replaced it with "There's a Small Hotel," which is a lovely song, but not right for the moment in the film.

Of course, "My Funny Valentine" became one of Rodgers and Hart's all-time standards. In *Betty Garrett and Other Songs*, I sing it to pictures projected on the back wall of the stage to my own funny valentine, my own Larry.

But that was not the only song that was cut out of *Words and Music*. Just before the end, Mickey Rooney wanders past a sleazy bar and sees the name of the girl who supposedly broke his heart years earlier on the billboard. He goes in and finds I have become a faded nightclub singer who is down on her luck and is on a tiny bandstand singing "It Never Entered My Mind."

I recognize him and come over to his table where we have one of those painful conversations where neither person knows what to say.

"How have you been?"

"Oh, OK. Wrote a little show."

"Oh, yeah, I read about it."

Finally, he gets up from the table, walks out into the rain, has a heart attack, and dies.

Again, it was just perfect for the situation, but when the studio people saw it, they said, "Oh, my God, that's so depressing! It's too sad. We can't do that." And they cut that song, too. I understood because it was depressing, but it was a shame because "It Never Entered My Mind" is another of Rodgers and Hart's greatest songs.

After a while, I discovered this kind of thing went on in Hollywood all the time. Larry and I used to go to parties where Judy Garland would get up and sing and invariably someone would ask her to do "Boys and Girls Like You and Me."

> *Boys and girls like you and me*
> *Walk beneath the sky.*
> *They love just as we love*
> *With the same dream in their eye.*
> *Songs and kings and many things*
> *Have their day and are gone.*
> *But boys and girls like you and me*
> *We go on and on.*

The lyrics are lovely and the tune is simply ravishing. When I asked Judy about it she said Rodgers and Hammerstein had written "Boys and Girls" for *Oklahoma*, but it had been cut. Later, she had sung it in *Meet Me in St. Louis* and it had been taken out again. Not long afterwards, it was our turn.

In *Take Me Out to the Ballgame*, there is a scene at a clambake where Frank Sinatra makes a fool of himself over Esther Williams but she is crazy about Gene Kelly. Then he walks over to me and we talk about how people don't always realize that another person is really the right one for them.

All of a sudden, Frank says, "Kiss me," and in that wonderful short-hand that exists only in the movies, we are in love. We go for a walk on the pier and he sings "Boys and Girls" to me.

There I was with Frank Sinatra, whom I had had a crush on for as long as I could remember and he was singing a beautiful love song to *me*? What a thrill. I wore a hot pink polka dot dress and had pink ribbons in my hair as we walked on the pier and when Frank finished singing, he kissed me. Then they cut it out of the picture!

All through the filming of the scene, they kept telling Frank he was singing the song too slowly and prodded him to speed it up. But Frank said, "No, this is a languorous, beautiful song and you can't rush it."

I listened to this argument and all I could think was, "They're telling *Frank Sinatra* how to sing a love song?"

Years later, I was on a television show with Dinah Shore and when she asked me what I wanted to sing, I told her the story about "Boys and Girls" and she said, "Great, that's what you'll do." So it was all set when one of the composers' estates said they had future plans for it and again it was cut!

And some time after that, our scene from *Ballgame* was supposed to be in *That's Entertainment III*, which included a lot of outtakes from MGM musicals. And believe it or not, it became an outtake one more time! Luckily, modern technology came along to save the day and Frank's version did make it to the laser disc of *Ballgame*.

But my favorite story about songs that ended up on the cutting room floor is not from one of my movies, it is from one of Larry's.

There is a scene in *The Jolson Story* where Jolson goes to a party and everybody says, "Sing us a song."

Jolson says, "All right, but I'm not going to sing one of my regular songs. I want to sing something from my childhood." And he sings a song entirely in Yiddish called "*A Chazzandl Oif Shabas*"—A Cantor for the Sabbath.

The song is about the people of a small European village who want to hear a famous cantor when he comes to a nearby town. But they can't all afford to go so they delegate three men—a tailor, a cobbler, and a teamster—to hear him and then report back.

The tailor returns and says the cantor sang the prayers as if he were pulling a needle through silk and pushing his steam iron.

Macht der Schneiderel,
Azai vif tee,
mit die nadel a tzie
. . . mit die bigeleizen
a forra horr

The shoemaker says the cantor sang as if he were pulling on leather straps and banging his hammer.

Macht der Schusterl, . . .
Azai vif tee,
mit die Petettsvay a tzie,
. . . mit die Hammerel a Kloppeler

The teamster says the cantor prays as if he were pulling the horse's reins and cracking his whip.

> *Macht die Ballagulla, . . .*
> *mit die Laitches a tzie*
> *mit'n beich a Schneit arein.*

And they each sing the refrain: "That's how he prayed!"

> *Oh, ho-o*
> *Vo-vo-vo . . .*
> *Hot er Gedavent!*
> *Hot er Gedavent!*

It is a charming song and was so wonderfully different from everything else in *The Jolson Story*.

Larry worked for weeks to learn the song phonetically and synchronize it for the movie and he was very pleased with it. But when they previewed the movie in Santa Barbara, the cards filled out by the audience afterwards showed they didn't care for "that song." It was also extremely long—seven minutes, I think—so they cut it out of the movie.

Larry was very disappointed, but the song was not wasted. He sang it in the shower almost every day of his life. After a while, I knew it pretty well myself and I am kind of proud of the fact that when I sing it to people who understand Yiddish, they say my accent isn't too bad. Of course, I might have had a little head start because "*A Chazzandl Oif Shabas*" was one of the most popular numbers Danny Kaye used to sing when he came up to White Roe Lake.

AFTER GOING to the premiere of *Words and Music*, I cried all the way home because I just hated the way I looked. I thought I came across looking like a giant next to Mickey Rooney and I did not like what they had done to my hair. The styles from that period were not attractive on me. Also, I thought my nose looked monstrous and was determined to do something about it some day.

But if I was disappointed in that picture, the next ones more than made up for it.

Come Up to My Place,
Baby, It's Cold Outside

The first time I see Frank Sinatra in *Take Me Out to the Ball-game*, he gets knocked out by a baseball. I rush out onto the field and carry him back to the stands, having just fallen madly in love with him. They were going to have a double do the scene, but I said, "I can do it."

"No, no," they said, "you can't carry Frank all that way."

"Believe me," I said, "I can carry him."

So I got in the middle of the huddle of people around Frank, they lifted him up, put him over my shoulder and I carried him off the field. Then I got to say my favorite movie line of all time.

Esther Williams, who owns the baseball team, comes up and says, "What's going on?"

I turn to a bystander and say, "Who's she?"

"She owns him," one of them says.

And I get to say, with a glint in my eye, "Can she *do* that?"

In a later scene, Stanley Donen, the movie's co-choreographer, had me put Frank on my shoulders during a number and swing him around. (He hardly weighed more than a feather in those days.) For the rest of the picture the big joke was that "Betty Garrett could carry Frank Sinatra any day."

Making *Ballgame* and *On the Town* at MGM was pure joy and Frank was an absolute delight to work with. He won my heart the first day on the *Ballgame* set when they had finished shooting a closeup of him over my shoulder. They were getting ready to move the camera for another shot when Frank said, "Wait a minute. What about my girl here?" And he made them reverse the camera angle and shoot my closeup over his shoulder, too.

107

There was that kind of sweetness about Frank, which contrasted with his tough talk that revealed his street-kid side. Gene Kelly did the choreography for *Ballgame* and *On the Town* and he was concerned about Frank's dancing ability so he made the steps as simple as he could when they were dancing together. When we saw the movie, though, we realized that Frank more than held his own. He danced up a storm.

But Frank was not always the hardest worker in the world and when Gene made his debut as a director with *On The Town* he got a little nervous at one point because we were running over schedule. Frank had been goofing off—just kidding around and not paying attention—but then he realized what was happening and stayed with Gene during the lunch hour to help him, acting as a stand-in while they set up the camera shots for the next scene. That was Frank, thoughtless one minute and then making up for it by doing something very kind the next.

I played Shirley Delwyn, a mobster's moll, in *Ballgame* and Brunhilde Esterhazy, a taxi driver, in *On the Town* and I spent both those movies chasing Frank. We rehearsed the musical numbers for a week or two and they were real rehearsals, just like in a Broadway show.

There is a scene in *Ballgame* where I chase Frank up and down the bleachers and sing "It's Fate, Baby, It's Fate." It was carefully staged by Stanley Donen, though the picture as a whole was directed by Busby Berkeley.

Busby had long been famous for his high "dolly" shots of huge chorus lines dancing in kaleidoscopic patterns. In *Ballgame*, he was determined to get the entire ballpark in one shot. The camera was mounted high on a crane so it could shoot down on the action below and Busby kept shouting "Back! Back! Farther back!" to the cameramen.

Gene Kelly, who stood there taking this in, muttered, "Yeah, back to 1930." By Gene's modern standards, Busby was hopelessly dated, but now when you see those scenes you realize what a showman he was.

I was astonished at how they came up with some of these shots. When we showed up for that scene in the bleachers, the ballpark was empty and there was a lot of junk left over from other movies in the back of the stands. "There are supposed to be crowds here," I said.

"Where are the people? And what about all that stuff in the back there?"

"Don't worry," they said. "It all gets painted in frame by frame," and they described an incredible process called Newcomb that they used to paint the crowds in the bleachers and cover up anything they did not want. Nowadays, of course, computers do it all much quicker and more easily.

The entire MGM lot was a magical place. You could walk from one street to the next and go from New York to China to a lake with the ship from *Mutiny on the Bounty* sitting in it. It was the same with the Columbia back lot. The Manhattan street where we shot *My Sister Eileen* was there, complete with a subway station, and the park where we shot the song and dance "Give Me a Band and My Baby" in the gazebo at night. The back lot at MGM is gone now—what a shame.

ON THE TOWN is a real classic that audiences will be watching forever, I think. It would have been better, though, if they had used all the original music from Leonard Bernstein's score and the original lyrics by Betty Comden and Adolph Green.

The only numbers they kept from the Broadway show were the opening song, "New York, New York," and "Come Up to My Place." The others were all written for the movie and frankly they did not measure up. I once heard Gene Kelly explain why they cut out those other great Bernstein numbers and his explanation made no sense to me at all.

He said that after a show opens on Broadway and the album comes out, the songs are old hat by the time the movie is released. This simply was not true of *On the Town*, which did not get a lot of play by disc jockeys so the songs were not overplayed. My opinion is that it showed a lack of respect for the audience's intelligence. The studio thought the songs were too sophisticated for moviegoers to understand. So they took out songs like "Lonely Town," "You Got Me, Gabe," and "Some Other Time," and replaced them with songs that in my opinion were not as good.

I do have to admit that one of the numbers they substituted, "Prehistoric Man," was pretty funny. We were all supposed to be at the Museum of Natural History, acting very silly and parading around to tom-toms as Ann Miller did a tap dance among the displays of stuffed animals. At one point, we knocked over a huge model of a dinosaur and that led to my favorite line in the movie. Two cops hear a call on their car radio to go to the museum where a dinosaur has just collapsed. "Oh, that's too bad," one of them says. "She was my favorite singer."

The atmosphere on the sets of *Ballgame* and *On the Town* was so loose and friendly that we thought nothing of hugging each other, pinching, or even giving a friendly pat on the behind. Until one day when we were shooting *On the Town* and I tried it with Frank.

"Don't do that!" he said to me very sharply.

"Gee, what's the matter with him?" I thought.

"Don't you know?" Gene told me when I asked why Frank was so upset. Then Gene told me about symmetricals, which Shakespearean actors used in their tights so their calves looked bigger. It seems Frank needed padding in the rear.

"If I were you," Gene said, "I wouldn't pat Frank on the behind while he's wearing his sailor suit."

One of the scenes everybody remembers from *On the Town* is when I sing "Come Up to My Place" to Frank while we are in my taxicab. We shot it in a cross-section of a cab with a process screen behind us showing a moving scene of a street so it looked as if we were traveling down it.

The cab was on springs and whenever I pulled on the brakes a few grips would give it a shake so it looked as if we were jolting to a stop. The music was all prerecorded, of course, which I hated because it took the spontaneity out of performing. But that was the test of an actor, trying to make things look natural while all these mechanical things were going on around you.

Frank and I sang another song at the top of the Empire State Building:

> *You're awful. Awful good to look at.*
> *Awful good to be with.*
> *Awful sweet to have and hold.*

Years later, I did a benefit where they asked me to sing "You're Awful" and after the first chorus, I stopped for a minute and said,

"You know what fans always ask me? They don't say, 'What was Frank Sinatra like?' They say, 'Was he a good kisser?' " Then, I sang:

> *He was awful. Awful good a kisser.*
> *For such a little pisher.*

Frank was there that night, but after he said a few words they whisked him off and I never got to see what his reaction was.

When they started making *On the Town*, only Frank, Gene, and Jules Munshin were actually supposed to go to New York for filming. They were the ones running around town while all the scenes with the women were shot in the studio. But Ann Miller was so unhappy when she learned we weren't going that she went to Arthur Freed, the producer of the movie, and cried real tears and said it wasn't fair. He relented so we all went and stayed at the Waldorf for a week. While the boys were working, we went shopping and to Broadway shows, saw friends, and had a ball.

The one New York scene where we *were* needed is the last one in the movie, back at the Brooklyn Navy Yard where the movie began. The three girls—Vera Ellen, Ann, and me—are waving goodbye to Gene, Frank, and Jules as they get back on the ship.

Something was not quite right about the scene, though, and it had to be shot again months later. We were scattered all over by then and somebody figured that since it was a long shot and you never saw our faces, they could use stand-ins. Every time I see the movie, I am reminded that that was *not* me at the end, because the woman wearing my costume and waving goodbye has the widest backside I have ever seen.

THE FIRST THING I had to learn about working with Red Skelton is that he never *stopped* working. Being funny was simply a part of his personality and he could never get away from it.

When we were making *Neptune's Daughter*, we would be rehearsing a scene and all of a sudden everything would stop while Red blew an imaginary feather into the air. You would swear you could see by his eyes that he was watching the feather fall and then, just as it was about to pass his face, he would inhale and swallow it. You could see the feather go right in his mouth and he would go through a dozen crazy expressions until it finally went down, by which time everybody would be on the floor laughing. Then we would go back to work.

Red and I became buddies on the lot. We hung out together and when we went into the commissary for lunch, the people at the writers' table, the producers' table, and the cast from the movie would fight over us.

"Come sit at our table," they said. "No, come sit at *our* table." Sometimes, somebody came over and actually grabbed us and made us sit with them. They knew Red was going to put on a show and they didn't want to miss it.

"Do whatever I tell you to," Red once said to me under his breath as we walked in.

"OK, Red."

"Hold out your hand," he said as we got to the writers' table. I held out my hand and he put a ball of ice cream in it! And then there were our matzo fights. They always had big boxes of matzo on the writers' table and we would each take a large piece and duck down behind it like we were in a fort while we snapped little pieces off the top at each other. Pretty soon the whole commissary would be staging matzo fights. It was like summer camp for eight-year-olds and we all loved it.

One day, Red and I got into an argument about acting schools. "Acting teachers ruin actors," Red said. "You don't need teachers. You do what you feel."

Having gone to acting school and studied with people like Sandy Meisner, I was insulted. I pointed my finger at him and said, "Red Skelton, if you took acting lessons, you'd be one of the great actors in this country!"

I realized I shouldn't have said it, though, because Red got up without a word and started to walk out of the commissary. I followed him pleading, "Red, please come back! I didn't mean it!" Finally, I got down on my hands and knees, threw my arms around his legs and said, "Please, please forgive me! I'll never say it again!"

By now the whole commissary was watching to see what Red would do. He just looked down at me and said sadly, "I thought I lost my buddy."

IF *NEPTUNE'S DAUGHTER* is remembered for anything—besides Esther Williams in one beautiful bathing suit after another and Red's hilarious attempts to get on a horse—it will be for one of the great movie songs of all time.

I don't remember what other songs were nominated for the Academy Award that year, but "Baby, It's Cold Outside" was the winner then and it's a winner now. I know it will always be my personal favorite.

>   She: I really can't stay.
>   He: But baby it's cold outside.
>   She: I've got to go away.
>   He: But baby it's cold outside.
>   She: The evening has been.
>   He: Been hoping that you'd drop in.
>   She: So very nice.
>   He: I'll hold your hands. They're just like ice.

The funny thing about it is that Frank Loesser did not write the song for *Neptune's Daughter*. He and his wife, Lynn, had been doing it at parties for years and considered it their signature song, their personal property. It was not for sale.

For years, singers asked Frank to let them use it in their nightclub acts, producers begged him to put it in Broadway shows, and the studios tried to get it for the movies. But Frank always said no. If you wanted to hear it, you had to be at a party where he and Lynn were performing.

But when we made *Neptune's Daughter*, Frank finally gave in. Ricardo Montalban and Esther Williams sang it while he was trying to seduce her, and Red and I sang it while I was trying to seduce him.

>   Red: My sister will be suspicious.
>   Me: Gosh, your lips look delicious.
>   Red: My brother will be there at the door.
>   Me: Waves upon a tropical shore.
>   Red: My maiden aunt's mind is vicious.
>   Me: Gosh, your lips look delicious.
>   Red: Well, maybe just a cigarette more.
>   Me: Never such a blizzard before.

I had known Frank Loesser from my *Laffing Room Only* days in New York. He was in the army then and not connected with the show, but it was the first time Burton Lane had ever written any lyrics and I always had the feeling Frank might have helped him a little. The song about the Boston Tea Party, with the marijuana jokes I was too naive to understand, always sounded like a Frank Loesser idea to me and I wonder if he might not have slipped it to Burton.

The set of *Neptune's Daughter* was where I first met Gerry Dolin, who became my musical director and friend for many years. Gerry went on to do arrangements for performers like Eleanor Powell, Esther Williams, and Eartha Kitt but when I first met him he was Frank Loesser's assistant.

Gerry had been the musical director for *Where's Charley* and he always claimed he was the one who wrote the great bum-ba-bum-ba-bum introduction to "Once in Love with Amy." They were trying to figure out how to get into the song, Gerry said, and he just played around on the piano until he came up with it.

My favorite Gerry Dolin story is about the time they were getting ready to record the soundtrack for *Neptune's Daughter*.

In those days, they just didn't think to use a person's voice unless they were "a singer" so Jack Cummings, the producer of the movie, came to Gerry and said, "Find some singers in the studio who can be the voices of Esther Williams and Ricardo Montalban in 'Baby, It's Cold Outside.'"

Gerry was friendly with Esther and Ricardo and he thought they had nice voices and could sing their own songs. So he rehearsed them, made a recording, and took it to Cummings.

"I think I've got just the people to dub for Esther and Ricardo."

Cummings heard the record and said, "That's fantastic. They sing so well and they sound just like Esther and Ricardo."

"It *is* Esther and Ricardo," Gerry said. Cummings was so mad he never spoke to Gerry again.

Esther, Ricardo, Red, and I were all excited when we were asked to sing the song at the Academy Awards presentation that year, but I guess I overdid things a little at the afternoon rehearsal.

There is a bit of business in the movie while Red and I are singing where he starts to put on his coat to leave, but I get into the other sleeve and then do a sudden turn and send him flying through the air onto a couch. It had all been worked out very carefully, but this time

I turned so violently that when Red fell on the couch he pulled me over on top of him so hard it knocked the breath out of me.

I was lying there on the floor gasping for breath with a whole group of people gathered around me like a football huddle to see if I was all right. I looked up and saw the actor Paul Douglas with a cup of coffee in his hand peering over the top of the huddle.

"What's the matter?" he said. "Her cup too tight?"

N O T   L O N G   A F T E R *Neptune's Daughter* was finished, Frank Loesser called and asked if I would do him a favor.

"I'm working on a number," he said. "Can you do a Brooklyn accent?"

"Shuah," I said in my best Brooklynese.

"Great," he said. "Do you think you could come over?"

"Of cawse," I said and the next thing I knew Frank was handing me a song about a woman who kept getting sick because her boyfriend would not marry her.

"Frank, this is hilarious," I said after I had sung it once. "What's it from?"

"They've adapted some Damon Runyon stories into a show," he said. "I'm doing the music and I thought this song was perfect for you."

I recorded the song, Frank revised it on the spot and then I recorded it again. This went on for some time and when I went home I played the tape for Larry and told him about this fabulous show Frank was working on.

Some months later, we saw *Guys and Dolls* in New York, and after Vivian Blaine sang "Adelaide's Lament," Larry turned to me and said, "If you ever do that again, I'll kill you. He picked your brain!"

It was true that Vivian had sung the song with the exact inflections I had used when I recorded it for Frank, although in fairness it really was about the only way it could have been sung. And Vivian was magnificent in the part. But Larry was furious.

"He was taking advantage of you."

"If I don't feel people are taking advantage of me, then they're not."

It was an old argument Larry and I had all our lives together.

O N   T H E   T O W N was the last movie I made with my old nose. Ever since I came home crying about how I looked in *Words and Music*,

I knew that one day I was going to have to do something about my nose, but I did not know it would be my obstetrician who would talk me into it.

Leon Belous was Dottie Bridges' obstetrician and when I became pregnant with Garry (we named him Garrett Christopher) I naturally inherited Dr. Belous. We were talking one day and he said, "You know, I think you should do something about your nose. Your face is so delicate, but your nose is not. It's just not in keeping with the rest of it. It needs to be fixed just a little bit."

That was what finally convinced me. My nose was all right for the stage—it was very straight and looked fine in profile—but there was a wide table on top that was distorted when the cameramen took three-quarter shots. It looked as if there were a bump and I got tired of having them scurry around and say, "Move Miss Garrett's key light over here. *No, no, no,* move it over here."

I would think, "Jesus, it must look just awful. What am I killing myself for? Just have it done and that will be the end of the problem."

I guess I was still intimidated by being around so many gorgeous ladies at MGM, too, so shortly after Garry was born I went in and got my new nose.

I was always a little surprised that nobody at the studio had ever suggested I do something about it because MGM had the most elaborate makeup system imaginable. There was a mimeographed chart of a generic face that was used by every makeup man, who marked it according to corrections he felt should be made on each actress. Shading here, shading there, eyes made up this way, throat made up that way, and so on.

Each picture then became completely different depending on the woman's natural coloring and contours. This line over Lana Turner's eyes, this direction for Ava Gardner's eyebrows. Everybody had her own chart so it did not matter which makeup man you got. He just looked at the chart and knew exactly what to do.

My regular makeup man was Keester Sweeney—I love that name—and he had his work cut out for him because my chart had so many marks it looked like the road map of the United States. Keester had to make it darker under the cheekbones and down the side of the neck, then highlight my cheeks, forehead and chin. And shade the nose, *shade the nose*! Keester earned his money when he made me up.

The studios spent forever trying to make everybody's face conform to a certain kind of look, a certain idea of what beauty was. Again, it was Judy Holliday who changed things, who showed that a leading lady could have a look that did not necessarily correspond to traditional ideas of glamor. And then, of course, Barbra Streisand came along and that was the end of every actress in Hollywood needing a Barbie Doll nose.

I have often wondered if I made a mistake. My joke is that if I had my old nose I could be playing Queen Elizabeth or Medea or Lady Macbeth!

All the time I was making up my mind about my nose, Larry never said a word. I did not find out how he felt until we went to Europe shortly afterwards. In every museum we visited, there seemed to be pictures of Jesus or Roman statues that had my old nose.

"See," Larry said as he pointed to one of them, "that's a beautiful nose."

A few years later, we built a creche and Larry spent hours constructing a beautiful barn and stables while I made the people out of clay. Every Christmas when we take it out, I realize that Joseph has my old nose and Mary has my new one.

MGM HAD its own recording company in those years, but it was not a big organization like Decca or Capitol and it did not do a lot of promotion so it seldom had any big hits. The studio never showed any real interest despite the fact it had good singers under contract and the rights to the sound tracks of all those popular musicals.

There was a lot of freedom in recording for MGM records, though. Jesse Kaye, who ran the operation, let us do pretty much anything we wanted. Sy Miller, my accompanist at the time, and I would come up with our own arrangements and Jesse would always say fine. I preserved "Ok'l Baby Dok'l" for posterity and did a couple of songs with Jimmy Durante. One was "The Pussy Cat Song" in which Jimmy sang:

> *Come yout, Come yout, Come yout, my purrty kitten,*
> *We will serenade the moon,*

And I answered:

> *Nyot nyow*

Then Jimmy sang:

> *Come Yout, (purrrrr) Come Yout (purrrr),*
> *Come Yout, my purrty kitten,*
> *We will sing a little tune,*

And again I answered:

> *Nyot nyow*

Those purrs were mine, too, by the way, rolled R's and all. What is remarkable about this song is that at least ten years later Jimmy and I were both working in Chicago and were invited to perform at a special event. As soon as I walked in, Jimmy looked up and sang, "Comeyowt, comeyowt, comeyowt my purrty kitten. . . ." He remembered the entire lyrics of the song, which I had forgotten by then.

While Jimmy and I were making the record, a friend told me my favorite story about him. He was rehearsing a show in New York called *Jumbo* and had a number with two big tall showgirls.

Jimmy had the reputation of never doing any off-color material. He would not tell a dirty joke on stage or say a dirty word. At one point in this number, he had to turn to one of the girls and say, "You're nuttin' but a parasite."

Jimmy stopped the rehearsal and said, "Oh, oh, I ain't gonna say that line. That's doity."

The director came over and said, "No, Jimmy, there's nothing wrong with that."

"Durante don't do doity material and I ain't gonna say that woid," Jimmy said. "It's a doity woid."

They stopped everything and called a conference in which the director, the writers, and the producer all crowded around and tried to convince him.

"Jimmy, parasite is not a dirty word," someone said.

"Listen," Jimmy said. "I've *been* to Paris and I've *seen* dem sights and they're doity."

AFTER *TAKE ME OUT TO THE BALLGAME,* Gene Kelly and I recorded a version of the title song, but for some quixotic reason

Sy Miller said, "Let's do it in four-quarter time instead of three-quarter time." The song is kind of kicky that way, but nobody is used to it. I've been told that every once in a while they play it at ballparks, but I doubt that anybody is crazy about it because it just doesn't sound like the good old waltz-time "Take Me Out to the Ballgame."

Larry and I made a couple of records together, too, using some of the songs we sang when we made personal appearances around the country. I also recorded a song called the "Humphrey Bogart Rhumba."

This is the Humphrey Bogart Rhumba
'Cause Humphrey Bogart is the star we admire
But if you do not care for Humphrey Bogart,
Then name it after any star that you desire.
Mickey Rooney, Errol Flynn, Jennifer Jones or Gable . . .

They really were writing songs like that back then. There was the "Hedda Hopper Tango" and the "Walter Winchell Samba" so why not the "Humphrey Bogart Rhumba"?

We had a problem when we made this song, though. We needed somebody to imitate Bogart's voice for just one line at the end and we could not find anyone whose imitation we liked. Larry happened to be working on a set right next to where Bogart was filming and they got to talking at lunchtime.

"They're looking for somebody to do a real good imitation of you," Larry said.

"Why don't I do it?" Bogart said.

"Gee, would you?" Larry said.

"Sure," Bogart said. "Tell me when the recording session is and I'll be there."

I was all excited and told Jesse Kaye, "Humphrey Bogart is going to come down and make that record with me!"

"He's just kidding you," Jesse said. "He won't show up." But at eight o'clock that night, the doors to the recording studio flew open and there was Bogart—with a trench coat over his shoulder.

In those days, they cut records directly on discs instead of using tape so there was no such thing as editing. If you made a mistake, you went back to the beginning and started over. Well, every time we got to Bogart's line, his hands were shaking so badly that he blew it. It took a while before we realized that the cool Humphrey Bogart was actually nervous! He wanted to get it just right! I loved him for that. It took several more takes until finally we got me singing:

> *No matter what you may say,*
> *It's sti-i-i-ill the Humphrey Bogart Rhumba.*

Then Bogart says, in his best gravel voice:

> *All right, everybody, let's dance.*

AFTER *THE JOLSON STORY,* it appeared there were no limits to Larry's career. He made *Down To Earth*, a charming musical with Rita Hayworth, and a couple of swashbucklers, *The Swordsman* and *Gallant Blade.*

He was on the cover of many fan magazines, which sent reporters swarming around our little house in Nichols Canyon to write about the two of us. This was a more benign journalistic era, one where they took pictures of the happy young couple in the kitchen and out on the town and wrote kind stories dictated by the studios. Larry was a presenter at the Academy Awards and the Bobbysoxers of America named him their Man of the Year. Then Harry Cohn decided to do another Jolson movie and Larry's troubles began.

Before the first Jolson movie, Columbia had insisted that Larry sign a seven-year contract and he balked. He had a few years left on his original contract and wanted the right to choose his own parts in the future.

"If you don't sign this contract, we not only won't give you the Jolson picture, we'll ruin your career," Harry Cohn said. "You'll go back to doing bit parts." And sure enough, Larry got a call to report for a one-day stint as a cab driver in a Boston Blackie picture, the lowest form of B movie on the Columbia lot.

Larry had already done *Counter-Attack* with Paul Muni and *The Renegades* with Evelyn Keyes and did not feel like a B-movie actor anymore. He felt he was working his way up, so for the studio to tell him to get ready for a Boston Blackie picture was a real insult.

But Lou Mandel said, "You just go ahead and answer that casting call" and Larry did. He walked into the costume department, was given a cab driver's hat, and walked out.

But finally, Larry had to give in. It was either sign the contract or not play Al Jolson. He did not get much of a raise—from $500 to $750 a week—and when you consider how valuable *The Jolson Story* was to the studio, it was ridiculous. So when Columbia decided to make *Jolson Sings Again* without raising his salary, he and Lou sued, saying he had signed the contract under duress.

The lawsuit was very painful, particularly because Larry thought that some of the studio people told outrageous lies on the witness stand. His one ally at Columbia was Virginia Smith, the secretary for Max Arnow, one of the top executives. Ginny secretly kept Larry informed about what was happening and even wanted to testify for him. But Larry knew that would have meant her job and told her not to. Her support meant a lot to us, though, and I stayed close to Ginny until she died.

The decision in the case turned out to be extremely important in Hollywood and in legal history. The judge, William Mathis, said he had to give the decision to Columbia because Larry should have sued before he signed the contract. The judge obviously did not understand the movie business.

However, Judge Mathis went on, he had studied Larry's contract and nowhere outside of major league baseball did he find one that was more inequitable, because the options were only on one side. If such contracts were ever really tested in court, he said, they would surely be overturned.

So the judge made a Solomon-like decision: He gave the basic decision to Columbia, but he took away its right of enjoinment. This meant the studio could enforce its contract and make Larry work for it, but it could not stop him from working elsewhere.

At first, the Columbia executives were delighted and said, "We won! We won!" But when they thought about it, they realized they had won the battle but lost the war. They quickly settled with Larry, raised his salary considerably, and made arrangements to start doing the second Jolson picture, which was another huge success. So in the end, everybody got what they wanted. Until the next crisis came.

A COUPLE OF YEARS LATER, it was my turn to experience first hand what Larry had gone through. MGM had just started production on *Annie Get Your Gun* when Judy Garland got sick and they needed a replacement right away.

Not only was I right there on the lot, I had already shown what I could do with the role in the screen test with John Raitt that Lillian Burns had arranged my first year at the studio.

Dore Schary was running MGM by then and he called me in and told me the part was mine.

"Wonderful," I said. "I love that show." Which was certainly true. I think *My Fair Lady* and *Annie Get Your Gun* are the most perfect musicals I have ever seen.

"Of course, we'll want you to sign another seven-year contract," Schary said.

I still had three years left on my original contract so that meant being tied up for four more years after that. Also, my salary for the movie would start at $1,500 a week even though I had worked my way up to $2,500 after having been in five MGM musicals. To Schary's credit, he said, "You can't do that to the girl!" So the salary cut was not part of the deal.

"Look," I said, "if you don't think I deserve this part, then don't cast me. But if you do think I deserve it, don't make me sign another four years of my life away."

The arguments went on for two agonizing days as they raked me over the coals and pressured me. I wanted the part very badly, but I was not going to sign away another four years of my life for it.

"I know what can happen," I said. "I sign another seven-year contract and make this picture and maybe things are going good for a while. Then I have a little slump, which happens to everybody, and when another picture comes along that I want desperately, you're going to say, 'Here, sign another seven-year contract.' "

"Oh, we wouldn't do that to you," they said.

"What do you *mean* you wouldn't do that to me?" I said. "You're doing it to me right now."

"We have people like Spencer Tracy who have been at Metro all their professional lives and they're happy here," they said.

Spencer Tracy probably would like to go somewhere else once in a while, I thought. I loved Spencer Tracy—I always thought he was one of the great movie actors of our time—but he was a slave to MGM and I'll bet that is one of the things that made him an alcoholic. I could not help comparing his career with that of Fredric March, who kept his freedom and made lots of movies but was able to work on the stage and do anything else he wanted. He was always my idea of an actor who was not dependent on what somebody else wanted him to do.

Lou Mandel encouraged me to stick to my guns, too, but I had the best example right at home.

"I don't want Betty to get in the same position her husband was in," Lou said. "I'll tell you what. If you haven't made your money back on her over the next four years, we'll pay it back to you." That was often Lou's way of doing business.

But it wasn't really the money that was at stake. It was the studio's belief it had to be in total control of you. MGM kept saying I was being offered the chance of a lifetime and that my lawyer was ruining my career. But I felt Lou was urging me to do exactly what I should have done.

The real villain of the piece, as far as I was concerned, was the William Morris Agency. My agent was a little guy named Sammy Weisbord and he kept encouraging me to hold out, too. What I did not know was that William Morris also represented Betty Hutton, who made a lot more money than I did. Betty got the part and the agency got a higher commission.

Things were different in those days because even though you had a contract with the studio, your agent had to get in there and pitch you for pictures. It was not like you worked at MGM and they used you for whatever part you were right for; your agent still had to work for you.

But because you were under contract and on his client roster, he did not really have to worry about you too much. You were getting paid, he was getting his commission, and that was all that really mattered. In a way, he became an agent in absentia and you hardly ever saw him except when he took you to lunch once a year and gave you a big pep talk about all the different things he was working on for you.

Once at our annual lunch, Sammy said to me, "There's a darling little picture coming up with Robert Walker Jr. It's a straight part, not a musical, and I think you're going to be wonderful in it."

I sat there thinking, "Yeah, sure," and not taking him any more seriously than I had all the other times he had something just right for me that did not turn out.

But two months later, much to my surprise, they called me in and said they were ready to start shooting.

"Look," I said, a little embarrassed, "is there any way that maybe this lady could be pregnant?"

"WHAATT!!" they said.

"I think I'll be about five months along when we start this picture."

"Didn't your agent tell you about this picture?"

"Yes," I said, "but I didn't believe him. He says these things to me all the time."

And that was the end of that.

My favorite story about Sammy is when I tried to interest him in representing Lloyd Bridges after his contract with Columbia expired and he was scrambling a little bit for work.

"Do you want to represent the best actor in Los Angeles?" I asked. I really meant it because to me Bud is a *great* actor.

Sammy's eyes lit up. "Who? Who?"

"Lloyd Bridges is looking for an agent."

"Oh, he's been around too long."

"So what?" I said. "He hasn't had a chance to really show what he can do."

"Well, his eyes are too close together," Sammy said.

"His *what*?" I just had to laugh.

Shortly afterwards, Bud got the lead in *Seahunt* and became about the biggest star in television at the time. And he has gone on to do fabulous work ever since. The man is eighty years old and still going strong. For years, I hoped that every night when Sammy Weisbord went to bed he said to himself, "His *eyes* are too close together! What a jerk I am."

In the long run, I never really regretted not playing Annie. Larry and I took our act to the London Palladium and the British provinces for the first time shortly afterwards and that opened up a wonderful period in our lives we would have missed if I had stayed at MGM. Working in Britain also became a lifesaver in the dark days that lay ahead.

Lou Mandel always said Larry played three important roles in the Hollywood of his era. He was the star of a very successful movie and its sequel. He was the key figure in a precedent-setting lawsuit. And he was the man in the middle when the shit hit the fan.

I Don't Think This Is
American Justice

Who knows why witch hunts get started? The only thing that's certain, I think, is the hunters have a secret agenda. Three hundred years ago in Salem, it was the church wanting to control the minds of the people. In the 1930s and '40s in Hollywood, it had a lot to do with labor unions.

The Motion Picture Association, an organization of studio heads, was frightened by the fact that writers, directors, and actors had begun organizing. Studio heads were powerful men used to having their own way and they did not like the idea of giving up any of their control.

The two traditional ways of breaking unions are to say they are run by gangsters or by Communists. Gangsters have a way of getting even, though, and the political climate in the country after World War II lent itself more to Red-baiting anyway.

And so the day arrived in 1947 when a man appeared at our door in Nichols Canyon with an ominous piece of paper. The House Un-American Activities Committee was beginning its hearings into "subversive activities" in Hollywood and Larry had been summoned.

Of the nineteen men who received those first subpoenas, Larry was the only actor. The others were screenwriters and directors who were not nearly as well known and we wondered why the committee had chosen him from all the actors in Hollywood who had been active in progressive causes. We always thought there could have been two reasons. The first is that *The Jolson Story* had made Larry the hottest young star in the country. The second is that Ronald Reagan might have been responsible. We had no proof of this, but Larry always felt it was possible.

Reagan was president of the Screen Actors Guild, which had been preparing for negotiations with the studios for a new contract. Larry was a member of the SAG board and had been appointed to a committee formed to survey the financial status of actors in Hollywood. The committee spent six months doing research and came to a conclusion that is common knowledge now but was shocking then: The average actor does not make a living wage. Even after you included all the movies' highest-paid stars, those who made millions of dollars, the average wage was below the poverty line.

Larry was told Reagan was very angry because this was not at all what he wanted to hear. He said the report was nonsense, and literally, I think, threw it in the trash can. He then made a deal with the producers that we are paying for to this day.

Actors get no residuals when their movies are revived on television and in the theaters. And though it was clear even back then that electronic recording devices would exist one day, they get nothing from video store rentals either. A small amount of money does go into a SAG fund, but whereas TV actors receive residuals performers in movies do not.

Reagan did almost exactly what he did to the country years later. Every time he would make a speech about how nobody was starving in America, I couldn't help but compare it to how he had refused to acknowledge the truth about his own profession.

Reagan was still president of the union when the House Un-American Activities Committee was choosing its victims and I have always wondered if the committee asked him who the dangerous characters were in the Screen Actors Guild and if he was still angry enough at Larry's report to single him out. Larry had been made a candidate for the SAG board by petition of the membership and not by the nominating committee. That might have also made him a suspicious character in Reagan's eyes.

But although Larry went to Washington with the original group of nineteen who had been subpoenaed, he just sat and watched as the ten men who appeared before the committee were asked the famous question: "Are you now or have you ever been a Communist?"

As they had agreed ahead of time, they all cited the First Amendment, which guarantees freedom of speech and assembly, and refused to answer. And in the end, Alvah Bessie, Herbert Biberman, Lester Cole, Edward Dmytryk, Ring Lardner Jr., John Howard Lawson, Albert Maltz, Sam Ornitz, Adrian Scott, and Dalton Trumbo were cited for contempt and went to jail.

During the hearings, Larry and I talked on the phone every day but we were afraid to say much because we were certain our phones had been tapped. All we could really do was wait and worry. And then, just before Larry was to take the stand—just before he would have become the eleventh member of the Hollywood Ten—the hearings were postponed.

It was a tremendous relief, of course, although we were still very nervous. J. Parnell Thomas, the chairman of the committee who later went to jail himself for padding his payroll, said, "This is only the beginning" and promised the hearings would resume one day. So we never felt completely at ease, especially as the Communist-hunting atmosphere around the country kept getting worse and worse.

When Larry came home, he told me how Bertolt Brecht had apologized to the other witnesses for not being able to take the First Amendment because he was not an American citizen. He simply said, no, he was not a member of the Communist Party and then left the country.

About the only laugh we got out of those hearings came from Larry's story about sharing a hotel room in Washington with Dalton Trumbo. A number of teen-age girls who had been smitten with Larry in *The Jolson Story* came to the door when he was out and Dalton took their names in a very courtly manner. Larry would sign autographs for them when he returned, he promised.

With all the attention focused on the ten who did testify, Larry's subpoena had not received much publicity and his career did not seem to be affected. He made more movies at Columbia while I started work on *Big City*.

I was a little concerned about how George Murphy, who played the cop who fell in love with "Shoo Shoo Grady" (me), would react. George was a pet of the Motion Picture Alliance for the Preservation of American Ideals and, as a friendly witness before the committee, he had testified that he always scrutinized his scripts for "Communistic content." But on the set, we never discussed politics or the fact that Larry had been subpoenaed. George was always the perfect gentleman and treated me with kindness and affection.

In the courtroom scene where I had to cry on the witness stand,

George was particularly nice to me. My first closeup happened to be at the end of an exhausting day of shooting. A star would have asked for the shot to be postponed until the next day when she was fresher, but I certainly didn't have that kind of clout. George could have gone home and let me read the lines to some grip standing next to the camera, or even a blank piece of cardboard being held up to show me where to look. But he not only stayed, he had the electrician shine a little light on him so I could see him even though he was out of the shot.

And when I did my tearful monologue during the closeup, he cried, too. One look at him and it was easy for me to cry. Not many big stars would do a thing like that for a newcomer. I hated George's politics, but he was a very nice man.

One day, a tall, good-looking man came to our house, showed credentials that said he was with the FBI and asked if I knew a certain woman. I was taking a life drawing class and she was the woman who posed for us in the nude. She had a cute little body—nice voluminous boobs and a round behind—and was so easy to draw that I loved sketching her. The FBI agent asked if I knew if she had any Communist connections.

"I don't know anything about that. She just came and posed."

"Well, are we talking about the same person? Do you have one of the pictures you drew of her?"

I went to find my sketch pad. "That's what she looks like," I said and I handed him my nude studies of this round little body. I had never drawn her face. I could laugh about it later, but it was a scary experience at the time. Nobody had ever asked me if I thought somebody was a Communist.

Later, I went to a big rally—for Spanish War Orphans, I think—where Katharine Hepburn was speaking. There was a familiar-looking man just sitting there, sort of lurking. Finally I realized it was the FBI agent who had come to our house. After a while, I began looking for him at every political event I went to and, sure enough, he would always be sitting in the back row taking notes.

The next time I heard from the FBI, they wanted me to go to the Los Angeles office. I was told they had reliable information that I was one of the leaders of the American Communist Party.

"What?!" I just stood there with my mouth hanging open.

One of the agents asked me: Had I ever been to such-and-such a meeting or made such-and-such a speech? Had I ever met this person or that person?

"Look," I said. "This is ridiculous. I never made that speech and I never heard of these people."

Finally, they handed me a newspaper clipping with a picture of four people in it. One of them was a woman named Betty Gannett, who apparently *was* one of the party's leaders. Maybe, they seemed to be suggesting, I was trying to disguise myself by calling myself Betty Garrett instead of Betty Gannett.

Luckily, Betty Gannett did not look at all like me. The agents passed the picture back and forth, looked at it, looked at me, and shook their heads. Finally, they dismissed me and I left, trying to figure out what had happened.

The only explanation I could think of went back to 1944, when I first came to Los Angeles. At the Clover Club, my billing on the sign outside ran vertically, from top to bottom, with very long letters that were hard to read, particularly the Rs and Ts. Some of my friends took one look at the sign and started calling me Benny Gannett. Maybe it got around that Benny Gannett was really Betty Gannett disguised as Betty Garrett and was a dangerous character.

But despite the fact Larry and I were never completely comfortable because of the threat the hearings would resume, our lives and our careers seemed to get better and better. I made those wonderful MGM musicals and was looking forward to more. Larry went from one starring role at Columbia to another and in 1950 he made *Love Is Better Than Ever* opposite Elizabeth Taylor at MGM. We took our singing and comedy act to theaters in several cities and then to the Palladium in London and all over Britain where *The Jolson Story* had been a huge hit and the audiences simply adored Larry.

We were the successful young Hollywood couple who were very much in demand at show business parties and all the big charity affairs. And when Garry was born in 1950, it seemed as if all of our dreams had come true.

And then, in February 1951, a man appeared at our door with the dreaded subpoena from the House Un-American Activities Committee again. We knew Larry would have to testify this time.

IN THE FOUR YEARS since the first hearings had been held, everything had changed. To begin with, there was the example of the men who had defied the committee and gone to jail. Larry and I saw their personal devastation when Edward Dmytryk, a director who had been one of the Hollywood Ten, came to our house with his wife and young son after he got out of prison.

Eddie looked beaten and Jeannie was on the verge of tears the entire time. Their son was ultimately discovered to have a nervous disorder and they never knew if it might have been caused by the trauma of what they had been through. It had taken a terrible toll on them, and Larry and I were heartbroken to see their pain.

Another difference was the fact that the atmosphere in the country had completely changed. When the first group of subpoenas went out in 1947, many of Hollywood's biggest stars had challenged the committee. They signed petitions, flew to Washington and held press conferences, and appeared on a radio show called "Hollywood Fights Back" that was full of impassioned speeches about what it meant to be an American.

Judy Garland, Humphrey Bogart, Gene Kelly, Lucille Ball, Charles Boyer, William Holden, Fredric March, Edward G. Robinson, and dozens of others spoke of the dangers to civil liberties the hearings represented. It was an exciting moment and it gave us hope that the entertainment community could stick together, rally the public, and shame the committee into just going away.

That hope did not last long. Even before the first round of hearings ended, the studios began to pull individual stars aside and tell them to lay off. Right-wingers in the press kept up the drumbeat of anti-Communist hysteria and the studio heads got together in New York and adopted a policy of regulating themselves.

Nobody was sure exactly what this meant. Would people who had been identified before the committee be kept from working in Hollywood? What about those active in left-wing causes generally? There were rumors everywhere, and everybody was nervous. So when the second batch of subpoenas went out four years later, that previous outpouring of unity and support had dissolved into silence.

The fact that the Korean War was being fought then changed things, too. Anyone who could be tied to leftist politics, even if it had been decades earlier, could be painted as a traitor to the American fighting man and some veterans organizations began threatening to boycott movies they considered suspect.

The committee had also gotten smarter. Instead of calling writers and directors the public did not really know, this time it went for the box office and brought in movie stars to grill, some of them in closed hearings. Sterling Hayden, José Ferrer, Lucille Ball, Edward G. Robinson, Lee J. Cobb, and others testified in 1951 and 1952. But Larry was called first and I am convinced that was the reason his career was affected more than anyone else's.

The thing I remember most about the days between the issuing of the subpoenas and the beginning of the hearings is how confused everybody was. Nobody seemed to know what to do. Citing the First Amendment certainly did not work—the Hollywood Ten had done that—and there was a difference of opinion about how to proceed.

A writer friend came to our house one night and said he had been talking to a number of people who had also been subpoenaed. They had agreed to take the Fifth Amendment, he said, which meant they would refuse to testify on the grounds of self-incrimination, and it would be best if everybody took the same stance.

"Look," Larry said. "What the hell's to stop us from all saying, 'Yes, we joined the Communist Party. So what? It was legal.' If we all did it, if we all stuck together, what are they going to do?"

But the writer just laughed and said, "Oh, no, that will never work. That's being naive."

"What do you think?" I asked Larry after he left. "What are you going to do?"

"I don't know," he said. "I just don't know."

Larry and Lou Mandel went around and around about what he should do. They had never had any reason to talk about what Larry's politics had been back before they met and when Lou found out how minimal his involvement had been, he was appalled.

"It's ridiculous for you to be singled out this way," Lou told him. "You were not any great muck-a-muck in the Communist Party. Just about every thinking person in the United States is involved on one side or the other. What the hell are you taking all this blame for?"

It was this attitude that made Lou argue against taking the Fifth Amendment. Even though it says people do not have to testify against themselves, he said, if you do invoke it everybody thinks you are guilty of something terrible.

"Why should you do that?" Lou said. "You did something that was perfectly legal and there was no reason you shouldn't have."

Lou had another belief, too, and it came down to respect for the law. If a law is bad, he said, you try to change it, but while it is the law you have to obey it. No matter how wrong we might think the committee was, it had been appointed by the government to conduct this investigation. To go against it, Lou said, would be breaking the law.

So why shouldn't Larry say he was there obeying the law? Why shouldn't he as a loyal American openly and honestly answer the committee's questions? Why shouldn't he testify that, yes, he had been in the Communist Party but he had never been particularly active and that he had not attended meetings for years. Which was true. There had been a general disillusionment after the Hitler-Stalin nonaggression pact early in the war. It had come as a terrible shock to all the people who idealized Russia, and Party membership had fallen way off.

Why shouldn't Larry say he was willing to testify about his own involvement but he did not want to implicate anyone else? This was a completely different position than anybody else had ever taken and it was the position Larry chose.

The irony of it was that this man who was accused of being "un-American" was as loyal and patriotic as any congressman sitting across the table from him. My son Garry once said to me, "I have never known anyone who had greater respect for his country, its history, and its laws than Pop did."

SOME TIME AFTER Larry testified, he told me something I had already suspected.

"You were on the committee's list, too," he said. "I think the only reason you weren't called is that you were pregnant. Badgering a pregnant woman wouldn't have painted a very sympathetic picture for the committee."

"What would I have said?" I asked him. "I refuse to answer on the grounds it might incriminate me and the baby?"

Garry was only a few months old when I discovered I was pregnant with Andy. We had not planned on having another baby so soon and as it became more and more likely that new hearings were going to be held, that was one more thing to worry about.

"You know we're facing the possibility I'm going to have to go to Washington again," Larry said. "This may not be a good time."

We discussed it at great length, but I wanted another baby very badly so we decided to go ahead. When the subpoena finally came in late February, it was a month before Larry was to testify and two weeks before Andy was due.

Because I had Caesareans with both boys, Larry arranged for private nurses around the clock and when I got to the hospital the same ones who had been there for Garry were waiting for me.

"You don't seem as joyful as you were with your first baby," one of them said to me as I was settling in.

"You're one smart nurse," I thought.

For a woman about to give birth to a child she desperately wanted I was as depressed as I could be.

When Garry was born, I remember nursing him in the hospital, looking out at a beautiful sunset, feeling this incredible happiness and saying to myself, "Oh! I hope this doesn't last much longer. I can't stand being up on such a cloud." But by the time Andy was born, I was so worn down from worry I could only nurse him for a short time. I have always said the House Un-American Activities Committee dried up all my milk.

When Larry went to Washington, he was still undecided about what to do. The night before he left, we decided on a code. We were convinced our phones were tapped and we didn't want the FBI to know what Larry intended to do.

So we agreed he would send me a telegram before he testified indicating what he had decided to say. He would let me know whether he had decided to take the Fifth Amendment or to admit he had been a member of the Communist Party. I can't remember what the code was but the telegram never arrived.

As the opening day of the hearings grew closer, I became more and more disturbed when I did not hear from him. Not knowing what was going on was simply agony and I found myself getting angry at Larry again for his habit of not communicating his feelings to me in times of trouble. I could not imagine why he did not send me that telegram. I understood later, though. He still had not decided what to do.

133

The night before he testified, Larry and Lou prepared a biographical statement showing that he was as "normal" an American as anyone could be. He was a boy from Kansas who had grown up on a farm. He was a graduate of the University of Illinois. He was a husband and the father of two small boys. He was a good American citizen and had a right to his own political views.

Then Lou left and Larry sat in his hotel room and wrote some notes to himself on a yellow legal pad. He was preparing to be in the most important drama of his life and he was using his training as an actor in an attempt to express the truth. This is what he wrote:

1. Do not wear out.
2. Never lose my temper.
3. Did I speak to my lawyer? Yes. Did anyone tell me what to say? No.
4. Conspiracy? No. I've decided for myself.
5. Don't let "treatment" upset me.
6. Never refuse to answer. Answer by asserting Constitutional rights. (Never use "decline, I won't, refuse," etc.)
7. Defend not only personal rights, but defend motion pictures.

Number six was the big one, of course. He and Lou had decided he should answer the committee's questions. He would admit he had once been a member of the Communist Party and hope that would be that. But he was not on the stand more than half an hour the next morning when he found out it would not be enough.

After a few questions about Larry's background, Frank Tavenner, the committee's lawyer, began asking him if he had known other people as Communists.

"I will tell you everything that I know about myself because I feel I have done nothing wrong . . ." Larry said. "I would prefer, if you will allow me, not to mention other people's names . . . It is my honest opinion that the few people I could name would not be of service to the committee at all. I am sure that you know who they are."

And for a moment, one member of the committee seemed to agree with him.

"How can it be material to the purpose of this inquiry to have the names of people when we already know them?" Congressman Francis Walter of Pennsylvania asked Tavenner.

After four years of investigations, Walter was saying, the committee had the names of everyone in Hollywood it suspected of being Communists. What was the purpose in bringing in more witnesses to repeat them?

But Tavenner said the committee was entitled to receive "proof of the information which it has in its files" and Walter let it go.

A little while later, John Woods of Georgia, who had become the chairman of the committee, asked, "How could it possibly reflect against the members of this group (Communist Party members) for the names to be known, any more than it would if they belonged to the Young Men's Christian Association?"

Larry realized this incredibly naive question was the end of his hopes that he might be let off the hook and as that realization began to sink in, all his plans to remain cool and in control began to unravel. At that moment, he sensed where things were leading and he began speaking from the heart.

"It is doubtful whether, after appearing before this Committee, my career will continue," he said. "It is extremely doubtful. For coming here and telling the truth . . . There were other things open to me that I could have done and I chose not to do them."

The rest of the morning session was devoted to the committee asking Larry about other people and Larry desperately trying not to answer. When they broke for lunch, Larry and Lou decided he should appeal to the committee one more time.

Much of what he said that afternoon was absolutely spontaneous. They were the things that had been going through his mind over and over for months. All the agony, the worry, and the frustration came pouring out. The careful preparation about what he wanted to say became part of what was almost a stream-of-consciousness monologue that revealed his most private feelings.

But this was not a part in a play. It was his career—it was the life he had built for himself—and he could see it was getting away from him and he was powerless to stop it.

First, Larry spoke of his family and his loyalty to the United States. "My people have a long heritage in this country," he said. "They fought in the Revolutionary War to make this country, to create this government, of which this committee is a part. I have two boys, one thirteen months, one two weeks. Is this the kind of heritage that you would like to hand down to your children? And for what purpose? . . . Don't present me with the choice of either being in contempt of this committee and going to jail or forcing me to really crawl through the mud to be an informer. For what purpose? I don't think this is a choice at all. . . . I don't think this is American justice."

The committee reacted to this challenge almost as if it had not heard it. Even when Larry compared the hearings to something that might take place under Hitler or in Russia, there was none of the shouting and gavel-banging that had marked the hearings four years earlier. I have always believed the members were not prepared for Larry's testimony and did not know how to respond to it. They had expected him either to refuse to answer, as the Hollywood Ten had done, or to be another "friendly witness" and willingly name names.

But here was a cooperative witness, one who was admitting his membership in the Communist Party and was not challenging the committee's authority, asking for its understanding. This was something new. I think the committee also sensed how honest Larry was being and was afraid he might win the sympathy of the American public in a way the Hollywood Ten had not.

Larry knew better, though. I sometimes think he was the only one in the hearing room who understood exactly what was happening and how it was going to end. And after he had revealed his thoughts and emotions and could instinctively tell that it was not going to do any good, he got mad.

"It may have been a mistake in judgment," he said. "This is debatable. But my two boys, for instance—I would rather have them make the same mistake I did under those circumstances than not feel like making any mistake at all and be a cow in a pasture. If a man doesn't feel that way about certain things, then he is not a man."

And then, just before the end of the afternoon session, he repeated the phrase that has been most associated with him ever since.

"I don't think this is American justice to make me choose (to) . . . be in contempt of this Committee . . . or crawl through the mud for no purpose," he said. "You know who these people are. This is what I beg you not to do."

"I know who they are, maybe you are entirely right," Congressman Woods answered, "but I still think it is within the province of the committee to determine how far they will go."

And that was that. Yes, the committee already had the names, but it insisted on hearing them listed again by Larry.

At 4 P.M., the hearings went into executive session. There was some sparring back and forth between Lou and Congressman Woods and then Larry was handed a list of names. Nothing I have ever heard or read about his testimony makes this clear. When Larry said the names of the people he knew to be Communists, he was not volunteering. He was reading.

"They gave me this list and it was just ridiculous," he told me later. "Gregory Peck was on it, for Christ's sake. And Jimmy Cagney, Humphrey Bogart, and Lucille Ball. They threw in every name they could think of, Communists or not. Of course, John Howard Lawson was on it." Everyone knew Lawson was a famous old radical who had publicly announced his Party membership, had cited the First Amendment, and had gone to jail with the Unfriendly Ten.

But Larry went down the list with Tavenner. It was a moment that haunted him the rest of his life.

The fact that what he did was so misunderstood was one of the things that hurt so much. And it was the one thing that never ended.

About fifteen years after Larry died, when I was performing in the New York stage version of *Meet Me in St. Louis*, Lou Mandel and I went out to dinner. Lou was hard of hearing by then and had a tendency to talk quite loudly. He began shouting over and over again as we sat in the restaurant.

"Betty, you know, he did *not name names*! *He did not name names*!"

I just sat there thinking, "Lou, be quiet. Everyone can hear you."

Fortunately, the only other people in the restaurant were Milo O'Shea, who was in the show, and his wife, Kitty. I apologized to them as we left and they said, "It's all right. We understand."

It was forty years later and Lou was still suffering the way Larry had until the day he died.

When that final session was over, Congressman Walter told Larry, "I think you could get some comfort out of the fact that the people whose names have been mentioned have (already) been subpoenaed, so that if they ever do appear here it won't be as a result of anything you have testified to."

"It is no comfort whatsoever," Larry said.

Immediately afterwards, Larry finally called home. We were still afraid to talk much on the telephone, but I did not have to ask him how it had gone. I could feel the pain in his voice.

"I've got to have some time away," he said. "Lou and I are going to go to Florida. We're going to lie on a beach or something."

"Florida?! My God, Larry! Why Florida?"

I was angry and hurt because I wanted him to come home. I was dying to know what had happened and I wanted to be able to help. But Lou took the phone and said they both needed to get away for a few days where they would not have to face anybody. Larry was in terrible shape, Lou said. The last thing he needed now was to have to go over it all again. Even with me.

So I did not try to talk him out of it and later I was glad. Larry was simply a wreck and really did need some time completely to himself. I was so involved with my newborn son that I did not have much time to sit around and worry anyway. And the next day's newspapers answered all my questions.

Larry got more coverage than the Korean War. The headlines stretched across the top of the front pages, every paper ran pictures of him testifying with tears in his eyes, and there were long accounts of his appearance before the committee. There was also a story that I had collapsed and was in bed with a "serious emotional condition," which was untrue, but other articles were all too accurate.

"Larry Parks Loses Film Role" one of them said. It had taken Columbia only a few hours to cancel his next movie role.

The studio was cautious in explaining what it had done. Larry was out of *Small Wonder*, it said in a statement, not because of his testimony but because the hearings might delay the start of the movie. This was nonsense, of course, because Larry's appearance was over. But it gave Columbia some breathing room while it gauged the public reaction to his testimony.

For a day or two, the public response was sympathetic. Congressman Charles Potter of Michigan, a member of the committee, said he hoped "the movie industry will not seek reprisal against a man who cooperates with this committee, who was a member of the Party and left when he realized the political implications of Communism. I hope he has the best box office he ever had."

Harold Velde of Illinois said he felt Larry deserved "a badge of honor for his great contribution to the Un-American Activities Committee and to the American people."

And when even John Wayne supported him, my heart leaped with hope.

John was the president of the Motion Picture Alliance for the Preservation of American Ideals and one of the most militant conservatives in Hollywood. If he defended Larry, I thought, maybe the public would be in his favor, too. Maybe it would prove Columbia was running scared for no reason.

"I'm sure they'll give him a second chance," John said the day after Larry testified. "The American public is pretty quick to forgive a person who is willing to admit his mistake. I think it's fine that he had the courage to answer the questions and declare himself."

But then the one power in Hollywood no one could overcome where public opinion was concerned weighed in. Not even John Wayne could stand up to Hedda Hopper.

"I feel impelled to speak the minds of the mothers of the 55,000 casualties in Korea," Hedda told a meeting of the Motion Picture Alliance. . . . "Why put so much emphasis on one career? Do we know what the careers of those 55,000 might have been had they not been cut short? I believe the life of one soldier fighting for our freedom is worth all the careers in Hollywood.

"Parks said he felt he had done nothing wrong. I feel awfully sorry for him, and I am wondering if the mothers and the families of those who died will be happy to know that their money at the box office will continue to support those who have been so late in the defense of our country."

John Wayne then stood up at the meeting and apologized for saying Larry would ever be welcome back in Hollywood. One apology was not enough for Hedda, though. Just to make sure everybody understood there would be no forgiving Larry or anyone defending him, she chastised John again in a column that appeared two days later:

"I was shocked as I read the statement of our president, John Wayne, which would imply that he voiced the opinion of our Alliance. If it did—we should so express ourselves. It is not my opinion. I suggest before we let the traditional theatrical charity govern our reason that we consider whether the mud of an informer is worse than the mud of Korea, mixed with the blood of our 55,000 boys whose luck ran out before they came to fame in Hollywood or anywhere else."

By then, you would have thought Larry was responsible for the Korean War. He was through as a movie star. One studio head was quoted as saying this was very different from the scandals that actually helped the careers of Errol Flynn and Robert Mitchum. "Sex and narcotics," he said, "are a whole lot different from Communism."

Of all the speculation that took place in the days immediately after Larry's testimony, an article that appeared in *Variety* hit closest to home. I do not know who wrote it, but as I read it now—more than four decades later—I think he got it exactly right:

"Although all but Hollywood's most rabid anti-Reds appeared ready to forgive and forget the action taken by a young actor of 25 under conditions 10 years ago, the situation is not that simple, insiders agree. Fact is that despite an exec's emotional urge toward forgiveness, when it comes right down to hiring Parks, he'll probably prefer to skip him. That's the viewpoint already volunteered by one film executive.

"There's no urgency to hire him as long as there's any sort of taint attached to his name. As a result, it can be expected that a producer given a choice of names for casting will prefer to skip Parks in favor of a number of other male leads with equal marquee power. Action may even be partially subconscious, but practical filmmakers are certain Parks is going to be hurt."

The speed of Larry's fall from grace—the fact that it happened literally overnight—was a godsend for the people who testified after him. By going first, Larry had shown what the rules were now, and what the price was for being honest. Subsequent witnesses quickly realized they had to look for other ways to save their careers.

Some of those witnesses informed on people they knew to be Communists willingly, at times almost cheerfully. There was no talk of "crawling through the mud" for them. Others arranged for their testimony to be taken in private and not released as Larry's had been. Larry was an object lesson for nearly all of them and they learned their lesson well.

"I think of Larry Parks (who) consigned himself to oblivion," Sterling Hayden wrote in his autobiography. "Well, I hadn't made that mistake. Not by a goddamned sight. I was a real daddy longlegs of a worm when it came to crawling. . . ."

The committee's attitude changed, too, I think. It had not meant to destroy Larry, it had only wanted to use him to boost its own importance by starting off the new round of hearings with the most visible witness possible. But when it saw what happened to him, I'm convinced that it lost its nerve.

How many people could they destroy by forcing them to repeat the same old tired names? Besides, there were so many cooperative witnesses lined up just waiting to make them look good. So when other people took the stance Larry did—when they said they did not want to name names—they were not challenged.

When Lillian Hellman wrote her famous letter about not cutting her conscience to fit this year's fashions, for instance, the committee let her get away with it. It simply did not want to go through its experience with Larry again so Lillian was not cited for contempt or threatened with a prison sentence and became a heroine of the left. I wonder if she ever stopped to think how much of her good fortune she owed to Larry.

Not long after Larry testified, we were out in the front yard when Lena Horne, who lived up the street, drove up, and stopped to chat. After talking to Larry for a minute, she turned to me and summed up everything that had taken place.

"Larry's taking the rap for a lot of us."

Dragon Country

In the years that followed, we never heard anybody say, "Don't hire Larry Parks. He's blacklisted."

Lou Mandel always said that if he could find somebody who admitted it, he would sue. But it was always a faceless edict. There was never anyone actually giving orders, never anything official. It was something that just seeped into the Hollywood air like some sort of evil ooze.

An odious book called *Red Channels* listed the names of anyone suspected of ever having belonged to any "subversive" organizations and it would have been laughable if the book had not been used to destroy so many people.

I had a friend whose name was in the book by mistake—he had never joined or supported any political organizations—and when jobs started drying up he knew he was being blacklisted. Somebody told him if he went to the *Red Channels* publisher and convinced them he had never been a Communist they might clear his name.

"We can't do anything for you," he was told. "If you confess that you *were* a Communist and you want to recant, maybe we can help you."

That is the kind of insidious nonsense that went on and once it started there was no end to it.

After a while, Larry and I realized we were a three-blacklist family. He was on the list, I was on the list, and *we* were on the list.

Larry had hoped that working in television might be a way of staying in the public eye until the political climate improved. So when he was hired to play Al Jolson on a show about a lot of famous performers getting together in heaven, he was delighted. But all of a sudden, the role went to somebody else. The reason the producers gave was that Larry was not right for the part!

About the same time, I got a call from Paul Roberts, an old friend who was directing concert versions of musical comedies on the radio.

"Betty, are you on the blacklist or something?" he said, sounding terribly upset.

"Probably," I said, although by then I knew I was. When Sammy Weisbord at the William Morris Agency said he could no longer represent me, I did not have to ask him why.

"I want you to be on my show," my friend said. "We're doing some of your songs from the movies and they say you're 'unacceptable.' I'm going to quit if they won't put you on."

"*Please* don't do that," I said. "It isn't worth it. Promise me you won't quit."

Then there was the time Larry and I were hired to do some numbers on the Arthur Murray television show. I had been on it in the past and they were enthusiastic about having us on together.

We went to New York, attended one rehearsal, and then were told we were off the show. Nobody seemed to know who made the decision, but it seems "they" had suddenly discovered there were too many people on the show. They paid our salaries and our expenses and sent us home. This sort of thing happened more than once.

And then, of course, there were the calls that never came.

Years earlier during the war, when I was in *Something for the Boys* on Broadway, Ed Sullivan, who was a New York newspaper columnist then, put on many USO shows. I was in practically all of them and though we remained good friends, he never asked Larry and me to be on his television show once we were on the blacklist. I often thought that being on the *Ed Sullivan Show* would have helped us a lot.

THE MOST SERIOUS EFFECT of the blacklist on our lives, however, was not professional. It was personal. From the moment Larry came back from Florida, it was clear we would never really be able to talk about what had happened in Washington.

At first, he was simply too wounded to be able to speak about it. It might have been good if we had tried, but it was just too painful.

We were not the kind of people who went in for at-home therapy, anyhow. We never sat down and analyzed ourselves. Instead, there was always a sort of silent understanding between us. We seemed to sense what the other was thinking and there was no need for a lot of heavy discussion. The image I had was that we walked hand in hand without a lot of conversation. So even if we had talked about it, we did not know how to get through the pain.

Larry used to accuse me of not wanting to talk about things, but that was the complaint I had always had about him. It went back to his not letting me know how sick his mother had been, to not calling me from Washington, to not wanting to come home right away afterwards. But he was right about me, too. Talking about painful things always upset me too much.

"I can't talk to you if you're going to cry," he said to me once. "You're just using your tears as a weapon."

"That's the way my emotion comes out," I said. "In tears. Yours comes out in yelling and if I can put up with your yelling, you can put up with my tears."

Larry put his arms around me and laughed as he recognized the truth of it.

We finally came to the realization that it was all water under the bridge and we should not dwell on it. We had our lives. We had our children. We had our careers, such as they were. Sitting around and rehashing such a painful episode just did not seem productive.

One short line from Tennessee Williams summed it up for me: "Dragon Country, the country of pain, is an uninhabitable country which is inhabited."

It inspired me to write a poem:

DRAGON COUNTRY

Oh, I have been in DRAGON COUNTRY!
I grow old in DRAGON COUNTRY!
No more virgin heart
To feed the Dragon's hunger—
No more youthful sword with which
To fight the fire-breather—
And you, my former Dragon-slayer,
Live in your own DRAGON COUNTRY.
So we stand atop
Twin hills of sighs
And signal to each other—

145

"One more day and still alive!"
Still alive
In DRAGON COUNTRY!

That was Larry and me, I thought. Signaling to each other from different mountaintops but still alive!

After a time, it became clear to us that the fallout from Larry's testimony was not going to subside and that we would never know what form it might take next.

One incident that was particularly disturbing to me occurred when Garry and Andy were little and we enrolled them in a cooperative nursery school in Hollywood. About fifteen families had gotten together and hired an excellent teacher with each mother agreeing to help out one day a week. The parents met regularly to arrange car pools and decide how the school should be run and we felt very good about the kind of environment we were providing for our children.

It was only later that the friend who recommended the school to me said she was afraid Garry and Andy might not be allowed in. Some parents disapproved of having their children associate with the Parks boys and there were some loud arguments about it.

It degenerated into people saying, "How are you going to punish two kids for what their father did?" and several parents objecting so strongly they actually withdrew their children from the school.

What was so ironic about this was the fact that Larry was the only father in the group who ever helped out as an extra teacher. When I was shooting *My Sister Eileen*, he took my days as the car pool driver and teacher.

"It's so cute," one of the mothers told me. "He goes around and pushes the kids in the swings, wipes their mouths off, blows their noses, and does all the things the mommies do."

"I'm lucky that Larry is that kind of father," I said. "He never draws any distinction between my chores and his chores."

I had another terrible experience when I was asked to serve on a committee with a lot of Hollywood stars for a big charity luncheon for the Motion Picture Home. We had an organizational meeting at Pickfair where the chairwoman announced that each table would have the name of a volunteer on it.

One of the women said she would like her professional name to be listed, but then she changed her mind and said, "No, I think I'd like to be Mrs. So-and-So," and mentioned her husband's name.

I thought that was kind of nice so when the chairwoman asked me if I wanted my name listed as Betty Garrett, I said, "No, I think I want it to be Mrs. Larry Parks."

As the meeting was breaking up, I ran into my old friend Ida Koverman, still Louis B. Mayer's secretary after all these years, and when I said hello, she gave me a disgusted look and said, "Oh, you're such a ninny."

What the hell was *that* all about? That night I found out. The chairwoman of the luncheon called to say they did not want me on their committee. They did not feel my "political associations" were appropriate for their charity.

I was humiliated and upset, of course, and Larry, who was listening to my side of the conversation, was just furious and took the phone from me.

"How *dare* you do something like this to my wife?"

"It wasn't me," the poor woman said, almost in tears. "I didn't want to do it. It was the head of the committee. I was just told to call you and tell you."

Sometimes, the opposite would happen. We went to a party once where somebody protested because Larry had been invited and the host, Stanley Prager, just lit into the guy.

"Listen, this is a friend of mine," Stanley said. "You don't have the right to tell me who to invite to my house. If you don't like it, you can leave." And he practically kicked the person out of the party.

But what hurt the most was being shunned by old friends, particularly people we had so much in common with politically. It became fashionable in left-wing circles to view Larry as a heretic even though his views had not changed and his testimony had hurt no one but himself.

These were people we had worked with, socialized with, and shared our triumphs and disappointments in show business with. They were people we cared about and who we thought cared about us. We had always considered having good friends to be such a blessing that it was painful to discover how fickle friendship could be.

"But we are all on the same side," I remember saying to Larry when some cruel remark by an old friend was reported back to us.

"They don't think so," he said.

Every so often I would run into someone we had not seen in a while and when I mentioned it to Larry his response was always the same.

"Was he pleasant?" he would ask, and my heart would break a little more.

One of the few prominent people on the left who went out of their way *not* to snub Larry was Dalton Trumbo, who told a number of people that he felt Larry had been treated unfairly. When Dalton made his famous speech about the HUAC investigations in which he said it did no good to search for villains or heroes or saints or devils because there were only victims, I am certain Larry was one of the people he was thinking of.

After Larry died, a number of people who had been friends told me they had misunderstood and felt badly about their attitude. While I appreciated the gesture it felt hollow because Larry was not there to hear it.

Fortunately, there were some apologies Larry was able to hear. One old friend who had rejected him very badly—he and his wife had literally packed up and left a friend's beach house when he learned we had been invited for the weekend—wrote us a letter when we were performing in England, where they were then living.

"I don't know whether you'll want to hear from me at all," he wrote. "I deeply regret the way I treated you and if you feel it in your heart to forgive me, I'd love to see you."

We called him and got together and were able to renew an old friendship.

There were also people who loved to report the latest gossip back to us. I guess it made them feel important. One of them once told me that a dear friend from my days at MGM had been going around saying, "I just love Betty and Larry, but it's really dangerous to be around them any more."

I thought it was so unkind of this person to tell me this even if it was true and I never confronted my friend about it. Even today, though, whenever I see her, I can't help but wonder if that is how she really felt about Larry and me.

Several years after his testimony, Larry had to suffer one final humiliation. If he tried to make peace with the committee, he was told, he might be able to work again. I can't be sure, but I think Lou Mandel

I was such a fat little baby I wouldn't even stand up until I was two years old.

My daddy, Curtis Garrett, and me, age 3. This picture was taken in St. Joseph, MO., during one of the summers he brought me to stay with my grandmother and his cousins on the farm.

On the farm with my father's darling cousin Katherine (Katty) Pike; my cranky grandmother Kate Garrett, and Hereford (Heppy) Pike, a deaf artist who drew pictures for me hour after hour.

The twins—Helen and Caroline Stone—and me in the middle at Neskowin Beach in Oregon. This must have been about 1925.

"Mother dear"
(Octavia Stone
Garrett) and me,
about eight years
old, in front of
the Clark Hotel,
Seattle, WA.

At Mary and Martha Cottage, I played the Virgin Mary in the Christmas show. I was all of nine years old in this picture.

I was Maid of Honor—which went to the girl selected as the "most improved"—at the Annie Wright Seminary's May Festival. Meige Guyles was the queen.

I met Danny
Kaye—here he is
with me and Betty
Rohan—at White
Roe Lake on the
Borscht Circuit in
upstate New York
in 1938.

I'm singing "I'm In
Love With a Soldier
Boy," the song Cole
Porter wrote for me
in *Something For the
Boys*, which opened
on Broadway in
1942. My soldier
boy is Alan
Flemming.

This is the kind of political activity that later got me in trouble as a "dangerous un-American."

Singing my show-stopping number, "South America, Take It Away" from *Call Me Mister*. I played a dance-hall hostess worn out from too many rumba-samba-congas with Alan Manson, Chandler Cowles, Howie Malone and Freddie Danielli. *". . . First you take it and you put it here . . ."*

Larry and I met at The Actor's Lab in Los Angeles where I did a comedy number about a starlet whose feet got stuck in the cement at Grauman's Chinese Theater. Helping him get me unstuck is Bert Conway and Larry, whose part was later played by George Tyne.

When Larry's mother showed me his baby pictures, I thought, "Wouldn't it be nice to have a little boy like that?"

Larry had a three-day growth of beard when we were married on September 8, 1944 because he was making *Counter-Attack* with Paul Muni. Columbia touched up the publicity shots it sent to the newspapers so he would look clean-shaven.

Our honeymoon on the beach at Topanga Canyon. When we walked down the beach everyone looked at Larry, not me!

As soon as the studio saw the power of Larry's performance in *The Jolson Story* in the daily rushes, it knew it had a hit on its hands.

Everyone thought Al Jolson coached Larry for the movie. In truth, after recording the songs, Jolson flew off to Florida. This is a posed publicity shot.

I was in *Call Me Mister* on Broadway when *The Jolson Story* opened at Radio City Music Hall. As a publicity stunt, they had me place Larry's billing before the title as opposed to after, a big difference in an actor's career.

George Murphy was the leading man in *Big City*, my first MGM movie. I played a nightclub singer and he played—what else?—an Irish cop.

Even walking to the set of *Words of Music* I towered over Mickey Rooney. I cried all the way home from the premiere complaining to Larry that I looked like a giant.

This dress is from *Words and Music*. Years later, my friend, Naomi Caryl, bought it at an MGM auction and gave it to me for my 60th birthday . . . and it still fit!

The joke on the set of *Take Me Out to the Ballgame* was Betty Garrett could carry Frank Sinatra anytime.

Red Skelton kept me in stitches the entire time we were making *Neptune's Daughter*. When the MGM executives watched the daily rushes, they would say, "Why does that girl come out laughing all the time?"

Oscar night, 1947. Larry was nominated for best actor along with Frederic March (who won), Laurence Olivier, Jimmy Stewart and Gregory Peck. I spent $350.00 for the Adrian dress and coat, the most I had ever spent for clothes. That's Glenn Ford in the background.

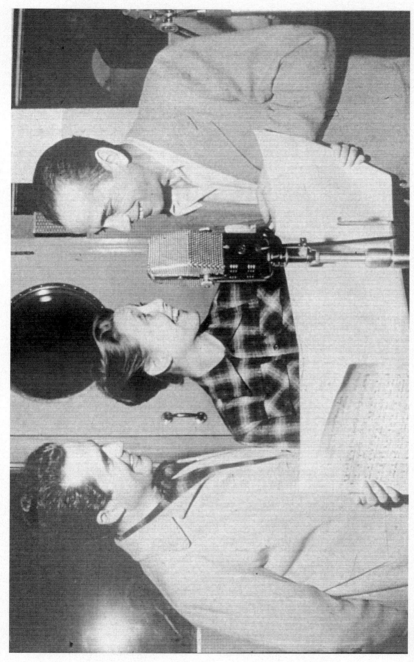

Recording "The Humphrey Bogart Rhumba." Who would have thought a big star would have been nervous about saying one line?

The day Larry testified before the House
Un-American Activities Committee, he was bigger news than the Korean War.

Mom was always there to babysit Garry, who was 9 months old here and obviously thought it was very funny.

Did you ever see two cuter little boys? That's Andy on the left, Garry on the right.

New Year's Eve 1950 at Louis B. Mayer's house. We jitterbugged until dawn and Larry drank so much champagne we had to call for oxygen when we got home. Garry was born 26 days later.

The christening of Garry Parks and Jeff Bridges took place at the home of Dr. Leon Belous, who delivered them. (Left to Right) Larry, me, Dr. Belous (holding Garry), Julie Belous (holding Jeff), Dottie and Lloyd Bridges, and 10-year-old Beau Bridges.

The Palladium in London was to British variety artists what the Palace in New York was to vaudevillians. This billboard is from our first engagement there.

Jack Lemmon, my favorite leading man outside of Larry. I always felt there was something about Jack that was like Larry—besides the hairline. A gentlemanly quality.

Janet Leigh and I felt as if we really were sisters by the end of the shooting of *My Sister Eileen*.

Marlon Brando, preparing to play Sakini in the movie version of *Teahouse of the August Moon*, received a few tips from watching Larry on stage.

Spoon River, which we developed at Theatre West, became a surprise hit on Broadway in 1963. That's me and Joyce Van Patten with Charles Aidman and Robert Elston.

Larry and I did a bus-and-truck tour of *Plaza Suite*. I think Larry enjoyed this part of the play more than any other.

My darling musical director, Gerry Dolin, would watch me as he played with such affection people used to think we were having an affair.

Mr. TLC, John Carter, who directed *Betty Garrett and Other Songs, No Dogs or Actors Allowed,* and *So There.*

Yeah! Cole Porter was amused by my hillbilly-boogie woogie gestures. I'm still doing them.

Larry got more and more handsome as he got older.

John Huston had a way of looking at you as if you were the only person in the room cocktail party in Munich for the cast of *Freud*.

I don't think
a caption
is necessary.

With my old
friend from
Theatre West,
Carroll
O'Connor. As
Irene Lorenzo,
the fix-it lady on
All in the Family,
I was the one
who took Archie
down a peg. To
this day, people
yell when they
recognize me,
"Give Archie
hell, Irene!"

Playing Edna Babish on *Laverne and Shirley* was my second regular part on the number one show on the number one network on television. (Left to Right) Me, Michael McKean, David Lander, Eddie Mekka and Phil Foster. Penny Marshall and Cindy Williams are in front.

After Larry died, work was the best healer. My favorite show was Barbara Damashek's *Quilters* at the Mark Taper Forum. It was almost a religious experience.

In *Breaking Up the Act* with Evelyn Keyes and Jan Sterling.

Betty Garrett in "Meet Me in St. Louis": "At this age, you don't turn down challenges. You take them. Because that's what keeps you young."

I think a Hirschfeld cartoon is the greatest honor a Broadway actor can get. My first was when I was in *Call Me Mister*. More than forty years later another was sketched of me in *Meet Me in St. Louis*.

Lou Mandel and me on my 60th birthday. Lurking in the background is Dick Davalos who was in *East of Eden*.

Life is like the seasons, after winter comes the spring. From left, Uncle Andrew, Gramma Betty, momma Karen, daddy Garret with Madison Claire Parks.

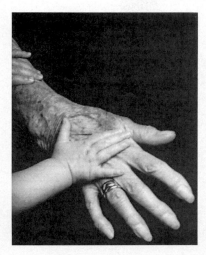

Two hands with 77 years in between.

probably encouraged Larry to do this. He saw some of the people who had testified before the committee getting jobs and was frustrated that Larry was still blacklisted. So he wrote the committee an apologetic letter and even agreed to speak before an American Legion meeting. He regretted both actions instantly.

I went with him to the Legion meeting and even though the speech he gave was noncommittal—something about every American's responsibility to his country—he just hated being there. The reactionary element was out in force that night and it turned his stomach to be around so many people who had supported the witch hunts.

"I will *never* do that again," Larry said on the way home. "It was *humiliating*."

Right around this time—late in 1953—Larry did get a job on a television show opposite Teresa Wright. "I feel like a man released from captivity," he told the newspapers, but in truth he was very uncomfortable.

The show was filmed at the Columbia Studios and I have always suspected that Harry Cohn was trying to open the door a little bit to Larry. But Larry's sense of pride made it difficult for him to accept lightweight TV roles instead of parts in important movies. Larry was very much one for dignity. Whenever he thought I was not behaving in a dignified way, he would call me on it and often we would have arguments.

"Dignity is something that comes from within," I would say. "It doesn't have anything to do with what you *do*. It has to do with the way you *are*. I feel I'm a dignified person and the hell with anybody else."

But Larry insisted on being treated in a certain way and I sometimes wonder if that did not hurt him professionally. Larry was offered roles from time to time, but they were either bad scripts or bad parts and he couldn't bring himself to do them. Perhaps if he had not had quite so much pride, he could have started over. Perhaps he was hurt as much by his own resistance to doing parts he thought were beneath him as by the blacklist itself. These are things I will never really know.

I do know that many years later when John Huston gave Larry his last movie role supporting Montgomery Clift in *Freud*, I got a glimpse of what could have been.

John literally ran into Larry on the street one day and he said, "My God! You'd be a perfect Dr. Breuer."

Larry had grown heavier and his hair had turned gray in the later years of his life and he had a beard that made him look very distinguished. So John cast him as Freud's mentor.

Larry was thrilled, of course, and when I saw the movie so was I. And a little sad. Larry was so good in the part, so relaxed and confident opposite Monty's fidgety portrayal of Freud, and the reviews he received were marvelous. It made me realize what a shame it was that he had not had the luxury of being allowed to age on the screen the way so many male stars do.

What good fathers Larry could have played. What good wise older men keeping their young headstrong partners in tow. What good villains, perhaps. What a waste that it never happened.

IT WAS EASIER for me to get used to not working than it was for Larry because I had my hands full with Garry and Andy. And I always had other projects—art, dancing, and Theatre West, which I had helped start along with some other actors in town.

After a few years, though, it became clear that we were going to have to get used to the fact that I would be able to work more in Hollywood than Larry. Singing and dancing and playing in television comedy sketches were right up my alley, something I would have naturally gone on to do anyhow.

But first there was the blacklist to contend with and while you could never beat it entirely, you could sometimes chip away at it and score small victories. Especially when you had the help of friends as good as mine.

Danny Thomas, my old pal from *Big City*, was the first to go to bat for me and I have always been so grateful to him.

"What have you been doing?" Danny asked me when I bumped into him one day after we had not seen each other for a while.

"Not much." I didn't have the heart to go into a lot of detail.

But Danny knew what was going on and hired me to be on two of his variety shows. James and Pamela Mason were on one of them and we did a sketch where they played a scene and then Danny and I did it backwards, which was terribly funny.

And there it was. One moment, I was not employable and the next moment I was making my debut on national television and nobody said a word. That was how crazy it all was. There was no rhyme or reason to any of it.

There was a fuss when I was hired to be on another show, though. It was a tribute to Ethel Barrymore and Carl Reiner was the master of ceremonies while Arnold Horwitt, an old friend from New York, had written some of the sketches. When somebody complained about my presence, they both threatened to quit and that was the end of it. I stayed in the show and never heard another word about it.

Several shows with Art Carney that were produced by David Susskind came after that. Knowing David, he may have hired me as much to make a statement as to hire someone he thought was right for his show.

In those days, they did television shows twice, once for the East Coast and once for the West Coast. They were done in kinescope and it's a shame that almost all of them have been lost. Many of the sketches we did were so inventive.

They were similar to what we had done at Tamiment and the Flatbush Arts Theatre and they were a forerunner, I later realized, of those takeoffs on the news they later did on *Saturday Night Live*.

On one of Art Carney's shows, we did a parody of the Miss America pageant that was ridiculously funny. The talent of one of the contestants was changing a tire, while mine was singing a song and accompanying it by playing one note on the violin after every couple of bars. At the end, I picked up my skirts and roller-skated away and as soon as I was off-stage there was a terrible crash. I was named the winner and when I came back to claim my crown, I had a big band-aid on my nose.

I loved being back at work and Larry was genuinely pleased, even though he remained on the outside for the most part. We had supported each other for all those years and we kvelled—in the old Yiddish expression—at each other's success.

That was something that never changed, on his part or mine. There was never any resentment or jealousy because we knew that so much of our circumstances had to do with the fact that his name was the one that had appeared in huge black headlines during the HUAC hearings.

Many people, in fact, were surprised to learn I had even been involved and I always thought it was so strange when people said things

151

like, "It was so wonderful of you to stick with Larry through all that mess."

"Why shouldn't I?" I said. To me it was like someone saying, "It's so nice of you to stick with your husband when he was having his appendix out."

In the interim, Larry had become very involved in the apartment house construction business he had gone into with Lou Mandel and as it became more and more profitable, I saw a whole new side of him.

A number of people were sitting around listening to Larry talk about one of his building projects one day when I said, "I think he really *likes* doing this."

I was teasing him a little, but bragging about how well he was doing, too, and I was shocked when all of a sudden he lashed out at me.

"Don't you think I'd *rather* be working as an actor?"

I realized that he had done it again. He had hidden his real feelings from me and lulled me into thinking he loved being a builder. I was wrong. His humiliation continued to eat at him. It always would.

Fortunately, in the early years of our exile there were places we could find work. There was no blacklist in Las Vegas, of all places, and we performed our nightclub act there. There was also summer stock and road companies of plays that traveled around the country.

And there was one of our favorite places on the face of the earth, a place where either they had never heard of the House Un-American Activities Committee or they did not care.

Thank God there was always Britain.

Second Chorus

Will Ye Nae Come Back Again?

Larry and I first played the Palladium in London shortly after *The Jolson Story* was released. American entertainers like Danny Kaye, Dorothy Lamour, and Danny Thomas had performed there with great success after the war, and when the movie became a big hit in Britain Lou Mandel arranged for us to take our nightclub act to London.

The Palladium was like the Palace in New York—the theater where all the big acts played—and after our engagement there we toured all over Britain. We went to Manchester, Birmingham, Glasgow, Edinburgh, Blackpool, Liverpool, Nottingham, Newcastle, and every little town that would have us. From Land's End to John o' Groat's, as they say, and then back to Glasgow and Edinburgh again.

This was such a happy time in our lives that even if it had not become difficult to work in our own country, we would have come back every chance we got.

Britain was still suffering terrible shortages of food and consumer goods when we first got there, but the audiences were wonderful and we made some great friends among the British performers who played with us. Vaudeville might have been dead in America, but what the British called "variety" was still very much a part of their entertainment tradition.

One of the first things that fascinated me was British humor. They think we are vulgar, but I have never heard more jokes about "boils" in my life. There was a comic who used to sing, "There's a rainbow 'round me shoulder and a big boil on me neck" and the audience would roll in the aisles. To me *that* was vulgarity.

I learned to love this humor, though. One of their favorite comics would come out and say, "I was feeling terrible so I went to the doctor and he gave me a complete examination. The doctor said, 'I tell you what I want you to do. I want you to drink a large glass of orange juice after a hot bath.' He saw me in the street a few days later and he said, 'Did you drink your orange juice?' and I said, 'No, I haven't finished drinkin' me hot bath yet.'"

Another act Larry and I became very fond of was the husband-and-wife team Stan and Ann White. Stan was this little man who came out on stage with a violin and some white pasty makeup with red lips and black patent-leather hair that made him look like a road-company Dracula.

"I should like to play Liszt's Hungarian Rhapsody," he would say. "I should like to play it, but I don't know it." Then he would put the violin up to his chin, start to play something, and one of the strings would go "Boinngg!"

Ann, who was this big handsome lusty woman, would go "HA! HA! HA! It broke." And Stan would say with a pained tone in his voice, "I know. I was there when it happened."

For the finale of their act, Ann would come out on stage carrying a big bass viol and wearing a World War I metal German helmet. She would walk over to a contraption that consisted of a pole on which was attached a 2 × 4 at right angles that held a large cymbal connected to a foot pedal. She would stand underneath, play the bass viol and work the foot pedal so the cymbal would come crashing down on the helmet: Ching! Ching!

In the meantime, Stan, in these awful-looking white wrinkled circus tights, would climb a ladder to a platform above the cymbal, stand on his head and play on a trumpet "Britannia Rules the Waves."

You can't hardly get acts like that any more!

Another favorite husband-and-wife act was a comedy knock-about dance team called Dickie and Yolanda.

They always began as if they were serious dancers, all very romantic. But the next thing you knew Yolanda would be sitting on Dickie's shoulders with her skirt over his face so he could not see where he was going. Then they would both fall down and start doing somersaults and all kinds of crazy acrobatics.

Dickie and Yolanda were a dear couple with a little boy and they saved money by traveling in a small mobile home. There was no john in the trailer and they had to go around with pockets full of shillings and pence so they could use the public showers and johns.

One night before a show, Yolanda was very nervous and when I asked what the matter was, she said, "My brother is out front and I know he's going to criticize everything we do."

"Why would he do that?"

"He and his wife do the same identical act Dickie and I do."

"The same act?" I said. "That's certainly unusual."

"That's not all," she said. "My sister and her husband have the same act, too."

It seems Yolanda's sister and her husband performed the dance act in circuses, her brother and his wife did it in cabarets, and Dickie and Yolanda played in variety halls. That way, they never had to compete with each other.

They had all grown up in the circus, she said, where her mother was a bareback rider. They were not allowed to do any of the dangerous acts like the trapeze or tightrope walking, but they were taught acrobatics and they all learned their comic dance act that trick for trick was exactly the same.

The idea of an entire family performing in the circus simply fascinated me and one day Yolanda told me the whole story.

Her family was from Romania and her grandmother was determined that her daughter was not going to grow up to be nothing more than a servant like most Romanian women. The grandmother scrimped and saved to give her daughter an education and as a result Yolanda's mother became the first woman lawyer in Romania.

Her first client was a man who owned a circus and came in to get a divorce. She got it for him and then married him, joined the circus, and became a bareback rider!

"My God!" I said, "how did your grandmother feel about that?"

"My grandmother never spoke to my mother again as long as she lived," she said. "But my mother loved the circus and she never had any regrets. We all had the happiest life in the circus."

Now, how could you not love people like that?

Another act I was crazy about was Vogelbein's Bears.

Vogelbein was a big craggy man who worked with three huge brown bears and one tiny little wife. Those damn bears could do *everything*. They would dance, they would stand on their heads, they would even ride bicycles around the stage. The stages in England are slightly raked—slanted toward the orchestra pit—and the bears would pedal their bicycles slowly upstage and then turn around and ride faster and faster downstage.

As they did their act, Larry and I loved to stand in the wings and watch the musicians down in the pit. When the bears were pedaling downstage, the whole violin section would lean away from the stage in unison and try to hide under their instruments. One night, one of the bears fell into the pit—right into the bass drum. You have *never* seen musicians move so fast!

At the end of the act, Vogelbein used to do something that drove Larry crazy. He would go over and give each bear a big hug and a kiss right on the mouth. Then he would turn around and kiss his wife on the mouth.

"That's disgusting," Larry would say, but even he had to admit it was a great act.

When we went back to Britain a couple of years later, the manager of the tour, a big, good-looking Scotsman with red hair and a wonderful Scottish burr, asked what acts we would like on the bill with us.

"How about Vogelbein's Bears?" I said.

"Och, lass," the manager said, "dinna ye hear? Vogelbein's Bears is nae mair."

"What happened?" I asked.

"Well, one nicht, after a particularly stirrring perrforrmance, Vogelbein hugged one of his bears and it hugged him back. Put him in hospital for three months."

"That's awful," I said, but right behind me I could hear Larry muttering under his breath, "I knew he'd kiss those damn bears once too often."

Our own act was the one we had performed back home. There had been a revival of the sort of thing they used to put on at the movie theaters years ago—live stage shows between feature pictures. Larry and I performed the act in Chicago, Cincinnati, St. Louis, Toronto, and Montreal.

These shows were well received because we had a real act whereas most movie actors making public appearances did not do much more than say hello or perhaps sing a song badly. "It's such a relief to see two Hollywood stars get up and really *do* something," the reviewers said and that always made us feel good.

Larry had a nice light baritone voice that blended well with mine and we sang "Anything You Can Do I Can Do Better" and a cute takeoff on "Baby, It's Cold Outside" called "Can I Come In for a Second?"

We did four shows a day, singing and dancing and doing some comedy material written by Bob Schiller, who later wrote the TV show *Maude*, and his partner that included an opening bit we were able to use in every city we went.

Larry would come out and in a very dry professorial sort of way recite some facts about the town we were in: the population, the major industry, the name of the mayor, important attractions, and so on. Then he would introduce me and I would start to recite some of the same statistics except I would get them all screwed up. He would get apoplectic and start shouting, "No! No! That's all wrong!"

Once, when we were playing Glasgow, Larry recited all the statistics and mentioned Willie Waddle, who was the city's big soccer star. Then I came out and said, "The population of Glasgow is so-and-so and they all waddle." This kind of silliness worked everywhere we went.

On one of our tours of Britain, we devised a clever gimmick for Larry. He would mention *The Jolson Story* and then say, "Everybody knows that Mr. Jolson sang the songs and I synchronized my actions to them. But people always ask me what *my* voice sounds like. So I thought I'd let you hear."

The next thing you would hear booming out over the loudspeaker was "When your sweetheart sends a letter of goodbye. . . ." "Cry" was the most popular song in the world at the time and Larry mouthing the words to Johnny Ray's voice got a big laugh.

During the blacklist, Larry also got very serious about dancing. He started taking ballet lessons three times a week—he looked magnificent in tights—and learned to do a soft shoe we could perform together while we sang "Side By Side." And then, the first time we toured Britain, he decided to go even further.

Our entire act consisted of things we did together, but Larry decided I should have a big solo number and sing "South America, Take It Away," my big number from *Call Me Mister*.

Lou Mandel had always insisted our act should be balanced and we agreed so I said, "All right, but then you'll have to do something by yourself, too."

"Fine. I'll play the piano."

"You can't play the piano."

"I'll learn."

Except for some lessons when he was a kid Larry had never touched the piano, but when we got home he had our accompanist, Gerry Dolin, write a beautiful arrangement of "September Song" and teach it to him note by note.

"Now you put this finger here on this key," Gerry would say, "and this finger here and then you play these two keys up here. Now go home and practice."

And did Larry ever practice. He would go down to my mother's little house half a block from ours and he would practice four measures of the song over and over again six hours a day. He nearly drove my mother crazy. Then he would come back to Gerry, who would show him the next four measures.

Larry learned the whole song that way and he played it brilliantly. He even got to the point where he could look at the audience and smile like Liberace. I was astounded that he could learn to do this—he must have had some innate musical talent even he did not know about—and even more so when he decided to press his luck and learn to play a boogie-woogie number.

"It's very hard," Gerry warned him. "I know great concert pianists who can't play boogie-woogie."

"I want to learn it," Larry said.

So Gerry gave him a number to work on and he practiced it to the point where one night his whole arm became paralyzed. He thought he was having a heart attack and called the doctor.

"You don't suppose it's because you were practicing the boogie-woogie so much?" I asked him.

"I just thought of that. That's probably what it was."

Eventually, he got very good at that number, too, and for years afterwards he never got tired of playing it.

When our son Garry was about seventeen and had decided that music was his calling, he got hold of a copy of the boogie and learned it. Larry came back from a show on the road and on his first night home, Garry sneaked into the living room and started playing it. I remember Larry standing in the kitchen in the middle of taking a bite of a sandwich with his mouth hanging open, then swearing.

"The little son of a bitch! He plays it better than I do." After that, we always called it "The Gerry-Larry-Garry Boogie."

Next, Larry decided he wanted to be able to accompany me singing a number so Gerry taught him a simple accompaniment to "Foggy Foggy Dew."

For a long time, that was his entire repertoire. He could play "September Song," "Foggy Foggy Dew," and the boogie-woogie number, but if anyone ever asked him to play something else he had to pretend he had a headache.

Larry was extremely nervous when he made his debut as a piano player. We were in Britain and he still felt he needed to practice so everywhere we went he rented a piano or walked into a music store and asked if he could use one for an hour.

A few hours before our first performance, I came into our room and found him sitting on the bed almost in tears.

"I can't do it," he said. "Why did you make me do this?"

"Larry, I didn't make you do it. You wanted to do it."

"But you kept pushing me and telling me I was good. I'm no good and I can't do it. I'm too nervous."

"Look," I said, "if you make a mistake, it's not the end of the world. Nobody dies."

And in the end, he did the numbers and got through them without any serious mistakes. From then on, I think he even enjoyed it.

When we got home from that tour, in fact, he was so hepped up he decided he was going to play a number we could sing together. Gerry arranged a version of "Shine On Harvest Moon" where Larry would play and I would sing, then he would play and sing a kind of patter and then we would put them together. At the end of the number, he would stand up and do side kicks while he was still playing the piano!

By then, our act had an entire section that involved Larry, me, and the piano. And all because Larry never seemed to be happy unless he was challenging himself, proving his strength.

We made excellent money on these tours—close to $10,000 a week, I think—so even though we had to pay our own expenses we did very well. But Larry had a chintzy side to him and just did not like to spend money if he didn't have to. So we didn't always go to big hotels when we were on the road.

Often, we stayed in what they called "digs," which were really just glorified boarding houses that were usually run by colorful old ladies who served breakfast and were great fun to be around. These were the places where the other variety acts stayed and they were just fine by me because we got to be with the performers more.

Then there were the strange English blue laws. You could do "concerts" on Sundays, for instance, but you could not do "shows." So we cut our dialogue down to the minimum to make it sound like a concert. We could announce the numbers, but we could not do any patter in between. It all seemed so silly but we had to go along with it.

The postwar food shortages in Britain also took some getting used to. Meat was in particularly short supply and we were told it was much appreciated as gifts. So we brought a little tin of ham for the publicity man from the London office of Columbia Pictures who accompanied us on one of our tours. He and his wife had just had a baby and we had all become quite close.

"We're saving it," his wife told me later. "I just take the knife and scrape off a little bit of it and chop it up for the baby. We don't eat it ourselves." It was so sad.

After a while, there were times when Larry and I, a couple of spoiled Americans, thought we were going to starve. Luckily, we became friendly with the owner of Isow's restaurant in Soho while we were playing at the Palladium and he would occasionally send over steaks. Only later, when we heard he had been arrested, did we realize he had gotten them on the black market.

Some of the places we played were still so depressed from the effects of the war that you could not help being touched by it. Stoke-on-Trent seemed like one of the dreariest places in the world to us. It was a pottery town and everything and everybody in it was covered with clay dust.

But despite the hardships, the British people had such a great attitude about everything. They never seemed to complain and always found something that made them happy. We played Brighton on a frightfully cold day and when we went for a walk along the water we could not believe people were swimming while we were wearing overcoats.

"Oh, lovely day," people would say as we walked past just freezing to death. "A lovely day."

It was that generous British spirit that Larry and I came to admire so much, particularly how kind they were to performers. Of all the experiences with the public we ever had in show business, we both agreed there was never anything to rival our first night in Glasgow.

For reasons I still do not completely understand, *The Jolson Story* was one of the most popular movies ever to play in Scotland. When it was first shown in London, it just sort of lay there but when it got to Scotland it exploded at the box office. Then they took it back to London and it became a huge hit there, too.

Today, *The Jolson Story* and *Jolson Sings Again* are played in Britain more than they are in the United States and I still get letters from people who say they see it every year. Some of them say they have seen it a hundred times!

On our first trip to Britain, Larry and I took a train to Scotland and the farther north we got the more impossible it was for us to understand the language. When we finally crossed the border, we were astonished to find people meeting the train at every station.

I do not know how they got the news we were on the train, but they would look in the windows and bang on them and even try to sneak inside. We could hear things like "Geesa fotey, geesa fotey" and we couldn't figure out what the hell they were saying.

Our friend the Columbia publicity man was with us and he translated. "They're saying, 'Give us a photo,' " so Larry would go out on the platform and give them pictures and sign autographs.

Then somebody would say, "Till yerwee weef tacum oot." We had no idea what that meant, either. "They're saying, 'Tell your wee wife to come out,' " the publicity man said. "Betty, they want you, too."

This happened at station after station. Then we got to Glasgow and it became even more incredible. A limousine was on the platform right outside the train. How odd, we thought, but when we looked down to the end of the platform we saw a high wire fence packed solid with people leaning against it and piled on top of each other.

We got into the limo, which made its way very slowly toward a gate that had been opened just enough for us to squeeze through. All of a sudden, the car became pitch black with people climbing all over it.

They were chanting "Laarry! Laarry! Laarry!" and their faces were squashed against the window as the driver tried to move through the crowd very slowly. We were worried someone was going to fall under the wheels, and when the car began to rock under the weight of so many people it became quite terrifying. Finally, the crowd let the car through and we drove slowly off with the chants for "Laarry" ringing in our ears.

When we arrived at our hotel, the crowds were even more enormous. They filled the streets and we had to make a dash through a crush of people to get to the door. We had almost made it when a girl ran up, grabbed Larry, and got his head in a hammer lock against her bosom. I could see him smothering in there and as he struggled to get out I turned into a tiger.

"You let go of him!" I grabbed her arms and almost threw her to the ground.

It was absolutely crazy and the only time in our lives we ever got a glimpse of what people like Elvis Presley and Marilyn Monroe went through.

When we finally got inside the hotel, we were taken in hand by a proper British butler who knew all the protocol and what was expected of us. The fans gathered below a balcony outside our window—we were on the second or third floor—and they stayed there all through one of those long Scottish summer nights that did not get dark until almost midnight.

Every so often, the butler would say, "It's time to go out now, Mr. Parks" and Larry would walk out on the balcony and wave to the multitudes as if he were the king of England greeting his subjects.

Then the butler would say, "Mrs. Parks, it's time for you to go out and throw them a rose." And I would go out and wave, throw a rose, and be the queen.

After a while, the crowd began to sing a song that was something like Auld Lang Syne. It was called "Will Ye Nae Come Back Again" and we stood there listening and waving with tears in our eyes.

Our hearts were full on a night we would never forget.

BY THE TIME we made our fourth trip to Britain, we could see the handwriting on the wall.

"I think this is the last time we'll be coming here," Larry said and I had to agree. The great days of British variety, which had begun to suffer after the war, were now coming to an end. The theaters had gotten seedier and the acts we had worked with were lucky if they were able to play more than a few weeks a year.

Television had taken over in Britain the way movies had years before in the United States and the sad part was that these performers could not participate in it. Their acts were very limited and had been the same for twenty years. If they put them on TV just once, that would cover an audience of many thousands—more than they had played to in years in the variety houses—and that would be the end of them. So most of them just quit and went into other businesses.

I know it could not be helped but I have often thought what a shame it is that Dickie and Yolanda, Stan and Ann White, Vogelbein's Bears, and all the rest of them will nae come back again.

NOBODY EVER BOTHERED to explain why it was unpatriotic for Hollywood to put Larry or me in a movie but it was all right for us to play Las Vegas. And we never asked. All we knew was that there was no blacklist there and we could make $10,000 a week doing our nightclub act.

We were delighted to get the work, of course, but there was always something a little spooky about Las Vegas. For one thing, you were never quite sure who ran the hotel where you were playing.

At the Desert Inn, there was a lovely white-haired old gentleman named Morrie who would sit at a table right outside the casino. As we walked by after the show, he would say, "Hey, kids, come on over and I'll buy you a drink." It turned out he was one of the owners of the club and he was so nice and grandfatherly that we could hardly believe what somebody told us when we happened to mention him one day.

"Don't you know who he is? He was the head of the Cleveland mob. They've put him here in charge of the Desert Inn."

We were sitting with Morrie one night when he reached over and patted me on the hand. "My wife is coming into town from Cleveland. I'm going to be busy for a while so would you guys take her out for cocktails? She just adores you—she saw *The Jolson Story* thirty times— and she'd get a big kick out of it."

"Sure, Morrie, we'd be delighted to."

By then, we knew that Morrie was going with one of the most gorgeous showgirls in the hotel and had put her up in a little cottage over by the golf course. He had just given her a birthday party that was right out of the old days in the movies. Every slice of cake had a $100 bill in it for each of the chorus girls and his girlfriend found a diamond bracelet in her slice.

The next day, we picked up Morrie's wife, a cute little lady named Jackie, who had once been a chorus girl herself. She had gotten a little plump and had dyed red hair and she was as jolly and as much fun as she could be in her mink coat and diamonds.

We went to the bar in the hotel and talked for a while and then suddenly she said, "I hear he gave *her* a birthday party the other night."

Ooops!

"That's all right," she said. "I know all about it. He's got her stashed along the golf course in one of those cottages."

Larry and I looked at each other and then she said, "You know what he gave her for a birthday present? He gave her a *washing machine.* You know what *I* got for my birthday? *A mink coat.* You know what I'm going to do? I'm going to take his dirty socks over to her house and say, '*You* wash them. You've got the washing machine.' "

I always wondered what would have happened if Jackie had known about the diamond bracelet.

After the show a couple of nights later, Morrie was at his usual table and his hand was wrapped in a napkin.

"What did you do to your hand?" Larry asked.

"I think I broke it," he said, and he opened up the napkin and showed us his hand, which was swollen to about four times its normal size. Larry helped him put some ice in the napkin and told him he had better let a doctor look at it.

We were walking outside the casino the next day when Jackie came driving up.

"How's Morrie's hand?" Larry asked her.

"Oh, the damn fool. He doesn't realize he's getting old. He still wants to do all the work himself."

"What did he do?"

"They caught a couple of guys cheating in the casino," she said, "so Morrie had them brought up into the office. But instead of letting the security guys beat them up he had to do it himself. So he broke his goddam hand. He's seventy years old, for Christ sake."

166

THE ONLY DIFFERENCE between the show we did in Las Vegas and the one we had done around the country before the blacklist was that it had to be shorter. The casinos wanted people to get back to the tables.

We tried to do some new things that involved making a comic out of Larry, but it did not work out. He was a fine singer and dancer and an excellent straight man, but telling jokes was not his thing. So we went back to singing and dancing, with Larry reciting facts about Las Vegas that I would then screw up.

This worked well at El Rancho Vegas the first time we tried it, but a couple of years later when we played the Desert Inn it was not as successful. Las Vegas was changing then—it was full of socko headliner acts—and ours was just too gentle and sweet. It probably seemed a little corny for the times and I think we began to be regarded as a kind of old fogey act.

We enjoyed going to Las Vegas, though, because it always seemed like a vacation. Garry and Andy were still babies so we would bring them and my mother, who would babysit.

One night, we made the mistake of celebrating Andy's fourth birthday at the Desert Inn. We let both boys come to the seven o'clock show and I announced it was his birthday and my mother led them up on the stage.

Larry picked up Garry and I lifted Andy and as the audience sang Happy Birthday, Garry waved and sang but Andy hauled off and socked me in the nose as hard as he could.

"Why did you do that?" I asked.

"I didn't want all those strange people singing Happy Birthday to me." He was absolutely furious with us for embarrassing him. Of course, he is the one who went on to become an actor.

WE HAD FINISHED the late show at El Rancho Vegas one night when the maitre d' came backstage.

"Senator Joseph McCarthy has just seen the show and he'd like to buy you a drink."

Larry just looked at me and I just looked at him.

"What do you want to do?" Larry asked.

"I don't want to have a drink with the old son of a bitch," I said.

But Larry had a kind of curiosity that surmounted everything. "I want to meet the bastard face to face."

So we went out and there, seated in this big leather booth, was Senator Joseph McCarthy. Smashed. The first thing he did was put his arm around Larry and say, "They giving you a hard time, kid?"

"*You're* asking *me* that?" Larry said.

"Let me give you a little motto to live by," McCarthy said. "*Bastardae non carborundum*. Don't let the bastards grind you down."

Then McCarthy, who was just swacked, said, "You want to see my operation?" And he pulled up his shirt and showed us a scar the way Lyndon Johnson did so famously on the cover of *Life* magazine years later.

We did not sit there long because we felt very uncomfortable, but I remember thinking this man was not serious at all about what he was doing. He had no convictions. He did not really care about patriotism or fighting Communism or any of the rest of it. He was just an opportunist who had latched onto something that got him a lot of attention. He could ruin people's lives one day and act like he was their best buddy the next. It was all the same to him.

Years later, when I was in *All in the Family*, I told Rob Reiner this story and he became incensed.

"How could you *do* that? How could you *talk* to that man?"

There was no way of explaining it, really. Maybe we should have gone over, spit in his eye, and left. I don't know. Instead, Larry and I bid our goodnights as soon as we could and went to bed.

The next morning, I walked out to the swimming pool to find my mother, and there in the pool was Senator McCarthy teaching my children to swim!

We got them out of there and took them back to the room. They never understood why they had to take a bath right after going swimming.

The Gardener

Back in Los Angeles, there was still no work for us, so shortly after the HUAC hearings Larry and Lou went into the apartment-building business. Lou knew Larry needed something to get involved in, something to make himself useful. The three of us formed a corporation and it was not long before we had apartment buildings all over town. They were two-story buildings with twelve to twenty units each and Larry supervised the actual construction while Lou ran the business end.

Of all the things Lou did for us, this was one of the most important because when our movie income was suddenly cut off, those buildings saved our lives financially. I still own the buildings, in fact, and I don't ever have to worry about working if I don't want to. It was just one more time when Lou did right by us.

Larry went into building the same way he did everything else that interested him—with great enthusiasm, energy, and resourcefulness. He got such a kick out of every part of construction and soon there was almost nothing connected with those buildings he could not do.

He painted, he fixed the toilets, he did the landscaping. Except for the electricity, which was the one thing he would not touch, he was as hands-on a builder as he could possibly be. He would get up early in the morning and spend all day at the apartments, doing every dirty job that came up. Every day, he would say he was going to try to beat the traffic and get home a little early but he seldom did. He was just too absorbed in his work.

Larry and Lou realized early on that the way to make the apartments really pay was not to build them and sell, but to own them and rent. That would give us a steady income over the years while the value of the property was increasing. So Larry became a landlord as well as a builder and that was the part he hated.

Collecting rent, trying to keep the apartments occupied, and dealing with abusive and destructive tenants made being a landlord seem like the lowest job in the world to him. But we were still blacklisted so we were grateful he could make a living. He would try to be careful about the people he rented to, but sometimes it was impossible to tell. Someone would look like a decent person when he signed a lease and then turn out to be terrible.

Once, Larry rented to a group of real tough biker types who must have been on dope and threw wild screaming parties every night. Larry knew he had to get them out of there, he just did not know how. Then he had an inspired idea.

One night when the tenants were not there, he went down to the apartment and removed the front door on the pretense there was something wrong with it that had to be fixed. But he never brought it back. You can live in an apartment that does not have a lot of things, but not one without a front door so the bikers packed up and left.

After a while, he started carrying a hammer in the back of his pants. "If some of those guys come at me," he said, "at least I've got something I can fight back with." That used to scare me and make me worry if he was late getting home.

There were other tenants who were not dangerous but could be difficult, too. There was one little old lady in particular Larry would visit once in a while because he could see she was lonely. He realized she was slipping when he walked by one day and she looked out her door and said, "Please, can you keep that cow from coming by here all the time? It keeps trying to get into my house." The apartment was in the middle of Santa Monica and there was not a cow within miles.

WHENEVER ANYBODY ASKED Larry how an actor was able to become a successful builder of apartment houses, he always told them it was easy. "I just pretend I'm making a B movie."

The philosophy was the same, really. Whether you are making movies or constructing buildings, the most inexpensive and efficient way to do it is to waste as little time as possible. Everything had to be planned down to the smallest detail and run according to the strictest schedule. Nothing could be taken for granted.

If a city building inspector was holding things up at one of his construction sites, for instance, Larry thought nothing of going down to the building department at 6 A.M., sitting outside on the steps, and grabbing the guy as he came to work: "You're supposed to come to my apartment this morning so the window framers can start this afternoon." Then if the window framers were late, he would go sit on *their* doorstep.

As a result, Larry was able to build apartment houses from the foundation to the roof in just six weeks. Other experienced builders in town found this incredible, but to Larry it was no big thing. If a movie with a large cast and crew and elaborate sets could be shot in a week, why couldn't a building be put up as quickly? In both cases, all you needed was a good producer.

I've always felt a little guilty about the fact that no matter how hard Larry and Lou tried, they could never get me to take an active interest in the buildings. Sometimes, Larry would drive down the streets they were on and point and say, "That's ours, and that's ours." I realized they wanted to get me involved, but I never did, and finally they gave up on me. Today, Milo, Lou's son, runs our corporations and the buildings, and I'm not exactly sure where some of them are. I never had much interest in owning property of any kind before. Except for those summers on the farm when I was a little girl, I lived in hotel rooms and apartments all my life.

The first place Larry and I lived after I moved from New York in 1946 was a little five-room house just above Hollywood Boulevard in Nichols Canyon. Having a house seemed like the most wonderful luxury. The land was as big as a postage stamp, but the house had a nice open feel to it, especially when we put in French doors that led out to a backyard that had seven avocado trees.

After Garry was born in 1950 and I was expecting Andy, we turned one room into a nursery, and when the boys got older they were allowed to write anything they wanted on the walls as long as they promised not to do it in the rest of the house. We made a number of other improvements over the years, and I adored that little house and loved showing it off.

One day, a woman came by to do the property tax assessment and said, "Now you haven't done anything to the house since the last time it was assessed, have you?"

"Oh, yes. We put in these French doors and we knocked out this wall." I took her around and showed her all the other work we had done. She was very nice about it, but she looked at me strangely.

171

"Well, we'll just say it has *about* the same value."

I thought this was odd until Larry came home and I told him what had happened. He hit the ceiling. "Don't you know the more you improve a house the more real estate taxes you have to pay?"

"Oh, I thought it was like income tax. If you can prove you did something to it, you get a deduction. I've never owned anything in my life bigger than a bottle of cologne. So how was I to know?"

THROUGH ALL THE TROUBLE and strife, the good times and the bad, the apartments gave us financial security and our home gave us comfort and joy. But the real refuge was our friends, the ones who were always there for us.

There were the Mandels—Lou and his wife, Ruth, Milo's mother, with her delightful sense of humor, so tragically destroyed by Alzheimer's at the end of her life. And Milo and Isabel, who seemed to bring forth another beautiful daughter every other year—four girls in all: Nicole, Denise, Suzanne, and Lori. We always spent Thanksgiving and Christmas together, and each year they add more grandchildren. By now, I've lost count.

Then, of course, there are the Bridges. Our lives have intertwined and stayed close, and we have helped each other through big and little crises. Dottie has written in her diary every day of her married life— what a book *that* will be—and every so often she will call me up and read to me about a day she, Bud, Larry, and I were together thirty or forty years ago, and about all the good times we had.

As for the bad times, well, that was *the* big test of friendship. Andy had just been born, Larry was still in Washington, the newspapers and television were full of the HUAC hearings, and the first people at my side were the Bridges. Of course, they had been involved in political activities, too, and were in danger of being called by the committee. Bud later testified in a closed session and I think he and Larry talked about that at some later time. But if there was any disagreement between them, it never stood in the way of their friendship.

I know Dottie still thinks we were irresponsible to join an organization like the Communist Party when we didn't know anything about it, just because friends we loved and respected were members. She thinks it was stupid to be martyrs to a cause we didn't understand. But I guess I'm still an old radical who thinks we were working for good causes that I continue to believe in today. At any rate, we don't get into it. Other things are so much more important, particularly the friendship and love our two families have for each other.

I know I have sometimes been accused of not expressing enough of my thoughts and feelings. Garry has said to me, "Ma, I don't know how you feel about certain things. How do you *really* feel about the blacklist? Angry? Frustrated? How?"

That needed to be answered and I thought about it a lot. Angry? No. To me, anger is a futile emotion. I think I can sum it up in two words: deep sorrow. Not for myself—I've survived, and my life is full of joy—but a deep sorrow for Larry that will be with me in my heart for the rest of my life. And, besides, I do express how I feel in the best way I know how—in a special lyric I wrote for *Betty Garrett and Other Songs*.

> *You wonder why I'm laughing,*
> *Well, it hurts too much to cry.*
> *So I'll sing my songs to you*
> *Till it's time to say goodbye.*

I THINK DOTTIE could be a therapist. I remember one incident early on in our friendship when we were visiting her and Bud. Dottie, who is so instinctive about these things, picked up on a tension between Larry and me, and she and Bud encouraged us to let it all out.

The problem was that when I left *Call Me Mister*, the cast gave me the most adorable Irish setter and I called him Mister. I brought him and a cat named Pepper out to Los Angeles with me.

This led to problems between Larry and me almost immediately. Larry thought I had really imposed on him by bringing a dog and cat back from New York without even consulting him, but I loved animals and could not bear the thought of giving them up. We had some terrific fights about it.

Anybody who has been around Irish setters knows they are either calm or crazy. Mister was crazy. He could not stand being out of my sight and at night when we put him outside he would bark and throw himself against the house until the neighbors were all up in arms. This was during the time when Larry's mother was so ill and we could not have a dog barking all night and disturbing her, too.

I did everything I could to calm Mister down. Sometimes I drove up in the hills and ran him beside my car, trying to wear him out. "He'll sleep tonight," I would think, but it didn't work. I even slept outside by his doghouse one night because that was the only thing that would keep him quiet.

As we told the Bridges this story, we all burst out laughing. Here Larry and I had lived 3,000 miles apart the first two years of our marriage with never a cross word. And now that we were finally living together, we were fighting about a dog! When we left Dottie and Bud we felt a lot better.

As soon as we got home, we went to check on Pepper, our pregnant cat. We had fixed a place for her in the back of a closet and when we got down on our hands and knees we saw she had delivered three little kittens. We lay there on our stomachs all night, looking at those kittens and thinking what a miracle it was.

Finally, dawn came and Larry and I just looked at each other and said, "What was all the fighting about?" The Bridges were great therapists for us that night and so was Pepper.

We had dogs and cats around us for years afterwards and I had to laugh when Dr. Belous, our obstetrician, told me I was pregnant the first time.

"Oh, Betty, you're going to be so happy," he said. "This baby will be better than any dog or cat you've ever had."

In the late 1940s, Dottie had a gorgeous baby boy. He was blond and tow-headed and so big that when he was six weeks old, he looked as if he were three months. He was simply an amazing child and when they named him Garrett after me, I was so touched.

Then, when he was four months old, Garrett died. At the time they did not know why, although since then Sudden Infant Death Syndrome has been investigated and identified. It is a cause very dear to the Bridges.

This was one of the most horrendous times in all of our lives. I still shake at the memory of seeing Bud, this big vital man, standing in a doorway, gripping the door frame, and sobbing as if he might never stop.

For a time, Dottie thought she might not be able to survive and even after she came out of it a little she said she did not want to think about having another baby. But Dr. Belous in his wonderful warm supportive way talked and talked to her and convinced her she should try again.

The next summer, we were at the beach house she and Bud owned when she told me she was pregnant.

"I'll tell you a secret," I told her. "I am, too."

"You *are*? Since when?"

"Since about a half hour ago."

She laughed and said, "How do you know?"

"Somebody told me that if you put your feet up against the wall afterwards, that makes sure it happens," I said. And it was true. At least it was true for me.

A little while later, Larry and I were driving down Sunset Boulevard and Lucille Ball pulled up in a car next to us.

"How are you guys?" she yelled over to us.

"We're fine," I shouted back. "I'm pregnant."

"Oh, you lucky bum," Lucy said. "Desi and I are trying."

"Put your feet up against the wall afterwards," I told her.

"Really?" she said.

"Yeah, it really works," I said.

Lucie Arnaz was born about nine months later and for years I teased Lucy that I should get some of the credit.

Dottie went into labor in December and on the way to the hospital she insisted Bud drive her by our house first.

Bud, as nervous as any expectant father, came knocking on our door, yelling, "For God's sake, come out here! Dottie wants to talk to you."

I went outside and there she was sitting in the car, panting through her labor pains.

"See," she said, "it's fine. It's fine. I just wanted you to see how easy it is."

"Bud, take her to the hospital," I said, worried stiff about her and yet so grateful to have a friend who even when she was about to give birth wanted to show me that what I would be going through two months later was no big deal.

Their son was born in December and ours was born in January. We had always intended to name a son Garrett after me, but we asked Dottie and Bud if it would be too painful for them. They said no, it would be a wonderful memorial to their lost son. So Garrett Parks and Jeff Bridges were christened together at the Belouses. Larry and I became Jeff's godparents while Bud and Dottie are Garrett's. When Andy came along, Lou and Ruth Mandel became his godparents.

Several years later, when Lucinda Bridges was born, that was *it* for Dr. Belous, this calm unflappable man who was so close to our families and loved us all as much as we loved him.

"I'm not delivering any more Bridges or Parks babies," he said. "It makes me too nervous."

BUD AND DOTTIE'S BEACH HOUSE was out past Malibu, about a mile north of the Ventura County line, although calling it a house is a bit of an exaggeration. Bud and Dottie had bought the land with Lewis Milestone and his wife Kendall—he directed *All Quiet on the Western Front* and other great movies—who put up a very elegant trailer.

But Bud and Dottie did not have much money so they bought a little one-room prefab shack at a building site and then took it apart and got Larry and a bunch of their other friends to help them throw the sections down over a cliff onto the beach. Then they all went down and put it back together again. I was doing a show in New York at the time so I missed all the fun.

The house had one small bedroom and a chemical toilet until years later when they added a little kitchen and a room in the back and a small john. Larry and I would sometimes go down there and sleep in the Milestones' trailer if they were not there. Or, if we went on the spur of the moment, we would bring our sleeping bags and Bud and Dottie would come out in the morning and find us lying on the patio.

We all got together and divided up the cooking and cleaning and other chores, but my job always seemed to be taking care of the children. And as the years went by, there were more and more children. I loved to do the same things they did, so Beau Bridges and the other kids who always seemed to be around would go out on the beach where we would swim, play games, and jump off the sand dunes.

The Milestones threw one party during which they wanted everybody to plant iceplant on the bank behind their trailer so we all brought things for a picnic and started planting. It was a very steep hill and after a while, Bud and I noticed we were the only ones planting while everybody else was eating and drinking.

At one point, Paulette Goddard came down to join us. She was wearing a big picture hat, a filmy blouse, and very stylish shorts, and she brought her chauffeur who was carrying a big wicker picnic basket. She opened it up and there was a bottle of champagne and jars of caviar. It was a typical Paulette Goddard entrance.

By the end of the afternoon, everybody else was just smashed down on the beach while Bud and I had terrible sunburns on our behinds because we had been up there working. I wore a bikini in those days and though it was modest by today's standards—all it really showed off was my famous belly button—it was new and sort of shocking. Even now, I have people come up to me and say, "I'll never forget that day at the beach where they had a big party and you got up on a platform in your bikini and sang a song."

Larry and Bud built a barbecue up at the house out of stones they had rolled up from the beach. It was a rickety-looking thing with a light hanging over it and they had loud arguments all the time they were sweating to put it together while Dottie and I just laughed at how these two great friends never could agree on anything.

The real fights, though, came after we had all been grunion hunting. Larry and Bud had different ideas about how grunion were supposed to be cooked. Larry thought they should be fast-cooked in oil over a hot fire with nothing on them except salt and pepper, while Bud liked them cooked over a slow fire in butter with a little sherry. They finally settled it by putting a line down the middle of the barbecue and for years Bud's grunion were always cooked on one side of the grill while Larry's grunion were on the other.

We turned the grunion hunting itself into a real ritual. The little fish came in with the tide and we would look in the paper to see what hour of the night they were supposed to be running. The Bridges and the Parks would sit by a fire until it was time, then we would all race down to the beach. When the grunion started swimming in, we would run along, shining a flashlight, picking them up, and stuffing them into sacks.

Our jeans always got sopping wet and so heavy that we could hardly run so after a while we made a House Grunion-hunting Rule: Everybody had to take their clothes off. As soon as we could see they were running, we would strip naked and run to the beach to hunt the grunion. Bud always seemed to have the flashlight and we used to accuse him of shining it more on the women than the grunion.

One night, Larry and I went to a party down the beach at Burt Lancaster's house, but the grunion were due at ten o'clock so we left at nine thirty. When we got back to the Bridges, Dottie came running out and said, "The grunion are already running. Hurry up, go on down to the beach."

So Larry and I raced down, stripping our clothes off as we went, just dropping them on the sand. We ran up over a sand dune shouting "Where are they? Where are the grunion?" only to discover Bud standing there with at least a dozen guests, all of them strangers. They had their clothes on, of course, and there we were stark naked.

THOUGH THEY WERE best friends, Larry and Bud were so different in many ways. Cooking grunion was not the only thing they disagreed on. In temperament, Larry was more like Dottie and I was more like Bud. On Sunday nights, when it was time for us to leave the beach and go back to the city, Bud and I always wanted to get in one more swim while Larry and Dottie would be sitting on the suitcases, grinding their teeth, and tapping their toes. They were both the practical perfectionists. We used to say if Dottie had married Larry, they would have killed each other, and if I had married Bud, we would have sunk into a pool of inactivity.

Larry and Bud always seemed to be in competition with each other, too, no matter what they were doing. They were out swimming in the ocean once and it turned into a sort of unspoken contest about who could swim farther from the shore. All of a sudden, they got caught in a riptide and realized they were in big trouble.

Larry swallowed his pride and turned to Bud and said, "I think I'm going to need your help."

Bud, who is a powerful swimmer, said, "That's funny. I was just going to ask *you* for help."

They started waving and shouting to us on shore. Of course, we couldn't hear what they were saying over the sound of the waves and just gleefully waved back.

Fortunately, they had enough sense to swim across the riptide and they made it back to shore, but the experience scared them very badly.

We spent the rest of that night sitting around the fire shivering and drinking martinis.

Larry, who was just exhausted and still a little frightened, finally got into his sleeping bag and I zipped him up until there was nothing showing but his nose and eyes. We all just sat there and sang him to sleep.

EVEN BEFORE Garry was born, Larry and I realized that our house in Nichols Canyon was going to be too small for us one day. We could not afford anything really grand, but Larry loved houses and he enjoyed looking even when he had no intention of buying.

There was one house in Holmby Hills up above Sunset Boulevard that he just adored. It was long and low and made out of adobe and looked as if it was right out of Mexico with aged beams supporting the ceiling of the porch and bougainvillea climbing all over it. Larry drove me up to see it several times and he always said, "This is my dream house."

Later, when I was making *Take Me Out to the Ballgame*, Frank Sinatra invited the entire cast to dinner one night and as we drove up Larry suddenly realized where we were.

"The son of a bitch bought *my house*!" he said. And sure enough, it was the house he had always wanted.

Frank was still married to Nancy then and when she showed us around we were stunned by how beautiful they had made everything. The walls were decorated with Utrillos—Frank's favorite painter— and Roualts and some of Frank's own skillful paintings, too.

Then Nancy took us upstairs to little Nancy's bedroom. There were two beds, each with canopies over them, ruffled bedspreads, and dozens of dolls sitting on them wearing dresses decorated with flowers.

"My God," said Larry, "what luxury!"

Nancy, worried that we would think her kids were spoiled, snapped back, "Don't worry. I deny my kids *plenty*!"

OUR HOUSEHUNTING went on for years. We knew we had to move when the boys were getting older because our house was getting more and more cramped and had just one bathroom. So Larry sent me out looking and I must have worn out ten real estate agents. I would find a place that was acceptable, but when Larry went to look at it the answer was always the same: He didn't like it. Larry had a list of things he wanted in a house just like the list he'd had of what he wanted in a wife. It had to have land. It had to be convenient. And it had to be cheap.

Dottie Bridges, who wanted us to move to Westwood where she and Bud lived, said, "Larry, you can't have *everything*," and she kept digging up houses for us to look at. They were beautiful houses, but usually with very small yards and Larry was a tree nut who insisted on having as much land as possible.

Occasionally, I would go out in the San Fernando Valley where there was some attractive property for not too much money, but Larry would not hear of it.

"I will *not* live in the Valley," he said. We had friends who lived down where it is flat and knew how hot it could get in the summer.

Just when I was about to despair of ever finding a house, a screenwriter friend named Bill Roberts and his wife, Helen, told us about one on a street near their house that had been on the market for a long time. It was in the hills above Studio City on the Valley side, but I could see this was different. The next time I went, I took Larry with me and the minute he saw it he said, "This is it."

"What about your vow not to live in the Valley?" I said.

"This is *not* the Valley," he said.

It certainly didn't feel like the Valley. The house was up a little hill from the street on a large plot of rolling land. It was surrounded by meadows, had a glade with a stream running through it, and there was even a hiking trail near by.

Much of it had been designated a wilderness area and the streets wound all through the neighborhood with cul-de-sacs that made it hard to get around if you did not know the way. That meant there would never be a lot of through traffic. And all the foliage, combined with the fact we were up the hill, made it ten to fifteen degrees cooler in the summer than it was on the Valley floor, which was only a few minutes away.

As Larry looked around, he could see the house and land had all the room we would ever need and that he would be able to plant as many trees as he wanted. Now all we had to do was convince the owner to sell us the house.

Bill told us the woman who owned it had gone through four real estate agents and they had all given up on her. The house would go into escrow and she would change her mind and back out. But Bill told us he would watch to see if the house went back on the market and so did our friends Shirley Robbins and Butch Baskin, who also lived in the neighborhood.

Shirley had gone to the Annie Wright Seminary with me while Butch had been a classmate of Larry's at Joliet High School. Not long after they met, Shirley told Butch quite proudly, "I know a movie star."

"So do I," Butch said. Were they ever surprised when they discovered the two movie actors they knew had married each other.

Larry and I knew nothing about this until one day we were at a party where Larry ran into Butch and fell into his arms at seeing him after all these years. I just stood there smiling when Shirley came up and said, "Betty, don't you remember me?"

"My God!" I shouted, "Shirley!" The reunion was complete. Only later did we find out that Butch and Shirley's brother had created the Baskin-Robbins ice cream empire.

One day, Shirley said she thought the owner of the house might be getting ready to put it back on the market. Knowing the woman's bad experience with real estate agents, I just knocked on the door and said, "Your neighbors said you were planning to sell this house. Could you please show it to me?"

The owner, a very nice man named Jack Smalley, took me through it and a little while later Larry and I both went to see it and found Jack's wife, Betty, in the greenhouse where she raised orchids.

"Oh, just what I've always wanted," Larry said, "a greenhouse." He started admiring her orchids, and that, I think, is what did it.

"The last couple that was here walked in and the man said, 'The first thing we have to do is get rid of the greenhouse,' " Betty Smalley humphed. "I wouldn't sell him the house."

It also turned out they had raised two boys close in age and here we were, a young couple with two boys thirteen months apart. So it all seemed just right to her and she and her husband sold us our beautiful house. I have lived in it for more than thirty years now and I love it as much today as I did the day we moved in.

Not long after we bought the house, Jack Smalley wrote us a letter.

181

He had been an editor for *Photoplay* magazine and had left us stacks of back copies that are treasures. He said he had meant to tell us something interesting about the house.

He had been writing a story for the magazine about Katharine Hepburn when she was making *The Little Minister*, and had visited her on location in this beautiful little glade with trees and a stream running through it. He had fallen in love with the area and a couple of years later he learned they were selling lots there so he had bought one.

"And that," he wrote, "is where your house is. It was the first one built in the area."

There were no houses on the hillside above us when we moved in and none next door, either. We were surrounded by woods and grass and Larry dammed up the stream near the bottom to create a waterfall and a small pond. We stocked the pond with trout and goldfish that grew so large they became almost like pets and we could not think of eating them. We planted watercress and I used to go down and pick it by the handful for salad.

As for trees, Larry was in his glory. He planted a weeping willow that bent over the stream and elsewhere on the property I think he may have planted just about every kind of tree that grows in California. The only ones he ever cut down were olive trees because it turned out I was allergic to them.

Larry also became a magnificent gardener. There was not a flower on the grounds he could not name and describe. He spent hours out on the grounds and was accompanied virtually everywhere he went by our dog Snoopy.

Snoopy was actually Andy's dog. We went to the pound on Andy's twelfth birthday and as we walked around, one little dog came over and stuck his nose through the cage and that was it. Andy knew it was his dog. I'll never forget turning around during the ride home and there in the back seat was this little boy with his new dog licking his face.

Snoopy was a mutt, mostly beagle, but I suspect he had some foxhound in him, too, because he had longer legs than most beagles. And he was as smart as any dog I've ever known. Andy always tells me I'm lying when I say this, but I would swear that dog housebroke himself.

"You didn't know how many nights I got up and cleaned the mess up," Andy said, but it was never obvious to us. And once Snoopy was housebroken, we never could see where he went. He was so gentlemanly I think he hid it in the ivy.

Snoopy taught himself tricks, too. He would lie down, sit up, stand up, and beg, or even dance and twirl on his hind legs on command. Or, if he wanted a bone, he would lie down, sit up, stand up, and twirl one after another without being asked.

The fact that Larry was outside gardening so much made him an object of curiosity among the children who lived in the area. There were always a lot of them around, including six or seven who lived on the top floor of a house across the street as if it were a dormitory.

Larry adored children to the point that when we lived in Nichols Canyon before Garry and Andy were born he would dress up like a monster on Halloween and go out and hide in the bushes to scare the neighborhood kids. He always did it in a way so they would know who it was, and for months afterwards they would come knock on the door and ask, "Can Mr. Parks come out and play?"

I never realized how much the children in our neighborhood came around when Larry was out gardening because he never made a big deal out of it. The only time I knew they had been there was when he would say something like "That little girl next door is the cutest kid" or "That little boy is so smart."

The family that lived across the street had one beautiful little girl who was retarded and became very special to Larry. The neighborhood kids teased her sometimes, but whenever they came over to play he made her the queen, put little wreaths of flowers in her hair, and had everybody dance around her. She loved Larry because he treated her like someone important and consequently the other kids in the neighborhood began to treat her better, too.

After Larry died, the girl's mother came up to me in the grocery store one day and said, "I can't tell you how much your husband meant to me and to our family."

Our home in the hills had an easement attached to the property that was too narrow for a street and we thought that would never change.

We were wrong.

Larry's big mistake was to clear an area on the hillside next to the house that went down to the street. It was like a jungle, so overgrown you could not even see through it, and by the time he was done it had become a lovely meadow. But as soon as he did that, somebody must have thought, "Hey, that's nice land up there." The next thing we knew, the Home Savings and Loan Company had bought the property, subdivided it, and started building.

I remember being out on the road in a play and getting the most heartbreaking letter from Andy saying the monsters had descended on us. Bulldozers were tearing up the beautiful hillside, filling in the stream, and building roads leading to little plots of land that were hardly big enough for the houses that would soon be looking down on us.

Later, Andy told me he organized some of the neighborhood kids to try to sabotage the bulldozers at night by throwing Kotex and sugar into the gas tank. Andy tells me now, years later, that the idea came from Larry.

"Dad didn't tell us to do it," he said. "He just told us how you could screw up a bulldozer."

They did not stand a chance, of course, and I was glad I didn't know about it at the time and that they didn't all get arrested.

One of the saddest things I ever saw happened when we were sitting outside one night and a deer and her little fawn came running out of the woods and stood on top of one of the cleared areas where they had probably lived. They were so frightened they went crashing down the road below us into my neighbor's greenhouse and knocked over all her pots and plants. They were looking for water that was not there anymore because it was trapped under the street the builder had paved.

The loss of that stream hurt the most. It began at a cliff above us and ran all year round, watering the entire area. Larry did everything he could to save it. He went to city officials and pleaded. He spoke to the workmen and asked them please to divert the stream over to our land. But nobody wanted to take the responsibility because it might disturb the building plans that had already been approved.

This was before the ecology movement had gained strength and I have always thought that if it had been just a few years later Larry might have been able to appeal to the authorities on the basis of saving natural water. The irony is that after the houses were built the stream kept popping up in people's backyards unexpectedly and became more of a nuisance than anything else. Even today, the stream flows out into the street.

Larry would have loved to see how Garry has taken over the care of the grounds today, planting ferns, making a brick path, an arbor, and a stone fountain with a waterfall. Sometimes I glimpse him through the trees mowing the lawn and I think "It's Larry." Of all my memories of Larry, the strongest is of him out in the garden.

Larry once visited me when I was on the road and he carried a fresh Tropicana rose, which was his favorite, all the way from Los Angeles. It stayed fresh for the longest time and even when it dried it kept its shape and bright orange color. I saved it and brought it home in a jar. It's still there with some other potpourri with traces of bright orange on its petals.

THE GARDENER

Everything grows for him.
His most typical gesture
A hand cupping a rose
And the soft touching of the petals
With his fingertips.
"Isn't this beautiful?" he says.
"That's a Tropicana . . .
And that other one
With the long stem
Is an Eiffel Tower
And that fat pink one
Is called the Helen Traubel . . .
Smell that dark red one over there . . .
That's Mr. Lincoln
Doesn't he smell sweet?"
And in the greenhouse . . .
Epiphyllum, Bromeliad, Dieffenbachia . . .
"Don't ever eat the leaf of a Dieffenbachia
It'll paralyze your vocal chords
But if you cut the leaf of an Aloe Vera
And put the juice on a burn
It'll stop the pain.

Taste the liquid
On the face of that Hoya blossom
Sweet as syrup, isn't it?"
And so he shows you the flowers and plants
And he touches them
And they grow for him

He embraces his sons
The way a man should embrace his sons . . .
Really holds them in his arms
Not afraid to show affection . . .
Fiercely protective against the world
But gently
And they grow for him

He holds me
With tenderness and respect and pride
And love that I can feel
And like the flowers
And like our sons
I too grow for him.

Family Matters

When we moved into the house in the hills, there was never any doubt that my mother would come with us. She had been fine in her own apartment just down the street from us in Nichols Canyon, but there was nothing suitable near the new house and we had plenty of room. I was also quite worried about her because of a drinking problem she had developed over the years. And after we moved to California it got worse.

Through all the shows and all the movies I was in, through all my friends and my marriage and my children, my mother was always there. And she was such a vital, intelligent woman that everybody loved her.

When I started working steadily in New York, she seemed to feel it was time to retire. Once, she took a job on the road for a sheet music company but she came back devastated and with a great sense of failure about it. I never knew what specifically had happened and she would not talk about it. I guess she felt she had bitten off more than she could chew. And when somebody stole her purse, she just seemed overwhelmed by things she would previously have taken in stride. She never took another job.

From then on, she did nothing except devote herself to me. While we were still in New York, she would wake me at noon every day. (If I was working in a show, I never got to bed before 3 A.M.) She would bring me a glass of hot water with lemon and honey and cook my breakfast. Later, she would cook my dinner and help me entertain friends after the show every night.

Still, she had too much time on her hands and cocktail hour started a little earlier every day until finally it got to the point where we would sit down to dinner and I could not eat because she was slurring her words.

I went to our family doctor, a wonderful woman named Dr. Clara

Gross, and said I was not feeling well, but it did not take her long to get me to tell her what the problem really was. "Send your mother in and let me talk to her," she said, and she talked to her not so much about alcoholism, but about what she was doing with her life.

Dr. Gross suggested volunteer work and my mother, who had always been comfortable around doctors and hospitals, said she would like to work in a hospital. Dr. Gross sent her to one, but even though she was not even sixty years old they told her she was too old. And that was the end, the final rejection, being told she was too old to help out at a hospital.

I saw then that her one great flaw was if anybody rejected her, she just gave up. I learned from that—there is no rejection that bothers me—but my mother had a gentle ladylike quality about her that I did *not* inherit. She would not stand up and fight.

After I was married, we never had an answering machine or a babysitter all the time my mother was alive. When we moved up in the hills, she sat by the phone all day long, played solitaire, and took our messages. She was always there to babysit until the night we came home and found her passed out on the floor with a big gash on her head. We read her the riot act, but we knew then we had to be careful leaving Garry and Andy with her.

We gave her a car, hoping it would make her independent enough to go out and see friends. But even when she finally passed the driving test, she was just too nervous to drive and I would always have to take her where she wanted to go.

When the boys were grown, in about 1970, Larry and I were in Kansas City doing *Plaza Suite* and my mother fell and broke her hip. Garry was with us, working as our stage manager, so Andy was home alone with her. There had been an earthquake and it had frightened our little parakeet Winkie so badly that he dropped dead in his cage. And Andy's dog Snoopy was sick and throwing up.

"You can't do this to me," Andy said when he called to tell us about my mother's accident. "You leave me here all by myself with a dead bird, a sick dog, and a broken grandmother."

I rushed home, of course, but I had to rejoin Larry back on the road and we could not leave my mother with Andy because she needed full-time care and physical therapy for her hip. So we decided the best solution was to put her in a nursing home where she could get the treatment she needed.

One of her greatest dreads had always been that we would just put her away somewhere and she was frightened that it was happening.

"Mom, it's just for a little while," I kept saying. "It's just until you learn to walk again. Do your exercises and the sooner you get better, the sooner you'll get home. As soon as we get back from the road, you'll be right back home with us."

She was suspicious, but the tour did not last much longer and I brought her home.

One blessing was she did not drink anymore because it just did not agree with her, although she smoked until the day she died. That was actually worse because she was always dropping cigarettes and we were afraid her bed would catch on fire. It finally got to the point where we would not let her smoke unless somebody was there with her.

She never got to the stage where she could walk without her walker, but she got around pretty well for a couple of years until she had a gall bladder operation. The anesthesia left her quite disoriented. She had the kind of walker she could sit in and often I would find her somewhere in the house, not knowing where she was.

I'd take her back to her room and she'd say, "Why can't I be in my own room?"

"Mother, you *are* in your own room."

"No, I'm not. I know what you're doing. You're putting me away."

I would argue with her and I would get very frustrated and we would both end up in tears. Then I realized I would simply have to learn to deal with the fact that her memory just was not there any more. Whenever she complained about not being in her own room, I would put her in her wheelchair and take her around the house.

"Here's the living room," I would say. "Here's the dining room. Here's the kitchen and now we're going down the hall into your room. See, Mom, you're in your own room now."

"Oh, well, I guess my old brain just isn't working," she would say and for just a moment she would come back to reality.

She started talking to imaginary people, too, and a friend told me not to argue with her about that, either.

"She's gone on to another plane," my friend said. "She's going back into her childhood and seeing people she knew, or maybe she's going ahead to some other place and meeting new people."

I am not a mystic, but that was a good way for me to look at it because it kept me from being angry at her when she was not all there. I learned to humor her and so did Larry, who was wonderful with her.

"Who are you talking to, Tavie?" he would say.

"Oh, that lady standing there."

"Well, what's her name?" and he would go along with her.

Once, Larry went into her room to bring her in to dinner and found her lying in her bed stretching her arms wide apart and then bringing them back together.

"What are you doing, Tavie?" he asked her.

"Well, I'm untangling this yarn." My mother loved to knit. Then she looked at what she was doing and said, "Oh, silly. I'm just imagining, I guess."

"Are you ready to come in to dinner?" Larry asked.

She said she was, but first she rolled up the imaginary ball of yarn and put it in her pocket.

One day my mother woke up blind in one eye. It was all very sudden and I took her to the doctor who tried cortisone and some other treatments, but they didn't work.

"Well, dear, you're just getting old," he said, which made her so upset and bugged me, too. What kind of diagnosis was that? We found another doctor, Glenn Dayton, who was much kinder and said, "There's nothing we can do for that eye, but I can change your prescription and give you much better sight in the other one. You'll be able to see everything you want to see." That's the kind of doctor I like!

It was not until many years later, long after my mother had died, that I finally found out what the trouble had probably been with her eye. I only wish I had not had to find out the hard way.

It began with headaches I simply could not believe. I had never had them before in my life, but these lasted forty-eight hours and there was no painkiller that seemed to help. My legs from the knees down ached so badly it felt as if I were standing in ice water. And my teeth hurt, too.

I also had aches and pains throughout the rest of my body, particularly just under my rib cage on the right side. I can't tell you how many times they x-rayed my teeth and my gall bladder and were unable to find anything wrong.

This went on for about six months and I lost weight because I could not eat and got weaker and weaker. It seemed as if I were in the hospital half the time. They ran brain scans, did a laparoscopy, in which they cut a hole in your stomach and insert a little camera to take a picture of your liver, and put me through every other incredible torture they could think of. One day, I had seven enemas because they kept taking me from one x-ray to another and they had to keep cleaning me out.

It was agony and I began waking up in terrible sweats. I had the boys bring my hair dryer to the hospital because I would wake up so wet there was no sense in changing to another nightgown. I would just get it wet, too. Instead, I stood there drying my nightgown and myself so I could go back to sleep.

The doctors kept coming back to my gall bladder because the pain was so intense in that area. But they simply could not find out what was wrong with me. Just when I was beginning to fear they would never know, my doctor, Robert Meth, called one day.

"Does it hurt when you comb your hair?"

"It's agony when I comb my hair." My hair was down to my behind then and putting a brush through it was torture.

"Do your teeth hurt?

"I've just come from the dentist. I thought I must have an abscess or something."

He kept asking me such strange questions that I finally asked, "Are you reading this from a book?"

"Yes, I got out my medical books and I'm trying to find out what the hell is wrong with you. I think I have a clue. I'm going to send you to a rheumatologist tomorrow. He deals with rheumatic diseases."

Fortunately, I had already had almost every test there was so they did not have to worry about my gall bladder or hepatitis or brain damage. The rheumatologist, a British doctor named Rodney Bluestone, ran a very simple test and then he came in to see me.

"We know exactly what's wrong with you," he said in his delightful British accent. "We're going to give you some medicine and you're going to feel veddy much better veddy soon."

191

"Oh, thank God," I said, and I broke into tears and just fell into his arms.

I had temporal arteritis, which is sometimes called giant cell arteritis. It is related to arthritis, but instead of being an inflammation of the joints, it is an inflammation of the lining of the arteries. In most cases, it is limited to the arteries in the temple, but mine was all over my body. Dr. Rinaldi, who was an associate of Dr. Bluestone, said I had the worst case she had ever seen, that she had never known anybody to have it in practically every artery of the body.

There are main arteries under the right rib near the gall bladder and in the legs and that is why I hurt so much in those areas. It had been so hard to diagnose because the only way to be certain is to do a biopsy of an artery. They clipped out one in my temple, and sure enough, it was inflamed inside.

Dr. Bluestone put me on Prednisone—a kind of synthetic cortisone—and within two days the headaches were gone and so were all the other pains. I took massive doses for more than two years and one result was that I blew up like a balloon. I had a big round moon face and became an entirely different-looking person.

"Betty, you can have a whole different career now," an actress friend, Maxine Stuart, said to me. "You can be this sort of plump character woman."

And for a while I was, but I was not at all unhappy about it. To finally know what was wrong with me and to be able to treat it was such a relief that nothing bothered me. I have been keeping a close watch ever since, but so far there has not been any recurrence of the condition.

Dr. Bluestone told me that one of the main dangers of temporal arteritis is that it can attack the nerves in the eye and cause instant blindness. And since the disease is not caused by a virus or bacteria, it is possibly hereditary.

The minute I heard this I knew it was what my mother must have had. It explained her sudden blindness and possibly her supposed gall bladder problem. To think that 60 milligrams of Prednisone could have spared her all that agony.

But despite her frailty and ill health, my mother always maintained her warmth and dignity and if we had people over, they all gathered around her. There was an inner elegance about her that I could never hope to attain.

As for Larry, he was very sweet to her—better sometimes than I was. When I would get mad and start fighting with her, he would say, "You can't treat your mother like that."

The kids made her happy, too, as they had always just adored her. She went to visit her brother in Oregon once and I took the boys to the airport to meet her when she came back. They were so excited to see her they ran toward her as she came off the plane.

Garry grabbed one hand and Andy grabbed the other—they must have been about five and six years old—and suddenly I looked down and saw Garry licking his grandmother's hand like a little cat. It was so primal and touching.

One day in 1973, some neighbors came by and we were all down at the pool laughing at something when I left to come upstairs and check on her.

"What on earth were you laughing at?" she said. "It sounded like you were having so much fun."

"It's their anniversary, Mom," I said, and I brought the neighbors up to say hello.

"We're all having a drink to celebrate," I said. "Do you want a glass of wine?"

"Oh, I'd love that," she said, but she just choked on it and finally said, "I can't drink anymore, but I'll toast you with a cigarette."

That night, I gave her a bath, cut her toenails, and put her to bed. Later, she had to get up and go to the bathroom and when I tried to help her out of bed, her legs gave way.

"Mom! Mom! Hold on! Hold on!" I shouted as I tried to get her standing again. "I can't hold you. I can't hold you."

"Don't be mad at me," she said, crying.

"Mom, I'm not mad at you," I said. "I'm just mad that you're sick, I don't want you to be sick."

Finally, I got her into the bathroom, but when I brought her back out she starting having a convulsive coughing spell and then she just went. I massaged her chest and I talked to her: "Mom, don't go. Please, don't go. Hold on!"

But I could tell she was gone. There is a moment when someone is not a person anymore and I could just see the essence literally go out of her. I went in and woke Larry and called the boys. She looked so beautiful with all the stress gone out of her face.

Everyone deals with death a different way and I remember how Garry sat the longest by my mother's bed as if he were communing with her before he finally let her go. She was a great lady.

MY FATHER'S COUSIN KATTIE from the farm also moved to California in 1946, shortly after I did. After being a farm girl in Missouri all her life, she just sold the farm when her brothers died and moved out to California to be near us. She was exactly the opposite of my mother, though, because she was totally independent.

She did not even have a Social Security number, but she went right into Bullocks department store in Westwood and, because she was a fabulous knitter, got herself a job in their knitting department and worked there for years. She bought herself a big car—she was about five feet tall and could barely see over the steering wheel—and she would just tootle around town in it. She took classes in yoga, art, astrology, investment, anything that interested her. Once, she took some classes in archaeology and the next thing I knew she was on her way to Egypt.

Kattie had a beautifully furnished little apartment in Westwood with some lovely furniture that I still have and she always spent the holidays with us. She would arrive every Christmas with a basket full of presents and became an important part of family celebrations. She had other relatives, but felt closer to us, I think. She had always adored my father and thought of him as a brother rather than a cousin so I became a niece instead of a second cousin.

After a while, though, I began to realize that Kattie's health was failing, too. Her friends told me that when she drove them to church or a luncheon she would drop them off and go look for a place to park. Then she would forget what she was supposed to do and drive home.

At one point, Kattie became very ill and when she went to the hospital her doctor saw there was a problem with the medication he had prescribed for a congestive heart condition. It had been working so well that when the problem recurred he realized she must either be forgetting to take her pills at all or was taking them twice. I learned a great lesson from that and have kept careful track of the pills I take ever since, but the doctor was worried about Kattie and said she must not be left alone.

A friend of hers, Dodie Fuller, and I decided she would be better off in a nursing home and we found what we thought was a very nice place in Santa Monica where I would visit her and we would sit and knit. But one day she fell and hurt herself and they began tying her into her bed or her wheelchair. I could not stand that so we took her back to her apartment and found a woman who was willing to live with her and act as her companion.

The minute we did that, she was fine. Her mind came back in the familiar surroundings and she was as happy as a bird. Kattie lived that way for almost a year and I visited her often until finally, on a very hot day, I found her lying on the couch looking kind of faded near a little air cooler on the floor that was not really cooling things off at all.

"I've had *such* an interesting life, haven't I?" Kattie said in her twangy Missouri accent.

"Yes, you have, Katherine."

She died that night and while I don't know whether she sensed she was going, I have always thought that's the way to go—saying, "I've had *such* an interesting life."

I ONCE TOLD Jack Lemmon a story about Garry and Andy and the next thing I knew he used it in an interview on a talk show.

When the boys were very young and we were still living in Nichols Canyon, we went for a drive over into the Valley. They had been in the car before, but as I saw these two little faces with their eyes looking anxiously out the window I realized this was the first time they understood they were traveling some distance.

"Where's our house?" Andy said as we drove up on Mulholland Drive.

"Well, it's back there around those curves," I said, "and when you get to Willow Glen you turn right and then you go down the hill until you get to Nichols Canyon and you turn right again and drive until you get to our house."

Andy thought about this for a while. "You'd have to have awful *long* eyes to see our house from here."

There was another silence and then Garry said, "Yeah, and they'd have to be *bent*." Jack Lemmon loved that story.

195

I'm sure Garry and Andy were no brighter or more adorable than anybody else's kids, but we were certain they were the most remarkable children alive.

Garry started walking when he was only nine months old. He just pulled himself up by the desk in the living room of our little house in Nichols Canyon one day and started to rock back and forth. Soon, he was putting one foot ahead of the other and walking across the room while Larry and I held our breaths. He never went through the crawling stage. We couldn't keep him in his playpen, either, and it got to the point that when Christmas came we let him have the run of the house and put the Christmas tree in the playpen.

Andy, on the other hand, never talked baby talk. From the beginning, he pronounced words perfectly and spoke in complete sentences. He is still the most verbal person I have ever known!

There was a time when Larry and I were sure Andy would be a lawyer because he could always get what he wanted. He often talked himself out of being punished and sometimes he would do it for Garry, too. He would argue so reasonably that we'd say, "Maybe we're being unfair" and reduce the punishment. It got to the point where Garry sometimes paid Andy to keep him out of trouble.

One time when Garry was about eleven or twelve years old he was invited to a party. Larry and I had plans for that evening and told him he couldn't go unless he arranged for an adult to drive him. So Garry offered Andy a quarter to find a way he could get to the party. It so happened that our plans changed and when we picked Garry up at school we told him we could give him a ride after all.

Garry was so excited that when we stopped to get Andy, he yelled across the schoolyard, "I get to go to the party!"

"You owe me a quarter!" Andy shouted back.

"But you didn't do anything!" Garry said.

"I *prayed!*" Andy said.

Another of my favorite stories is about the time we were getting ready to go to a party. Larry was taking a bath and I was sitting at my dressing table putting on mascara when Andy, who couldn't have been more than five, discovered a box of Tampax. He marched into the bathroom to ask Larry about it and, although I couldn't quite hear everything they were saying, I could tell Larry was explaining a little about the facts of life.

A few minutes later, Andy came in, rested his elbow on the side of the dressing table, crossed his legs, looked at me, and said, "What's this I hear about you laying an egg every month?" I promptly stuck a mascara brush into my eye!

At an early age, Andy was a bit of a showoff, singing out loud whenever we shopped for groceries and shouting Hello to strangers wherever we were. He got so much attention that Larry and I felt Garry should have something special about him that people would pay attention to. So we were delighted to discover that when he was no more than three or four years old he had taught himself to add.

That was his big accomplishment and when there was company we would say, "Garry, come show how you can add."

"What's three and four?" somebody would ask, and he would screw up his face, close his eyes, and say "seven" and everyone would applaud. After a while, Garry could add quite large sums.

Once, Garry had a bad case of the flu with a high fever and a terrible racking cough, and Larry and I literally walked the floor with him all night. At about three in the morning, Garry was wheezing and coughing when all of a sudden he chimed out, "Four and five is nine, five and six is eleven."

"Oh, honey, you don't have to do that," we told him, but I guess it made him feel better somehow.

As they grew older, each of the boys had one special experience that I thought influenced their lives dramatically.

With Andy, it began when, after taking prelaw courses at UCLA for more than three years, he quit just one quarter before graduation.

"Every day I go there, I hate it more and more," he told Larry and me. "I realized I was going to be a lawyer just to please you. But I don't want to be a lawyer. I want to be an actor."

Larry hit the ceiling and I had to remind him that he had done pretty much the same thing. He did get his degree at the University of Illinois, but he did not follow through on his plan to go to medical school. Instead, he became an actor almost immediately.

"But why couldn't he just get the *degree*?" Larry kept saying. "He only had one quarter to go."

"If you're going to be an actor," I said, "who cares if you've got a college degree?"

The truth is, Andy had been an actor almost from the moment he was born. He always seemed to be performing somewhere. He never missed being in a Cub Scout play, he memorized the entire score of *Once upon a Mattress* when he was thirteen years old, and Larry and I often used to hear him in his room reciting Shakespeare soliloquies. I have a feeling he will play Hamlet someday.

As a teen-ager, he was in a series of moralistic little dramas called "Plays for Living" about things like drugs and teen-age pregnancy that were performed at high schools, and he made a comedy album called "Sex, School and Other Pressures" for our friend Bud Freeman that was quite delightful. But by the time he left college, all Andy had done professionally was a couple of *Room 222* episodes and a *Man from Shiloh* on television.

And then, from out of the blue, he was asked to star in a movie. Norman Toback, who lived across the street, had always liked Andy and he was friendly with Leon Capetanos, a filmmaker and writer who was looking for a young man to be in his next movie. Norman suggested Andy and before we knew it, at the age of twenty he was playing a lead role in a film that was shot all over Europe.

The movie was about two young American students backpacking around Europe—it was called *Summer Run*—and the other student was played by Dennis Redfield, who is still one of Andy's closest friends. I thought the picture was charming, but it never really went anywhere. The shooting of the movie was like a grand tour—London, Paris, Amsterdam, and other great cities—and the company was put up in nice hotels, was chauffeured everywhere, and had all its meals catered by the movie company.

But Andy decided that was the sissy way of doing things so the next summer he decided he would do the trip all over again, only this time he really would rough it. We were quite worried about him because he was all by himself and we could tell from his letters how homesick he was and how much he missed the conveniences he had had before.

"I have a room where when I sit on the bed my knees touch the opposite wall," he said in one letter. "I finally took some money and bought a little radio because I couldn't stand being all by myself."

I have often thought how typical it was of Andy to do something like that, and how much it was like something Larry would have done—both of them proving their own strength.

Garry's experience was far more traumatic. When he was thirteen years old, he contracted Guillain-Barré syndrome, a rare disease in which the body's immune system attacks part of the nervous system. I first realized something was wrong when I took him a glass of orange juice one morning and it slipped right through his fingers. Then, when he tried to get up, he couldn't walk. His legs just collapsed under him. It scared the hell out of all of us.

We took him to the hospital right away where luckily our pediatrician, David Goldstein, set out to find what was wrong. He stayed up two nights and two days, watching Garry, reading up on all the symptoms and taking tests. Finally, he ordered a spinal tap, which confirmed that Garry had Guillain-Barré syndrome.

This is a disease that causes a traveling paralysis. It will travel up your right side one day, then down your left the next, and so on. For a while, half of Garry's face was paralyzed, which made it difficult for him to eat. The doctor would come in and say, "Can you whistle today, Garry?" Of course, you can't whistle when one side of your mouth is useless.

We were relieved to learn that the disease usually just goes away after a while, but until it does there is a danger the paralysis could travel to the heart or lungs so the patient needs to be near life-support equipment. That meant Garry had to stay in the hospital for several weeks.

During that time, he shared a room with a boy his age who had to have a leg amputated. This affected Garry very deeply and made him really think about his own condition. Often when I visited, he would talk about what he would do if he was paralyzed the rest of his life.

To give him encouragement, one of the specialists who was treating him brought him a model of an antique car and said, "Garry, someone gave this to me but I don't have time to put it together. Will you do it for me?"

That was just the kind of thing Garry loved to do and the next time I visited him he showed me the model and said, "That's what I could do the rest of my life if my legs are paralyzed. I could do things with my hands." It killed me to hear him talk like that, but at the same time I was proud of his spirit.

Eventually Garry completely recovered, but I have always wondered whether Guillain-Barré syndrome might somehow have destroyed an inner sense of security and confidence that Garry had.

Garry himself says that he seemed to lose a sense of purpose and started to lead a kind of reckless existence.

Larry and I were not aware of it except that he seemed to lose interest in architectural drawing and the piano and swimming, all the things he was so good at. Certainly none of us was prepared for the fact that by the time he was eighteen, he was a heroin addict.

It was the 1960s, and of course we were aware that almost everybody was experimenting with marijuana. Larry and I even tried it at a party one night, but since I didn't smoke I didn't know what to do and it didn't have any effect. But we figured the kids were probably using it, too, and we never thought it was a terribly serious thing. It was like the beer we had drunk as teen-agers, with our parents sort of half knowing and half not.

Garry once confessed to us that he had tried LSD a number of times, too. That alarmed us, but a lot of people were advocating it in those days and Garry even became its champion for a while. He claimed it was an experience everybody should have. Later, though, he said he was through with LSD. He said it was beginning to make him feel "flakey."

That seemed to be the end of it, but it wasn't. And since Garry had always seemed like such an ideal kid to us, we overlooked all the signs: the irritability, the secretiveness, the wild characters hanging around, the long sleeves in the heat of the summer, the loss of interest in his drawing and his music. So even though we should have known, the fact is we didn't.

It all came to a head when I was performing in a lengthy engagement of *Plaza Suite* in Chicago. Garry was not only using heroin by then, he was dealing, too. There were suspicious guys coming to his door downstairs in the back of the house at all times of the night and Garry had signed Larry's name on some checks. He knew he needed help and finally he got up his courage and told the one person whose help and protection he had always been able to count on. He told Andy.

"You have to tell Dad," Andy said.

"I can't," Garry said. "He'll kill me."

"Let me talk to him," Andy said.

So Andy went to Larry and pleaded Garry's case the way he had so often when they were little.

"Garry needs to talk to you about something," he said. "Please, please, don't get angry. Please listen to him. He needs your help."

Larry had a pretty short fuse sometimes, but to his credit he listened sympathetically as Garry told him the whole story and he reacted very calmly.

In those days, Synanon, a drug rehabilitation organization, had a good reputation, so Larry and Garry drove out to their headquarters on the Pacific Coast Highway. They talked to a man who told them the rules were very stringent. Garry would have to give himself over to Synanon completely for six months. He could have no contact with his family or friends and no involvement with any of his normal activities, which meant no drawing and no music.

Larry had a funny feeling about the whole thing and he sent Garry to sit out in the car while he talked to the man some more.

"What do you want to do?" Larry asked when he finally came out.

"Pop, please don't leave me here," Garry said.

"I have the same feeling," Larry said. "But if you come home there are things you've got to do—and I'll help you. You've got to stop seeing your friends, you've got to stay at home with me, and you've got to do what I say."

Garry agreed and Larry moved him up into our bedroom, which had twin beds in it. Larry found a tiny antique hand pistol that had no bullets and I don't think had ever been used. But he thought if any of the guys Garry dealt with came to the door he could at least pretend to threaten them.

There were nights when Garry was in really bad shape. Larry would get in bed with him and hold him as tight as he could to keep him from shaking. It was a frightening time for both of them, but somehow over the next few months Garry got clean.

Larry cooked nourishing meals for him, took him to the gym, and got him to exercise, lift weights, and get all the nervous energy out of his system. By the time I came home on vacation from the show, Garry was in great physical and mental condition.

Larry and Garry met me at the airport, which was unusual because Larry usually came alone, and together they told me the whole story. I was in shock, of course, but at the same time I was happy to see Garry looking so good and talking so openly about his addiction.

Looking back, what is so remarkable about all this is the fact that

Larry had very little tolerance for what he felt was weakness. But he loved Garry so much that he kept his cool throughout the whole thing and I think he did more than any therapist or treatment could have done.

Of course, it wasn't quite that easy; it took Garry a year to kick heroin completely. After staying absolutely clean for seven months, he started again and, though the addiction was worse than it had been before, this time he fought it by himself. Garry says it might have been easier if he had sought professional help but because he had licked it once with Larry's help and knew he *could* do it, he was able to prevail.

Larry was on the road this time and I remember taking Garry to the Bridges' beach house, looking out onto the beach, and seeing him digging his heels into the sand trying to read a book.

"Please don't tell Dad," he told me. "It'll kill him." I respected his wishes but I felt so helpless. All I could think to do was just *be* there and fortunately it was enough. Garry is rightfully proud that he won the battle for good.

Since that time, he not only hasn't touched drugs, he doesn't drink or smoke, and he is on a strict nondairy diet. He works out every day of his life, plays racquetball three or four hours, gives lessons, competes in tournaments, and has become the Western regional champion in his age group. He also is deeply involved in his music, composing and working on his piano and synthesizer until all hours of the night.

He has also helped innumerable friends who have had substance-abuse problems. He knows how to talk to them because he's been there. I hear him on the phone sometimes and one of the things he says is "I don't care if they *are* your friends. If they use drugs, they're killing you. You can't afford their friendship!"

Which I'm sure is what Larry used to tell him.

On The Road

*L*arry and I had just finished a tour of Britain one summer when Lou Mandel called with the most exciting news imaginable. Judy Holliday had gotten into a contract dispute with Columbia just as they were getting ready to film *My Sister Eileen* and they needed a replacement in a hurry.

They wanted me.

I would have been thrilled under any circumstances, but it was particularly important at that moment. A number of people who had been blacklisted, like Zero Mostel and Jack Gilford, were starting to get work again, especially on Broadway. So to have a major studio hire me to play a leading role in an important movie was a real breakthrough.

I think people were beginning to forget who had been made unemployable and even to wonder why anyone had ever cared. Of course, there was still a whole group of people out there who would write to the sponsors every time they saw someone they did not like on television. I think the studios cared only about what it would do to the box office. They had to be convinced that hiring one of us would not destroy a movie financially. In this case, I have always thought the person who did the convincing was Lillian Burns.

Lillian, who had been so helpful getting me started at MGM, had moved to Columbia where she had become Harry Cohn's right-hand woman. He was consulting with her a lot in those days and I'm sure she just told him, "I know the perfect person for this part." I will always be grateful to her, for I realized all over again how lucky I have been through the years to have so many friends do so many unexpected favors for me.

One problem with the offer was that Larry and I had signed a contract to do *The Fourposter* in summer stock after we got back from Britain. But Lou quickly got Pat Englund, a very good actress, to replace me and told me to hurry home and come to his office in New

203

York. I would sign the contract there, he said, and then fly to California for a meeting with Harry Cohn the next day.

I ARRIVED in New York exhausted after the trip from England and when I got to Lou's office I discovered that a contract was not the only thing I would have to sign. There was also a loyalty oath.

I took one look at it and very naively decided that I was not going to sign Columbia's loyalty oath, I was going to write one of my own. So I sat down and wrote what amounted to a justification of practically my entire life.

I kept writing things like "I don't regret a thing I have ever done" and "I am not ashamed of anything" and "This is the way I felt about things at that time" and on and on for page after page.

Lou kept coming in and saying, "Betty, we have to go. This has to be in the mail and you have to catch a plane."

"I'll be done in a minute," I told him and I kept writing and agonizing over every word.

It was ridiculous, of course, but I felt very strongly about it until Lou came in one last time and said, "Look, all you have to say is 'I am not a member of the Communist Party. I am a loyal American citizen.' " The whole statement was two sentences long. I signed it and rushed out to the airport for an overnight flight to Los Angeles.

I got myself all dressed up for Harry Cohn that morning. I wore a nice dress with a kind of bouffant skirt that had a lace petticoat sticking out underneath, but when I walked into his office his first words to me were typical Harry Cohn: "Your slip is showing."

The old manipulator was always looking for your vulnerable point, always trying to find a way to control you. But he picked the wrong girl that day because I was not feeling very vulnerable.

"Thank you very much," I said. "My slip is *supposed* to be showing. So should I go out and come back in again?"

There was no doubt about it. I was back in Hollywood.

MY SISTER EILEEN must have had the strangest progression from one form to another of any movie ever made. First, Ruth McKenney wrote some stories for the *New Yorker* magazine. They became the basis for a Broadway play with Shirley Booth and Jo Ann Sayers, and then a movie with Rosalind Russell and Janet Blair.

Next Rosalind and Edie Adams played the same parts in the musical version of the play *Wonderful Town*, which had music by Leonard Bernstein and lyrics by Betty Comden and Adolph Green. It was a big hit in New York so it was only natural that Columbia, which had filmed the play, should want to make a movie of it too.

But somebody connected with the musical wanted a lot of money for it and Harry Cohn said, "The hell with you. We own the property. We'll write our own music." And he brought in Jule Styne and Leo Robin to write a whole new score.

When we began, the movie seemed so promising. I was Ruth, Jack Lemmon was the magazine editor I try to sell my stories to and fall in love with, and Janet Leigh played Eileen. Bob Fosse, who played the soda jerk, did the choreography and he and Tommy Rall danced up a storm. Dear Richard Quine, who killed himself a couple of years ago, was the director and Blake Edwards wrote the screenplay.

We all had the happiest time making the movie. It took nine months to shoot (time enough to have a baby) and yet there was never any tension. Richard Quine was the kindest of directors with a terrific sense of humor, Janet Leigh and I were together so much we began to feel as if we really were sisters, and Jack Lemmon quickly became the favorite person I ever worked with other than Larry.

To illustrate the kind of guy he is, we were shooting a scene where Jack, as the publisher of a magazine, has invited me to his apartment under the guise of discussing a story of mine he has promised to publish. His real intention, of course, is to seduce me and he plies me with wine, gourmet food, and an after-dinner brandy all the while singing "It's Bigger Than Both of Us." The scene ends as, hypnotized, I watch him swirl the brandy in a snifter; he drinks it and then throws the glass into the fireplace.

We shot the scene in full, and everyone laughed at my reaction to his throwing the glass. Then it came time for my closeup.

"Don't throw the glass this time, Jack," Dick Quine said. "It's out of the shot. No one will see it. Betty, just pretend you hear the crash."

"Oh, no!" I pleaded. "Please let him throw the glass or my reaction won't be as real."

"You're an actress, you can make it real," Dick said, trying to shame me.

Jack could see I was distressed and gave me an almost imperceptible wink as the cameras started rolling. My eyes circled dizzily as Jack, off-camera, swirled the brandy in his snifter. I looked up as he lifted the glass and drank. Then . . . crash! He hurled the glass into the fireplace and I nearly jumped out of my skin.

Jack, wide-eyed and innocent, looked at Dick and said, "Oh, gosh. I'm sorry! It slipped out of my hand!"

They used my closeup in the finished picture and I have loved Jack Lemmon ever since.

Despite all the fun we had making the movie, we worked like dogs, which will not surprise anybody who has ever worked with Bob Fosse. When we were doing the dances, Bobby insisted on going over and over every step. It would be six o'clock at night, we would have been in the rehearsal hall all day, and he would say, "Let's do it just one more time." Two hours later, we would still be there.

The dance captain was Rickey Gonzalez who used to anticipate Bobby every time we finished a number by saying, "*Uno mas.*" After a while, we all started calling Bobby "*Uno Mas.*"

But nothing stopped him. One night we were shooting an outdoor scene in a gazebo and it was so cold we were all freezing. We worked all night and Bobby started going, "Phew, it's so hot," and got us fanning ourselves, loosening our clothes and going through this whole charade about how hot it was. At one point, somebody slipped us some brandy so by the time we finished the shot we were a little warmer— and a little potted, too.

But it was such a happy set that we all hated to see the filming end. On the last night, Janet and Bobby and Tommy Rall and I were all sitting around when somebody said, "Let's go home, get a night's rest, and come back and do it all again."

But the movie was not a raging success and I think there were several reasons. Jule Styne and Leo Robin were not chopped liver by any means and the music they wrote was nothing to be ashamed of, but it certainly hurt to lose those great songs from *Wonderful Town*. For instance, there was a really good comedy number for Ruth called "A Hundred Easy Ways to Lose a Man" and to replace it Jule and Leo wrote a song called "As Soon As They See Eileen."

I sang it with my hair in curlers as I was putting "frownies" and all kinds of beauty creams on my face. Then I walked outside and scared a little boy, who ran screaming from the patio. It was cute, but not the solid kind of comedy song that "A Hundred Easy Ways to Lose a Man" was.

There was also a wonderful song where four characters sit around on a first date with nothing to talk about. It was very funny in the show, but they played it as a straight scene without music in the movie, which was not quite as clever. And "We're Great But No One Knows It," which Janet and I sang as we were going off to work, could not make up for the loss of "Ohio," the great show-stopper from *Wonderful Town*.

Then there was the problem of the title. They could not use *Wonderful Town*, which meant losing the name of a hit Broadway show. And calling it *My Sister Eileen* made audiences think it was just a remake of the earlier movie with a different cast.

But I did not discover the biggest problem of all until we went on the road to do publicity. In town after town, we found the distributors did not want us to mention that it was a musical!

I was really shocked at this and when I asked why, they said musicals were not selling the way they used to. It was the first inkling I had that Hollywood's Golden Age of Musicals was coming to an end.

I had never stopped to think that musicals would go out of style, at least the kind they used to make. There will always be movies with musical numbers, of course, but I don't think they will ever again be made the way they were then: where suddenly there is a dance number or people just burst into song.

It was all very artificial and I think after a while audiences found it harder and harder to suspend their disbelief. We did not realize it while we were making the movie, of course, but we were taking part in the end of an era. There was no killing off *My Sister Eileen*, though. It's now on videotape and even today people come up to me and say how much they love the movie, which has become a cult film.

AT THE TIME, I did not worry about what the failure of the movie might do to my career. Although *Big City* was the only picture I had ever done that was at all dramatic, I had looked forward to doing straight roles one day. With all my training and experience, it seemed like a natural move to make. If only I had known what my next straight role would be.

I think Columbia was testing me when they cast me in *Shadow on the Window* with John Barrymore Jr. in 1957. It was an inconsequential little black-and-white melodrama, almost a B picture, and the studio might just have wanted to see if I would do it. When Lillian Burns brought me in to work with her on a few scenes, I sensed a kind of impatience, as if she were saying, "What are you doing this for? This is beneath you."

And when the picture got little attention—I never even see it playing on late-night television—Columbia dropped my option. Perhaps the studio was still worried about the blacklist or thought I was too strongly identified as a musical performer. Or perhaps, because I had been in two flops in a row, I was no longer a saleable property. Whatever the reason, I have not made a movie since *Shadow on the Window*.

There were other offers from time to time, but Lou Mandel did not want me to take them because he felt the parts were not right or not big enough. Occasionally, we fought about this and there were times when we became almost like father and daughter with Lou laying down the law and me rebelling.

"You just have to be patient, dear," he would say to me. "I know you want to work and your time will come. A good part will come along and they'll want you."

There were people who said Lou's brusque manner harmed my career, particularly his insistence that I would never audition for a role. There were a number of producers and directors who told me Lou yelled, "She's not interested!" or "How dare you!" at them and slammed down the phone when they wanted me to read. They would not try to hire me again, they said, because they did not want to deal with Lou. I would defend Lou to them by saying he was just being protective of me.

I'm sure I could have worked in smaller movie roles, and I would not have minded, but in the end I followed Lou's advice. I continued along the path I had always followed—letting things happen, letting other people tell me what to do next.

This was how I had gotten to New York, how I had gone to work for Orson Welles, Mike Todd, Vinton Freedley, Louis B. Mayer, and Harry Cohn. Sometimes, it seemed as if I was a spectator observing my own career from the sidelines. And if I had not had any great ambitions back before I came to Hollywood, I certainly was not about to develop any now.

In the long run, I think Lou was right. Larry and I could always go back to England. We could tour in our nightclub show. And Garry and Andy were young and I wanted to be with them. So there was something to be said for being choosy. I took very much to heart a marvelous formula Lou had for deciding whether or not to take a job.

There were three things to consider, he said: money, prestige, and artistic satisfaction. If a job had any one of them, you would consider it. If it had two, you would *really* consider it. And if it had all three, then it was the best job in the world for you at that time.

Maybe you needed money so you took whatever came along. Some of the lesser roles I took in television fell under the heading of prestige. It was a matter of being noticed in something successful. Artistic satisfaction meant a project was very important to your soul even if it did not pay well and might not get a lot of attention. I have always found this a wonderful way of looking at things because it helps me decide which roles to accept and which to turn down.

By the time I finally did realize my movie career was over, it did not seem to matter much because Larry and I had discovered so many opportunities in the theater by then. I had always loved being on stage and it was such a relief to discover that people out around the country did not seem as interested in blacklists and loyalty oaths as they were in Hollywood.

I don't think it ever came up in the local press—there were no editorials that said we shouldn't have been hired—and on the few occasions when a reporter did ask Larry about it he simply refused to answer. Sometimes, he even told publicists in advance that if the subject was brought up he would leave the room.

In the 1950s, that was probably the wisest thing to do but after Larry died I began to talk about it and I have ever since. If anybody asks me about the blacklist, I answer as honestly as I can. I think it is important that people know how ugly things were. Every once in a while, though, I listen to myself and think how Larry would hit the ceiling if he could hear me discussing it so openly.

THERE WAS A TIME when it seemed as if Larry and I performed in every modern husband-and-wife comedy or musical ever written. Over the years, we did *The Marriage Go Round, Tunnel Of Love, Cactus Flower, Plaza Suite, The Tender Trap, Anniversary Waltz, Send Me No*

Flowers, Who Was That Lady?, Bells Are Ringing, High Button Shoes, Goodbye Charlie, and others I'm sure I've forgotten.

Our engagements ranged from a few weeks in summer stock at places like the Famous Artist Colony Playhouse in Fayetteville, New York, the Avondale In-The-Meadows Playhouse in Indianapolis, and the Salt Creek Playhouse in Hinsdale, Illinois, to lengthy national-company tours of cities like Detroit, Chicago, Washington, and New Orleans. One summer, we actually did two plays at two summer stock theaters, one right after the other. We performed in one while memorizing the other and ended up exhausted!

I was so happy to see Larry enjoy performing again and we were both delighted by the fact the shows were so well received by the public and the critics. Larry had developed a fine light comic touch and we really did work well together. Our timing was so synchronized and we knew each other's moves so well that sometimes he would say to me, "I can tell what you're doing when my back is turned."

We did *Cactus Flower* in Chicago for four weeks once and just reveled in a couple of its uproarious scenes. You say a line, you get a scream. You say another line, you get another scream. We would come off stage and just look at each other and grin. Working in the theater doesn't get any better than that.

Looking back, it is hard to believe, but I actually played in *Plaza Suite* for two and a half years. First, I performed with Forrest Tucker in Chicago for almost a year, then I went on the road with Howard Keel for another nine months, and finally Larry and I did a bus and truck tour of smaller towns the major road company had missed for another eight or nine months.

Larry and I were really looking forward to the bus and truck part of the tour, which consisted of one-nighters or split weeks all over the country. The rest of the cast rode in a bus while we were given a mobile home to drive ourselves. This meant we would not need to pack or unpack and we had a refrigerator so we would not have to stop for food—or so we thought. Garry was with us as the stage manager of the show so he and Larry would take turns driving and relaxing and we would stop at hotels at night.

We started out in Massachusetts in the fall and we thought we were in heaven. The leaves were turning, the weather was beautiful, and the clam chowder at the old inn where we were staying was delicious. This is the way to live, we thought.

But we soon learned how mistaken we were. The mobile home turned out to have a very bumpy ride. It joggled so much that after a while you felt as if your back teeth were coming loose. This made it difficult to get up and move around and nobody could get much rest, either. The fact that the refrigerator never seemed to work turned our idea of not stopping at restaurants into a joke, too.

We also had problems with the fact that the mobile home was too big to park in underground garages and was not allowed in many parking lots because it took up two spaces. And it had to be balanced just so at night or the electricity would go off, which meant there was no heat and Garry had to give up his idea of saving money by sleeping there.

The tour itself made for a lot of wear and tear, too. We went to places like Tamaqua, Pennsylvania, which reminded me of Stoke-on-Trent because it was covered with coal dust instead of clay dust, and Dubuque, Iowa, and towns all over Texas and Oklahoma. We played ninety-six cities in seven months!

Whoever made a map of the routes from town to town might have thought Jackson Pollock had drawn the map of the United States. We made hops from Iowa to Texas and then back up to South Dakota, then down to Baton Rouge and up to Kansas City. There were blizzards on that part of the trip and one night, when Larry and I had flown ahead to do an interview, Garry almost froze to death on the road.

He was driving several hundred miles to the next stop when the electrical system in the mobile home went out. He got out on the road and tried to flag down the bus carrying the rest of the company, but they didn't see him and zipped right by. Luckily, Garry had bought a big sheepskin coat at the beginning of the tour or he would have frozen to death. Finally, he got a ride and stumbled into the hotel late that night.

In many of the towns, the hotel rooms were not only dingy, they were so exactly alike that after a while we were able to walk in with our eyes closed, hang up our clothes, and stumble into bed. There was this nightmare quality of "Where are we? What town are we in?" We made jokes that we were really dead and would be on this tour for eternity, traveling from one Holiday Inn to another, where all the rooms looked exactly alike.

Sometimes, our whole life revolved around "Where are we going to sleep? Where are we going to eat? Can we get a good meal?" If we came into a town without a good restaurant or a place to go after the show, we felt like crying.

Many of the towns we went to had new civic theaters and the residents were always so proud of them. "Wait until you see our new theater," the publicists would say. "It seats three thousand people and it's good for everything—concerts, ballet, opera."

When Larry saw one of these monstrosities, he would say, "You know the only thing this theater's good for? *Aida* with elephants."

Of all the small towns we played, Valdosta, Georgia, where we did *Plaza Suite*, may have been the most memorable. It is spelled Valdosta, but they call it Val*des*ta for some reason and a couple of days before we got there, we received an official-looking letter on the stationery of the Hallelujah Church Women's Theater Society of Valdosta, Georgia.

"Dear Mr. and Mrs. Parks," the letter said. "We do not allow any obscenity or profanity in any production under our auspices. Please delete same from your script or you will not be allowed to play here."

"What are we going to *do*?" I asked Larry. "Maybe we should go through the script and sort of censor it a little."

"No! This is Neil Simon! I'm not cutting one single semi-fucking-colon!"

But I was a timid soul and I went through it and cut out "Jesus!" in a few places and we went to Valdosta hoping for the best.

Opening night, Larry walked out and delivered his first line, which used to get a nice little laugh: "Three hours in the goddam dentist's chair!"

Nothing from the audience. Not a peep.

During the whole first act of the show, I try unsuccessfully to get one of my galoshes off so I limp around with one bare foot, which always got a few chuckles.

Nothing!

In the second act, Larry plays this ridiculous middle-aged movie producer who dresses like a hippie and I play this little itsy-poo middle-aged lady who thinks she is Betty Boop and talks in a high squeaky voice.

Still nothing.

The third act, where we play the parents of a bride who locks herself in the bathroom just before her wedding, was just as bad, and we went back to the dressing room not knowing what to think. We had played to unresponsive audiences before, but never one that just *hated* us.

Afterwards, we were supposed to go to a party given by the Hallelujah Church Women's Theater Society, but Larry said, "I don't think we can go, do you?"

"No, they'll stone us."

Just then, the hostess knocked on the door to pick us up and take us to the party and Larry pulled her into the room.

"Listen," he said, "I don't think we'd better go. We've obviously offended somebody. We got this letter that told us to cut out all the obscenities and. . . ."

"That old *bitch*!" the hostess said. "She's done it again! She's always doing that. She has no right to use The Hallelujah Church Women's Theater Society of Valdosta, Georgia, stationery for her own purposes.

"Besides," the woman said, "you must have felt how *warmly* you were received. We of Valdosta, Georgia, have the reputation for being the *warmest* audience in the whole United States!"

On that same tour, we played in Cleveland where a critic for the Cleveland Plain Dealer wrote one of my favorite reviews ever. I will never forget his name—Jimmy Valentine—and he wrote, "In the first act of 'Plaza Suite,' Betty Garrett walks funny. In the second act, she talks funny. In the third act, she *finally is* funny."

Usually, when a company breaks up after a tour like that, everybody is crying on one another's shoulders and saying, "Oh please, let's get together. I'm going to miss you all so much. Let's do another show together." But the day we finally left *Plaza Suite*, we had all been together so long, the only thing anybody wanted to say was "*Goodbye!*"

There were certain things about being together twenty-four hours a day on the road that Larry and I loved. On the nights we were performing, we would always go to dinner as soon as the best restaurant we could find was open because we did not want to be stuffed when we went on stage.

We would ask for a table that had good light, Larry would ask for "two Rob Roys with cherries straight up," and we would order dinner. Then we would look at each other, say "OK," and open our books and read. It was so relaxing to just sit and eat and read together although occasionally we would look around and wonder if people thought we didn't like each other very much.

There were other areas where we were not so compatible. Larry and I learned early on to go to the theater in separate cars, for instance. He always wanted time to relax before the curtain while I would arrive just in time to get my makeup and costume on and slide onto the stage with my opening line. We always had separate dressing rooms, too, because he was prone to bugging me by standing in back of me at my dressing table and asking, "Are you going to be ready?"

And Larry was an early-to-bed, early-to-rise type while I had always been a night owl who thought nothing of staying up until three in the morning. This always aggravated him, particularly when I was making *My Sister Eileen* and had a 6 A.M. call.

It was the night before Halloween and I was making costumes for Garry and Andy at 2 A.M. when Larry came storming out of the bedroom.

"Are you still *up*? You're going to look like shit tomorrow."

Larry had always had great admiration for Joan Crawford when she worked at Columbia. He told me how wonderfully disciplined she was, even to the point of sleeping in her dressing room when she was making a movie so she would look her best in the morning.

"Joan Crawford wouldn't be up at three in the morning when she had an early call!" he shouted at me.

"Joan Crawford wouldn't be making Halloween costumes for her children, either!" I yelled back.

It's just as well Larry wasn't around for *Mommie Dearest*. I don't think he would have gotten over the shock.

LARRY'S GREATEST TRIUMPH on the stage began in 1955 and it came about almost by accident. Burgess Meredith had been out on the road with *Teahouse of the August Moon* and we stopped backstage after the show one night to see him.

"You know, I'm getting ready to leave the show," Burgess said.

"It must break your heart to leave such a great role," Larry said.

"Actually," Burgess said, "I don't know when I'm going to be able to leave because they haven't got anybody to replace me."

Then, almost as if he were thinking out loud, he said, "You know, *you* could do it, Larry." And he recommended him for the part.

Larry played Sakini for almost two years in dozens of cities all over the country. It is one of the great comic roles in modern American theater, I think, and it was just perfect for Larry. So perfect that after a while he *became* Sakini.

Larry was five-feet-eleven, but somehow he made himself look like the little Japanese valet to a U.S. Army captain. He trained his hair, which was very curly and high on his forehead, to come forward in bangs and he wore it that way all the time because if he combed it back it was just too hard to comb forward again.

He also had to speak with a Japanese accent, which meant pretending to have difficulty with Ls. His first lines as the play's narrator, for instance, were "Rovery radies and kind gentermen."

But even this was not enough for Larry. There were only four or five American actors in the play while the rest were supposed to be Japanese. But the casting director could not tell Japanese from Chinese and hired some of both. As Larry got into his role, he found he enjoyed the company of the Asian actors and extras so much he started hanging around with them and even living in the same inexpensive hotels they did.

It seemed as though the Asian members of the cast had relatives all over the country and most of them owned restaurants so in every town they went to Larry ate Chinese or Japanese food. After a while, he began to learn a little of the languages and started talking like the Asian actors and taking on some of their characteristics.

When I visited him on the road, I would feel I was entering an entirely new world. Larry had this completely different manner about him and I would come away thinking I was married to a small Japanese man.

I took Andy and Garry with me on one of these trips when they were about five and six years old and Andy fell in love with the geisha at a Japanese restaurant. Her name was Chik and she was about twenty-five and he asked her for a date. She accepted and we went to a movie where he bought her a bag of candy and held her hand. There were times when I thought we were all playing parts in *Teahouse of the August Moon*.

In 1960, Larry and I returned to Broadway in a musical called *Beg, Borrow or Steal* that started off in the weirdest way. Bud Freeman, a writer friend, had written a musical with a composer named Leon Pober for a benefit for the actors charity SHARE.

They called their show *The Gray Flannel Briefcase* and it was a take-off on movies that dealt with social and political problems like *Gentleman's Agreement* and *Marty*. But they got into a disagreement with someone on the board of SHARE, and took the material away.

Bud brought the music over to play for Larry and me one day and we thought it was really fun. Bud said he had decided to record an album of it.

"An album of a show that has never been produced?" I asked.

"Why not?" he said.

I could not think of a reason and agreed to sing the part of a lady butcher who falls in love with a Madison Avenue executive.

The album turned out well, and Larry in particular got so excited about it that we decided to turn it into a Broadway show. Bud wrote a book—there had not really been one before—and put in a part for an attractive scoundrel who owned a New York coffee house, a perfect part for Larry!

Biff McGuire was a Madison Avenue executive while Eddie Bracken played the lady butcher's brother and Estelle Parsons was in the chorus. Billy Matthews, a good friend who had directed Larry in *Teahouse of the August Moon* and both of us in *The Tender Trap*, was hired as the director.

One of the backers was Harris Masterson, a man I had met on the *Queen Elizabeth* on one of my trips to Britain. (Larry had gone ahead to make a film.) Harris was an educated, attractive multimillionaire who lived in a mansion in Houston, but what I liked about him was the fact that he was a very good dancer. We danced our way across the ocean to London where I introduced him to Larry and we all became friends.

Several years later, Harris and his wife, Carol, were visiting us around the time of the *Beg, Borrow or Steal* auditions and when we told him we were looking for investors, Harris said, "How much do you need?" We told him and he came up with over half the amount on the spot.

The show was set in the beatnik era with flower children, coffee houses, poetry recited to jazz, Zen Buddhism, and so on. Larry grew a beard for his role and I recited poetry, did some African dances, and sang several beautiful songs, including "No One Knows Me," which was a sort of early feminist plea. Outside of that, I have no idea what the plot was supposed to be.

I thought the show really was working well and I continued to think so right up until it all started falling apart. First, somebody decided having a lady butcher as a character was kind of repulsive so they changed her to a health food store owner, which was not nearly as interesting. Then, as the show got in trouble on the road, Billy Matthews was fired as the director and that broke all our hearts.

It did not get any better after that and although a dance number where I beat on a drum with my behind stopped the show, it did not seem to warm the critics at all. The reviews were scathing. They lit on the beatnik aspect of it: "How *dare* they make those druggies attractive?" That sort of thing.

It was a very traumatic experience because we had all put so much time and money into it, but I will never forget Carol Masterson's reaction as we sat at Sardi's reading the reviews.

"Well, dear," she said to Harris, "What shall we do next? Shall we invest in another show or shall we buy a radio station?" That's being cool!

BEING ABLE TO WORK TOGETHER was the real joy of these years, of course, and I am glad to say Larry and I never took it for granted.

I remember so well when we were doing *Cactus Flower* in Chicago and I left to go to New York to rehearse *Plaza Suite*. It was difficult to leave.

Larry, who still had another couple of weeks in *Cactus Flower* with an understudy, put me on the bus to the airport. I reached out the window to him standing there on the sidewalk and I saw he had tears in his eyes.

"You'd think as you got older that it would get easier," he said. "But it gets harder and harder to say good-bye to each other."

I told him I felt the same way and then I realized I was crying, too.

The Spoon River Marauders

I f *Beg, Borrow or Steal* was a big disappointment on Broadway because we all had such high hopes for it, *Spoon River Anthology* was exactly the opposite.

The play was conceived as an exercise for an actors workshop in Los Angeles, but to our astonishment it took on a life of its own and swept us all the way to New York. It was as if we were Mickey Rooney and Judy Garland saying, "Hey, kids, let's put on a show" and the next thing we knew we were playing before packed houses.

It all began when Curt Conway, with whom I had worked years earlier in *Meet the People*, called one day to say he and a number of other actors who had come out to Hollywood from New York were getting together to form a workshop called Theatre West. They were starving for some real creative work, Curt said. Why didn't I join them?

Joyce Van Patten was in the original group, along with Charles Aidman, Scott Marlowe, Sandy Kenyon, Bill Berger, Carol Rossen, Bert Remsen, Maxine Stuart, Hannah Hertelendy, and a number of others. Curt was a marvelous teacher as well as an actor and director and the group grew from twenty actors to about forty and we met on Saturday mornings in a tiny theater at 666½ South Roxbury, which we named "Sick Sick Sick and a half." We would bring in scenes from plays, monologues, songs, or anything else we wanted to work on.

Occasionally, some pieces grew out of this that seemed ready for performance, but we were terribly snobbish when anybody suggested inviting the public. "Showcase" was a dirty word to us then. We were there to work on our *art*. Eventually, though, we realized that acting is not just for the performers, but for audiences, too.

Charles Aidman had always loved Edgar Lee Masters's poetic saga *Spoon River Anthology*, which tells the stories of hundreds of residents of a small Illinois town, and he adapted some of these for staged readings. Joyce Van Patten, Robert Elston, Chuck, and I started perform-

219

ing them and my friend Naomi Caryl Hirshhorn joined the group to produce them. When Chuck discovered what a lovely voice Naomi has, he decided to have her put a folksong frame around the poems that turned them into something quite magical.

Spoon River is not Great Poetry, but it is very actable. The characters all speak from their graves and they reveal themselves in so many ways that each poem becomes a little play in itself.

What Chuck did that was so clever was to take about fifty of the poems—Masters wrote more than two hundred—and arrange them so you got a real feeling of the people in the town and their relationship to one another. A man would speak and then a woman would appear with her poem and you would realize they are husband and wife. It may have started out as unconnected, but by the time it was finished you felt as if you had seen a play about this little town, Spoon River, Illinois.

We each did about twelve characters and creating them was one of the most satisfying experiences I've ever had on stage. Retaining the workshop atmosphere and developing our own concepts of the characters led to some fascinating ideas and Chuck was open to almost anything.

"I want you to try Yee Bow," Chuck said to me one day, referring to a Chinese boy who grew up in a laundry in Spoon River.

"How the hell am I going to do a small Chinese boy?" I said, but we figured out a way. My hair was quite long then, but I hid it under a black bandana and I reached down and pulled the long skirt I was wearing through to the back and tucked it into my waist so it looked like pantaloons. Somehow, I found the right accent and I became a small Chinese boy.

The rest of my characters were women and each of them had to be different from the others so I would pile my hair on top of my head or put it into a pony tail or use the bandana. We were never off-stage—we sat on benches with little shelves on which to put props like eyeglasses or a book. We would quietly make our changes while another actor was performing. It was really a test of our skills.

I played the town flirt, a fortune-teller who was quite mad, and a woman who went crazy and burned her house down when a drought killed all the cattle on her farm. I did a woman who had gone away to New York and become an actress—I played her like Tallulah Bankhead—and a schoolteacher who placed all her faith in one particular student. There was another woman whose life became so twisted because of her disagreeable husband that she got a twitch in her face.

One of the most affecting characters was Hannah Armstrong, a woman who ran a boarding house where Abraham Lincoln had stayed as a young man. She went to Washington to beg him to let her sick son out of the army and you could not help but be touched as she described her meeting with him at the White House.

> *And when he saw me he broke in a laugh,*
> *And dropped his business as president,*
> *And wrote, in his own hand, Doug's discharge,*
> *Talking the while of the early days,*
> *And telling stories.*

My last part was Lucinda Matlock, a woman who told of living in Spoon River for nearly a century, of being married for seventy years and of having twelve children, eight of whom died before she did.

> *At ninety-six I had lived enough, that is all*
> *And passed to a sweet repose.*
> *What is this I hear of sorrow and weariness,*
> *Anger, discontent and drooping hopes?*
> *Degenerate sons and daughters,*
> *Life is too strong for you—*
> *It takes life to love Life.*

Masters had based Lucinda Matlock on his grandmother, but as I read these lines they reminded me of a neighbor in Nichols Canyon, a Scandinavian woman named Anna Zuberano, who was like a second grandmother to Garry and Andy. So I gave Lucinda Matlock a Swedish accent in honor of Anna.

By the time we opened it to the public, *Spoon River Anthology* was about an hour long. Lamont Johnson, who ran the Center Theatre Group at UCLA at the time, came to see it and encouraged Chuck to turn it into a full production. So he adapted more of the poems and added another folk singer along with Naomi and we did a two-hour show for six weeks at UCLA where it was a great success.

Then things really got wild. A man named Robert Weiner saw the show one night and recommended it to Joseph Cates, who produced a show called *Celebrity Circus* for television. Weiner, who was Cates's assistant, was a bright, sensitive, strange man, while Cates was a rough sort of guy who was also working on a musical version of *What Makes Sammy Run*. I think he thought the idea of being associated with a play that appealed to intellectuals would give him a little class.

He might also have been thinking how inexpensive *Spoon River* would be to produce in New York. There were only six actors and a bare stage with just six benches. And since we had all agreed to work for half salary and pay our own expenses, he could do the whole thing for $13,000 a week, which was phenomenally cheap. Too cheap as far as Larry and Lou Mandel were concerned.

"You can't do that," Lou yelled at me when he heard how little I would make. "If you do, everybody will know you'll work for nothing and that's what you'll get—nothing."

They were also upset that when we did it at the Center Theatre Group we were listed alphabetically with no pictures of us in the publicity. Being treated like a star was never that important to me, but it was something Larry and Lou insisted on. I had been a star on Broadway, they said. How could I go there now in an ensemble performance at half salary and with alphabetical billing?

I got into tearful arguments with Lou about this, but he would not budge until finally I wrote him a letter. I have learned that I am much better at expressing my feelings about emotional subjects when I sit down and spell them out instead of trying to talk about them, which usually ends up with me crying.

"Lou," I wrote, "every one of these characters is my creation. They're like my children, like babies I have nursed. If anybody else does these parts, it will break my heart."

That won Lou over. "Why didn't you tell me that?" he said as if I had not been trying to tell him all along. "I understand completely, darling. Of course you'll do the play."

A few months later, when the New York reviews were unanimous raves, Lou was on top of the world. He blew up the notices and sent them out to everybody he knew. "This proves Betty is not only a musical comedy star," he told them, "but a great dramatic actress, too."

I had to laugh, but that was the kind of relationship we had. We really were like father and daughter. And Larry was just as pleased as he could be, too.

Jules Fisher, who has gone on to be a producer, got his first job as a lighting director on Broadway in *Spoon River* and the work he did was exquisite. Joe Cates promised us full salaries after he made his money back but even though what was supposed to be a four-week run lasted five months somehow that never happened. I think he knew we would stay with the show because we loved the material so much.

What upset us more than the money, though, was that there was so little publicity about the show around town. Cates was so caught up in producing *What Makes Sammy Run* that he did not pay any attention to us. There were no billboards on Broadway, no posters, and almost nothing in the papers.

At one point, Cates came to us and said we had a chance to do a TV show with Hugh Downs where we would each play several of our roles. If we would give back the $10,000 we would make from the show, he said, he would take out an ad in the *New York Times*. But Lou put his foot down.

"Since when do the actors pay for the ads?"

Cates was furious and said he would put my understudy in the TV show, and he had her stand in the wings where I could see her miming all my moves. But Actors Equity and the TV producer stepped in and said they could not do the show without *all* of the original cast. So I went on and Cates never forgave me. I never forgave him, either.

The fact that we were playing at the Booth Theater in Shubert Alley, where there were huge posters of every show in town except ours, really hurt. But then we saw there was one big blank space on the brick wall and we had an idea. One night after a performance, we gathered in Naomi Caryl's hotel room with stencils, some spray paint, and yards and yards of white poster paper.

At 3 A.M., Naomi, Joyce Van Patten, Robert Elston, Bob Doyle (the understudy), and I—the entire cast except for Chuck Aidman, who we were afraid would disapprove—went down to Shubert Alley to put up a huge poster that said SPOON RIVER. Larry, who loved any kind of conspiracy, was in town rehearsing a show. He became our lookout as I stood on Bob Elston's shoulders and tried to paste up a poster that kept falling down on top of me. Suddenly Larry saw a couple of guards come out of the New York Times Building on Forty-fourth Street next to Sardi's.

"I think those guys are going to come over here and arrest us," he said.

But instead of panicking, Larry very coolly walked over to the guards, told them what we were doing, and said, "Do you have anything we could use to paste the posters up? They keep falling down."

The guards thought it was hilarious and went back inside the Times Building and brought out some thick poster glue and strips of tape. We put up our poster and the next day every advertiser in Shubert Alley was up in arms when they saw they were sharing space with a hand-made poster nobody had paid for. We all played innocent and of course they tore the poster down immediately. But we were just beginning.

That night, we got some more stencils and paper that measured from two feet square to four feet square and cut SPOON RIVER on them. From then on, there were nights when we would gather after the show, look at each other conspiratorially, and say, "Time to stencil."

At 3 A.M. we would get in a cab in front of the hotel, drive down Broadway, and then stop around forty-fourth Street. We would stand in a little group as though we were talking, and somebody would drop a stencil on the sidewalk and spray it with red paint. Then we would stand by the wall of a building where somebody would hold the stencil up to the wall and spray some more.

After a while, the words SPOON RIVER were in red paint up and down Broadway. They were on the sidewalks, on the walls, outside the box offices of other shows. How they got there soon became a big mystery and the wonderful thing was nobody ever found out.

AT A MATINEE performance one day, the oddest thing happened. We were nearing the end of the first act when, from a box at stage right, I distinctly heard someone say "Bullshit!"

During the intermission, I asked Chuck Aidman if he'd heard someone say 'bullshit.' "

"Yeah, what was that?"

We came back out for the second act and the voice continued. It kept moving around the theater and every so often we would hear someone say "Crap!" or "Bull!" Finally, when Joyce Van Patten was doing one of her most sensitive and beautiful characterizations, the voice said, "Act it, Miss Van Patten! Act it!"

It was so upsetting that finally Chuck moved up to the front of the stage and said, "Excuse me, I must stop the show. There is someone in the audience who is very disturbing to us on the stage and I'm sure to you out there. Will he please leave."

And the voice called out, "The essence of drama is conflict, Charlie!"

With that, the great acting teacher Stella Adler, who just happened to be sitting in the second row, stood up, and said very dramatically, "Throw that man out!"

That inspired Bob Elston to jump off the stage, run up the aisle, and go smashing against a locked door he thought would take him to the heckler. In the meantime, we could see the ushers upstairs chasing the guy all across the balcony. Finally, he escaped and we finished the play.

We never knew what it was all about until years later when Joyce told me she had received a letter that read: "Dear Miss Van Patten. I am a member of Alcoholics Anonymous and one of our twelve steps is to make amends for any hurt that we may have caused anyone. So I want to apologize very deeply for interrupting your beautiful performance in *Spoon River*. Please extend my apologies to the other members of your cast."

Joyce never said if it was signed or not and as far as I'm concerned it doesn't matter. It's just a wonderful end to the story.

WE WERE all surprised and delighted when our four-week run in *Spoon River* just went on and on and I think it might have been extended even longer. But that November, President Kennedy was assassinated and we closed a few weeks later. People did not seem much in the mood for lyrical verse about small-town America any more and I could hardly blame them.

AFTER *SPOON RIVER,* Theatre West just grew like Topsy and became one of the focal points of my life. Over the years, wonderful actors like Carroll O'Connor, Richard Dreyfuss, and Beau Bridges joined us, either to perform or to work on things of their own. On the same night in workshop, somebody might do a scene from Shake-speare and somebody else might work on a play he had written him-self. The atmosphere was always stimulating.

We moved around from place to place until finally we settled in a nice little theater just minutes from our house where we now hold workshops and put on productions of all kinds. I developed *Betty Garrett and Other Songs* in workshop there and eventually became chair of the board of directors.

If I was not working in a play someplace else, in fact, I could always be found at Theatre West where we all pitched in to do everything connected with the theater—sets, costumes, building maintenance, cleaning toilets, you name it. Recently, for instance, some new seats became available from a theater in Long Beach and we all went down and picked them up and then spent days down on our hands and knees bolting them to the floor. You never saw Mickey Rooney and Judy Garland doing *that* in the movies.

"How come you make curtains for Theatre West and you don't make them for our bedroom?" Larry once kidded me. Or he would pretend to be very sad when I was leaving the house and say, "You're not going to Theatre West *again*, are you?" If he ever divorced me, he once said, he would name Theatre West as correspondent.

LARRY WAS EXCITED when John Huston asked him to be in *Freud*. It was an important picture, the part of Dr. Breuer was a large one, and Larry had always liked John so much.

"His motor's running," Larry used to say. It was his favorite expres-sion about people who had a kind of positive energy about them and it certainly was true of John. His motor was running all the time.

The fact that John cast Larry the minute he saw how gracefully he had aged was also very flattering. I think John had always been sympathetic toward Larry's situation and Larry was touched by that. He was in high spirits when he left for Germany.

Things got off to a wild start when Montgomery Clift was delivered to Munich in handcuffs. Evidently, he had had so much to drink he had made a fuss on the plane and had to be restrained when they took him off.

Poor Monty was really quite deranged in the last years of his life. He was drinking heavily, was addicted to some kind of drug, and I think there was still something wrong with him from a terrible car accident he'd had a few years earlier.

I visited Larry in Munich during the filming and Monty reminded me of people who are suffering from a hormonal imbalance. Suddenly, their faces become very coarse and their eyebrows get bushy. It is almost a Dr. Jekyll and Mr. Hyde transformation. Anyone who has seen pictures of Monty when he was young and compared them to the way he looked just before he died could see he had undergone a gross change. Everything had thickened—his face, his nose, his lips. It was almost like he was suffering from lupus and I think there was something wrong with him mentally, too.

Susannah York, the beautiful young British actress, played one of Freud's patients in the movie and Larry thought she was absolutely wonderful, so good and disciplined. But when Monty arrived, they started running around town, staying up all night, and arriving on the set without knowing their lines. Larry was disgusted with both of them and when I stood and watched them do the forty-eighth take of one scene together I could see why.

Monty in particular just could not remember his lines at all. They would write them on the floor for him and he would forget to look down. After a while, they took some of Monty's lines and put them in Larry's mouth. "You mean to tell me you think babies have sexual feelings, Dr. Freud," Larry would say. And Monty would say "Yes." It was just pathetic.

One day, they were shooting a scene where Freud breaks down. Monty had a couple of martinis at lunch and came back worse than ever. Somebody on the crew made some remark about what a big jerk he was and Monty heard it and was terribly hurt. He was completely falling apart when they started shooting that afternoon, which just happened to be perfect for the scene.

When you see that moment on the screen you think "My God, what an actor this guy was!" but the truth is he was in tears because he had overheard somebody say something mean about him. This is not to belittle the great talent Monty had shown earlier in his career, but later he became a truly tragic figure.

Monty's condition played right into John Huston's hands because John seemed fascinated by neuroses. There was a dream sequence where Monty was supposed to be crawling up the side of a mountain and they built a sort of rocky obstacle course on the floor. Monty crawled across it as they shot the scene sideways so it would look like he was climbing.

The rocks were jagged, which made it difficult for Monty to propel himself, and John made him do it so many times he was bleeding. Monty kept protesting and John kept saying "Do it again" to the point where it became almost sadistic.

It was not long before the shooting was far behind schedule and John and Monty were blaming each other. They threatened to sue each other and at one point they both had psychiatrists on the set trying to prove the other one was crazy.

Larry sided with John, of course. "John is crazy," he said, "but Monty's *really* crazy."

LARRY GOT some nice reviews for his performance in *Freud*, but the movie was not a success at the box office and there seemed to be no public curiosity about his return to the movies after all this time. The most virulent days of the blacklist had ended—nobody was keeping lists of "subversives" any more—but so had the opportunity for a lot of people to go back to work. They were like anybody else who had been out of the business for a long time. The question was how do you get back in? In Larry's case, you didn't and *Freud* was his last movie.

That was the least of his problems, though, because not long after we returned from Germany, he began to develop the health problems that continued in one form or another the rest of his life.

Somebody in the cast of *Spoon River* had discovered a great cheap seafood restaurant on Eighth Avenue in New York—a whole dinner cost $3——and one day we went over and stuffed ourselves. Larry was mad for raw clams and oysters and had a whole plate of them.

During the show that night, Joyce Van Patten was terribly sick and kept going offstage and throwing up in the wings. She would get through each poem just fine, but then she would go to the side of the stage and upchuck. She would come back, act out her next poem, and then go off and be sick all over again.

This is a miracle that happens to actors, I think, something almost like hypnosis. There have been times when I have had the stomach flu with all the symptoms but as the curtain was going up, I could literally feel the peristalsis stop. Then, when the show was over, I would run for the john.

Six months after Joyce's awful case of food poisoning Larry was on the road when he began feeling ill. At first, he was not particularly concerned because he often got sick on the road. If it was not the stomach flu or laryngitis, then something else would be bothering him. This was clearly a reaction to stress and it often happened when a show was about to open. I, on the other hand, am always at my healthiest at times like that. It is afterwards that I fall apart.

But when Larry did not get any better this time, he went to a doctor and learned he had hepatitis. The incubation period for the disease, he was told, was six months and we counted back trying to remember if he might have gotten a flu shot with an infected needle somewhere on the road. But then we realized where he had been six months earlier. It was the day Joyce had been so sick, the day he had eaten all those raw clams and oysters.

What we did not realize was just how debilitating hepatitis can be and how it can lead to deep depression. Poor Larry was so miserable that some days he just seemed to be at the bottom of a well.

"What can I get you, honey?" I once said to him when I came into the bedroom.

"Nothing. I'd jump out the window except it's only one story high."

Eventually, Larry recovered but his health was never the same. He had always been such a great one for physical exercise, for going to the gym and lifting weights. But now he was gaining too much weight—he was an excellent cook and had what amounted to an addiction to food—and his blood pressure began shooting up.

Larry had had rheumatic fever as a child and had been rejected by the army because of his rheumatic heart, but even when his doctor begged him to have some tests done he would not take his condition seriously.

Once, I came home from an extended period of summer stock and was delighted to find that Larry had lost ten or fifteen pounds. He looked just great and at first all he said was that the doctor had put him on a strict diet. But finally, he told me the truth. He had had a heart attack.

"Don't bother your mother with this," he had told the boys. "She'll quit the show and come home and that wouldn't be good."

229

Well, of course, I would have left the show—it was typical of Larry to try to spare me—and thank God for my friend Naomi Caryl, who learned of his condition and appeared every day at our house with food for him and whatever else he needed. Larry never forgot that. By the time I did get back, he looked good and felt good, and I was delighted when he kept to his strict diet. I cooked him things like fish with herbs and no salt, which were good for his heart, but it was not long before he began to complain. "I'm from Kansas and I never *saw* a fish until I grew up."

After a while, his way of dieting was to have a glass of juice in the morning, starve himself all day, wolf down dinner, and then eat the rest of the evening until he went to sleep. I would come into the den and he would be eating a can of salted nuts. Or I would find an empty can of nuts under the couch in the morning. It was just crazy.

Unfortunately, I am not a nag like some women I have known who keep a tight rein on their husbands' eating habits. If only I could have been.

Archie, the Girls, and Ted Friggin' Williams

Bernie West and Mickey Ross, two of the writers on *All in the Family*, loved to tell the story of the time years earlier when they came backstage to see me after an American Youth Theatre revue in New York.

Bernie and Mickey had a comedy act together and Bernie, who was in the show with me, said, "Oh, you've got to meet Betty."

They knocked on the door and came in and I said, "Hello, how are you?" as I sat in front of my dressing table stark naked from the waist up.

They were shocked, but I just had no sense of modesty at all when I was younger, especially after my days at the Latin Quarter. I would never do something like that today, but that's for reasons of vanity not modesty.

Bernie and Mickey were not the only ones connected with *All in the Family* I had already met. Sometimes, it seemed as if I knew everyone on the show before I got there.

Norman Lear, the producer, had been a twenty-one-year-old publicity man on *Call Me Mister* and he confessed he had had a big crush on me then. Carroll O'Connor was a member of Theatre West long before he became famous as Archie Bunker.

Don Nicholl, who was the head writer, was British and he and his wife, Gee, had interviewed Larry and me in London when they were working for a newspaper. They were a dear couple and we had all fallen in love with each other.

Rob Reiner is the son of Carl Reiner, who had stuck up for me on the Ethel Barrymore radio broadcast by saying he would quit if they did not let me on the show. Jean Stapleton was in *Bells Are Ringing* on

231

Broadway when Larry and I took over for Judy Holliday and Sidney Chaplin during their vacation.

About the only person involved with the show I didn't know was Sally Struthers, and we quickly became so close they had to separate us during rehearsals. We both loved to do crossword puzzles and we would sit in the corner and giggle until they finally had to make us sit on opposite sides of the room. Sally is just the cuddliest, most adorable girl and when we see each other today the first thing we do is throw our arms around each other and say "Girlfriend!"

All in the Family was well established as the top-rated show on television by the time I joined it and they were in the process of creating two new characters. The Jeffersons, who were the Bunkers' black neighbors, were moving—Sherman Hemsley and Isabel Sanford were actually starting their own show—so they decided to move in Frank and Irene Lorenzo, an Italian man with an Irish wife, next door. I was asked if I would come in to discuss the part and I was all set to go when Lou Mandel said no.

"I don't think it's dignified for Betty to come into the office to see you," he told them. "She'll receive you at her home."

I don't know where Lou got these ideas sometimes—I would never dare to say "I will not come to your office, you'll come to my home"— but by God they all came and sat in my living room and we talked. I was pretty close to getting the part, they said, but in the end they chose Sada Thompson who had just won a Tony in New York for her multiple roles in *Twigs*.

I could understand why they chose her because she had a completely different look than I did. Not plump exactly, but sturdy and that is what they were going for. Unfortunately, Sada was used to the stage where they did a lot of rehearsing and she did not like the pressure of doing the show in front of an audience before she felt completely ready. By the time they had shot one episode, everybody realized it was a mistake and they came back to me.

I was out of town doing *The Price* in summer stock and rushed back on a moment's notice to reshoot the show they had done with her. All of a sudden, I was Irene Lorenzo and that was the beginning of three very happy years in *All in the Family*.

The hardest thing to get used to in a television series was the fact that I didn't always have much to do. I wasn't one of the central characters so I didn't appear in every show, and even when I did there was always a lot of waiting around.

Some actors who are used to the stage find this very difficult to adjust to and Norman understood. He had a great sense of fairness and would let people go without any pressure. His attitude was that he did not want anyone around who was unhappy. When Sada wanted to leave, he agreed and later he did the same thing with Vince Gardenia, who played my husband. Vince was a lovely man, but he would just sit in a corner and grump and grumble.

"I'm so uncomfortable here," he told Norman. "I like to be in a play or a movie where I'm an important part of things. I feel very uncomfortable hanging around here all week long to do one little scene."

So after just one season, Norman let Vince go with his blessing. The only problem was they never explained on the show where he went. One moment, I had a husband and the next moment he was gone.

"We've got to say something about Frank," somebody would say and they would put in a line where somebody would ask, "Have you heard from Frank?"

"Oh, yes," I would say. "He's on the road selling toilet seats. He'll be home soon."

But when it came time to shoot the show, there was always too much script so something had to be cut. And they always cut that line so Frank's disappearance was never explained.

It really got strange when a little relationship began to develop between me and one of Archie's co-workers, Stretch Cunningham. Stretch was played by Jamie Cromwell, who years later was nominated for an Academy Award when he played the farmer who dances for the pig in *Babe*. Stretch was obviously much younger than I was and kind of a big goof.

There was thought of building a romance between a young man and an older woman, but then Irene was married and where was Frank? So nothing ever came of it. But when we would do things together fans would write and ask, "What is this? Are they dating?" Again, it was never explained.

Irene was a fix-it lady and the one Catholic character on *All in the Family*. Some issue relating to Catholicism would almost always come up when I was on, such as the time my sister the nun came to visit and caused all kinds of consternation in the Bunker household.

Most of the time, however, I was the anti-Archie, the one woman on the show who could cut him down. I guess the audience loved her for that because I still run into people who say, "Give Archie hell, Irene," calling me by the name of the character I played more than twenty years ago.

Norman and the writers were very smart when it came to the terrible things Archie said. They never allowed him to say anything anti-Semitic, anti-black, or really vicious without a rebuttal. There was always someone around who made Archie look like a fool for saying such things and one of my purposes in the show was to have a zinger ready to put him down. And there was always some twist in the plot that made you see what a bigoted man Archie was.

That was the difference between *All in the Family* and *Till Death Do Us Part*, the British series on which it was based. Don Nicholl, who had worked on that show, too, said the father in it was far more vicious than Archie.

But Carroll made Archie more human and that made things even touchier. He would say these terrible things yet somehow you would always think, "But that's a nice man." I think it was more realistic that way because there are "nice" people in the world who are anti-Semitic and anti-black because they're ignorant. They don't know any better and that makes them scarier—and more dangerous.

Not everybody understood how the show was constructed, though. One day, I was shopping in the Farmer's Market next door to the CBS Studios when a darling little lady recognized me and came up to me in tears.

"Why do they let Archie say those terrible things about the Jews? You must do something about it."

I tried to explain—"What we're showing is how stupid it is to say those things"—but she didn't get it at all. All she heard were the words Archie was saying.

The funny thing about Carroll's success playing Archie is that for as long as I had known him, I could never remember him doing comedy. I had seen him play Claudius in *Hamlet* at Theatre West workshops and in the movies he was almost always cast as a heavy. He had been an English teacher, had worked in the theater in Dublin, and at

Theatre West he developed plays he had written himself. I performed in a couple of them and when we went out for drinks afterwards he was always jolly and amusing, but he never played any comic roles.

Where Carroll got the character of Archie, I don't know, but of course it was simply brilliant. And he became very hip to who Archie really was and strict about not doing anything he felt was against Archie's character.

Personally, Carroll could not be more different from Archie. He is very intelligent, quite liberal in his politics, and soft-spoken.

But his wife, Nancy, said to me one day while we were watching a rehearsal, "You think he isn't like Archie? Let me tell you something. Every morning, I cook him a hard-boiled egg. You know how sometimes you have trouble peeling a hard-boiled egg? Well, the other morning he got an egg he couldn't peel. I walked into the kitchen and there he's got it in his hand and he's growling at it and squeezing it. Finally, he goes 'AARGH!' and squeezes it so hard the egg goes all over the kitchen. Now isn't that something Archie Bunker would do?"

Carroll was mad at Nancy for telling me that story, but I think it makes him sound adorable.

Carroll often did a lot of rewriting of his own part. Just about everyone on the show—particularly Jean, Rob, and Sally—came to know their characters so well they could almost write their parts themselves. The show had brilliant writers, of course, and they would allow us to sit in at story conferences and make suggestions, which was very exciting to me.

Jean is one of the most generous, cheerful women I have ever met. I have never known anybody who was so positive, so up about things all the time. Ever since playing Edith, she has had to strive to get beyond that image and since it was such an indelible character you can see how it would be hard for her.

But Jean has a great deal of dignity about her and I think she has been quite successful in changing her image. People came to accept her as something other than a dingbat. She did an Eleanor Roosevelt that I thought was wonderful and a short operatic version of a Ruth Draper monologue called "The Italian Lesson." Jean has quite a lovely voice, which surprised me after hearing her sing the duet with Archie that opened *All in the Family*.

I love what Rob Reiner has done with his career, too. Every movie he makes is completely different from the last one and when I remember him from those days I can't imagine where it all came from because he never showed any interest in directing our show. He was interested in writing, though. There always seemed to be somebody on the set he was writing with or who was trying to get a show produced. I not only admire Rob's work, I like him tremendously as a person.

Rob was the only member of the cast who could go to lunch with me at the food stalls in the Farmers Market, where I loved to eat. Carroll, Jean, and Sally could not go because they would be mobbed. People would just gather around and literally prevent them from eating. But all Rob had to do was leave his toupee back in the studio and nobody knew who he was. I was always glad I never had that kind of celebrity, although one day a lady behind a coffee counter did recognize me.

"I admire you so much," she said. "I know everything you've ever done." She started talking about *All in the Family* and then she went on to name every movie I had made, every Broadway show I had been in, and on and on.

"Thank you so much," I said. "I'm flattered you remember all these things. It makes me feel so good."

"Oh, yes, I just like your work so much." Then she pounced like a bird of prey. "Tell me, have you made any commercials?"

"Gee, no, I'm sorry," I found myself apologizing. I guess all you have to do to become *really* important is make a commercial.

DON NICHOLL CALLED me in one day and said, "Would you have any objection to playing a woman who had an operation for breast cancer?"

"I'm an actress," I said. "I'll play whatever you want. Why are you asking me this?"

"Well, some actresses might feel squeamish about it," he said, "and I didn't want you to feel that way. It's going to be our Christmas show."

"Well, Merry Christmas!"

"No, no, don't worry. It's going to be very tasteful and very funny."

A tasteful, funny show about breast cancer? This I had to see.

The script called for Edith to go in for a breast examination and to be afraid she might need a mastectomy. This led to a wonderful scene where we talk and I reveal that I had had breast cancer. Immediately, we lose eye contact and she begins looking at my chest.

"Don't bother looking," I say. "You can't tell which one." But for the rest of the conversation, she keeps trying unsuccessfully *not* to look down. It was such a delightful and meaningful little scene that cancer societies began showing it at meetings and fund-raisers.

There was another show where I beat Archie at pool, which drove him nuts, and one more where I was made his foreman at work. I even got to play the ukelele in one episode and sing "Bye, Bye, Blackbird."

One of the nice things Norman Lear did was guarantee your contract whether you were in every script or not. Most of my contracts were for thirteen weeks, but if I did not do thirteen shows I still got paid for them.

This was different from *Laverne and Shirley* where I had to be in every show because I was being paid for them. Very often, the script called for me to do dumb things that had nothing to do with the plot and could just as easily have been cut out. And if the show ran too long, they *were* cut out. Sometimes, I did nothing more than come into a room, say "Hi," tell a joke, then say "Bye" and leave. Rue McClanahan, who was playing a similar role on *Maude*, started calling us the "hi-bye girls."

Needless to say, I enjoyed *All in the Family* more because in almost all the shows I did I was an important part of the plot. But finally the year after Gloria had her baby they got into that aspect of life at the Bunker house and my role was phased out.

I HAVE FRIENDS who confessed to me they could not bear to watch *Laverne and Shirley* when it was the most popular show on television because it was "so juvenile." Years later, the same friends would watch the reruns and come up to me and exclaim, "They're funny!" and I would say, "I told you they were."

And I still think many of the episodes are absolute classics. The writing may not have been as innovative as *All in the Family*, but there was some wonderful physical comedy, which, of course, I've always adored.

Another actress was already playing the landlady on *Laverne and Shirley*, but they had decided to replace her—sound familiar?—at about the time someone on the writing staff saw me performing *Betty Garrett and Other Songs* in Westwood. The next thing I knew I was on the show that had succeeded *All in the Family* as No. 1 in the country and that was on the network, ABC, that had replaced CBS as No. 1.

I had a hard time at first because I came into the show without any real idea of what they wanted. "Think of something that's kind of a signature for yourself," one of the writers said to me, "something that is easily identifiable with you, like the big L Laverne always wears on her sweaters."

The first season, I tried everything—piling my hair up inside different wigs, wearing a variety of clothes—but I just could not get a handle on who this woman was supposed to be.

Then in the second season they brought in a costume designer who put me in high-heeled shoes, too much jewelry, flashy clothes, and big earrings, and did my hair in a kind of chignon with fluffy bangs and a crazy ponytail hanging out. All of a sudden, it was as if a light bulb came on in my head. That was when Edna Babish-De Fazio was truly born.

I saw Edna as this sort of jazzy, middle-aged lady clomping around in ankle-strap shoes, wearing clothes and jewelry that were not in good taste for someone her age, and who was generally kind of dizzy. But she had the same sort of sensible element in her that Irene Lorenzo did.

Irene Lorenzo and Edna Babish were my age, but I have always loved playing older ladies, starting with the eighty-year-old dowager who sang the hymn to Park Avenue in *Call Me Mister*. Now that I *am* an old lady it ain't funny any more, but I hope I give a good performance—I've been rehearsing for it all my life.

I began to wonder why I have this fascination for elderly people and I think it might be because I missed having them in my life. I had only one grandmother who lived—and I didn't like her—so it is almost as if I created a whole bunch of older people to be my grandmother.

I have been guilty of being in shows where older people are put down because that can be very funny sometimes. But I don't think I ever played an old lady who was not feisty. Those are the parts I like, the people with a lot of piss and vinegar.

It is sad, I think, to see actors trying to stay the same all the time. I don't believe in that and I carry on a crusade with people my age.

Lying about your age and trying to pretend you are younger gives fodder to the whole idea that you can't be attractive or active and involved when you get past a certain age.

I'm here to prove you can be, I tell people. I'm seventy-eight years old and I took a tap-dancing class last night, I have a boyfriend, and I can still crawl around and clean the seats at Theatre West. I don't think people my age should give up and I don't think the public should relegate them to an old ladies home, either. My heroine is Maggie Kuhn, who founded the Gray Panther movement.

PEOPLE ALWAYS ASK me if Penny Marshall and Cindy Williams, who played Laverne and Shirley, got along. Well, I have never seen two people work together as well as they did. Their improvisation was incredible, their ability to take a situation and just go with it. They were like Laurel and Hardy to me, a truly funny creative team.

But there was a lot of tension between them because Penny's brother Garry was the show's producer—and one of the nicest people I have ever worked for—and her father was the executive producer. I think Cindy always felt Penny had an edge on her and was sort of fighting all the time to keep her position in the team.

Basically, it was like a marriage. They had their differences, but they worked really well together. When Penny's marriage to Rob Reiner broke up, Cindy was there for her, calling and getting her out of the house and being a true friend.

And after I had known them a while, I came to love both of them. Cindy is the world's biggest animal nut so we have a lot in common, and Penny has a vulnerable side that makes her very dear to me. She has a wonderful sense of humor, but she always has a kind of downlook as though she is thinking "God, the world is just so difficult."

Like Rob, Penny went on to become a movie director, but in her case I was not surprised. She directed a couple of *Laverne and Shirley* episodes and her ideas were brilliant. She would very quietly say things like "Why don't you do this, you know. . . . " And you would think "Wow, that's a good idea," and you would do it and it would get a big laugh. Or Penny would say, "Don't do that. Maybe if you went over here. . . ."

It got so I would do anything she told me whether I thought it was right or not because I thought she knew film and she knew actors and she knew directing.

Though I never felt I had enough to do on the show, there were some lovely moments that occasionally made it worthwhile from a creative standpoint. After Edna's character had been established, it turned out she had a retarded daughter who came to visit in one episode. She developed a kind of a relationship with Lenny, one of the goofy guys who lived in the girls' building, that was very sweet and touching.

During the course of the show, I talked about my daughter to Penny and started to cry. Everybody was stunned—I'm not sure they knew what to do, really—and Penny said, "This is a record for *Laverne and Shirley*. It's the first time we've had tears on the show."

I played the ukelele in one episode and that was a hysterical show for me. I sang a song called "Plenty of Gin" that was written by a friend of mine named Bill Woods. It was full of tongue-twisting lyrics and during the performance I could not get through the song without bumbling the words. I don't know how many times they had to stop the cameras and start over.

Of course, the studio audiences love it when you goof up so when I finally got through the whole song without a flub, the audience went wild. If you see the episode on TV, it looks as if "Plenty of Gin" was the biggest thing ever to hit *Laverne and Shirley*. But they were just relieved I got through it!

Edna really came into her own when she started going out with Laverne's father and later married him. Frank De Fazio, who was played by Phil Foster, was kind of an Italian Archie Bunker and Edna was in the same position Irene had been, always bringing him down to earth.

There were a couple of shows where Frank and I were courting and the wedding itself was very funny. Frank had waited too long to book a church and the only one available was a black gospel church. So here is Frank with his Brooklyn accent, along with Laverne and Shirley and Lenny and Squiggy, in a gospel church where the choir breaks into song every two minutes, which scares the hell out of our party.

The part of the preacher was particularly comical because of the way he read the service and I was delighted when they cast Charlie

240

Murphy, an old friend of mine, in the role. There was only one problem: Charlie is white.

I don't know what was in the minds of the writers or the casting people but by the time they got to the dress rehearsal, somebody woke up and said, "There's something wrong here. There wouldn't be a white preacher in a black gospel church."

By then, Charlie had alerted his friends and family all over the country that he was going to be on the biggest show on television so when they replaced him with an honest-to-God black preacher he was heartbroken.

Everybody else felt terrible, too, and Penny and Cindy said, "We've got to find something for Charlie real soon and hire him again."

A couple of shows later, they found a part and called him in. On the first day of rehearsal, he showed up in blackface and we all fell down laughing.

Finally, after seven years, *Laverne and Shirley* was going to call it quits. There was a big wrap party in the commissary and everybody was crying on each other's shoulders and saying good-bye. But then, just as we were all weepy and nostalgic, the strangest thing happened: They announced the show would go on for another year.

They had shot two endings (just in case) and Cindy was teetering back and forth about whether the show should end or not. Penny just said, "I'll do whatever you decide," and in the middle of the party Cindy decided. The show *would* go on.

"What happened?" I asked Penny.

"Cindy had a dream that her aunt came to her and said, 'You must go on another year.'"

I had already signed to do a play called *Supporting Cast* in New York with Jack Gilford, Sandy Dennis, Joyce Van Patten, and Hope Lange so I said I was sorry but I would not be available for the final season. It was a little disappointing, especially when *Supporting Cast* was not a success, but I'm rather glad I was not around. I understand the last year of the show was not a pleasant one.

Cindy was pregnant and had been promised she would only have to work a certain number of hours and I guess there was a lot of sniping back and forth. Finally, she walked off the set and even sued Paramount. It was a little sad to see a show that had been so much fun to work on end that way.

Probably the best thing about my television roles was they opened doors that would never have been open to me now. Nobody expects me to be "perky" Betty Garrett anymore—I used to hate that adjective anyway.

Television reaches so many people and here I was being seen by a whole new generation, one that had no idea I had been in shows on Broadway and had made some great movies. I would rather be remembered for some of the things I did that were bigger and more important, but being known for *Laverne and Shirley* was certainly not bad when it came to "promoting my stock." If I did a road show or *Betty Garrett and Other Songs*, I could command a good salary because I was well known from television whereas it has been a long time since Broadway and the movies.

And there were other benefits, too. It was very nice to drive onto a studio lot, have the gate man say, "Good morning, Miss Garrett," drive into my own parking place, and go to my own dressing room that had a refrigerator, a typewriter, and a telephone. I would hole up in there, learn three or four lines, walk out and do my bit, then go back in the dressing room and lie down if I wanted to. I used to take all my correspondence over to the set and I had a little arts and crafts setup where I would make Christmas presents. It all got very cozy and I got very lazy and very lacking in creative ambition. I finally woke up one day and realized I was getting dangerously comfortable with this.

And yet there could be creative rewards in television, too. I did a couple of *Murder She Wrote* shows with that all-time gracious lady Angela Lansbury. She made every show a pleasure to do and I understand it was her idea to use some of us old-timers as guests—a smart move because it added interest and a generous one because it gave us jobs.

One of the most delightful guest appearances I made was on Beau Bridges' show *Harts of the West*. Of course, I had known Beau since he was a baby and he and I had had those great times jumping off the sand dunes at the Bridges' beach house. Years later, Beau confessed that when Garry and Andy were born he was really hurt because I paid so much attention to them he thought I didn't love him anymore.

"Oh, Beaubie," I said, "how could you think that? I loved you *so* much." And I still do.

I got Beau into Theatre West when he was nineteen years old and it was over the protests of my fellow members. "We are all professional actors here. He's not old enough or experienced enough." But finally they agreed to take him on a trial basis and I had to tell him he was only in on probation.

It was typical of Beau to say, "Oh, that's OK. I wouldn't want to hang around if I wasn't good enough."

Beau and I did some scenes from *The Corn Is Green* and he not only did a great acting job, he mastered a Welsh accent. The group fell in love with him and now we are all as proud of his great success in the movies as Bud and Dottie are. We feel the same way about Jeff, my godson, who was also a member of Theatre West for a while.

Harts of the West was about a city person who has a heart condition and gives up his business and moves to a small western town, where life is supposed to be less stressful. To win acceptance there, he decides to compete in an annual wagon race and hires as his second a man who has won the race every year before.

But then he finds out the man has recently died and his widow turns up to help him win the race instead. Beau will have none of that and enters the race by himself so the widow decides to run against him. It was a great part because I start out as a sweet old lady wearing a little hat with violets on it and turn into a tough old broad who of course beats him in the race.

I had a commitment in Miami judging a high school talent contest while the show was being shot and by the time I flew down on a midnight plane, spent three days judging video tapes, and arrived back on location at King's Canyon at six in the morning, I was beat. My asthma was acting up, too, but there I was climbing hills and standing in the back of the wagon, whipping the horses, and jogging alongside. By the time we were through, I was really sick but it turned out so well Beau submitted me for an Emmy award. I didn't win but I was touched he would do a thing like that.

Another show that was fun was *The Good Life* with John Caponera and Drew Carey. I played John's mother-in-law and there was an episode where my daughter talks him into taking me to a baseball game.

I keep obstructing his view by standing up or ordering popcorn when a great play is taking place so he becomes annoyed with me and I get all in a huff and leave. When I don't come back, John becomes frantic and looks all over the ballpark until finally he goes home and there I am.

"Where were you?" John says.

"Well, you were so unpleasant, I decided to go up and watch the rest of the game in the press box."

"*You* know somebody in the press box?"

"I've had friends up there for years. Ever since I dated Ted Williams."

"You dated *Ted Williams*?"

"Oh, yes, we were good friends and went out all the time."

"Weren't you married to my wife's father then?"

"He was overseas," I explain, "and it was all very innocent. And besides, it was Ted Friggin' Williams."

Well, as soon as the network censors got a look at that line, they told me I couldn't say that. Of course, the writers expected that so they changed it to "Freakin'," which really sounds almost the same.

As usual, they shot the show twice, at the dress rehearsal in the afternoon and then again in the evening. Just before the dress rehearsal, the writers came to me and said, "Go all out in this one, OK?"

So when we got to that line, I said, "And besides, it was Ted Fuckin' Williams."

Well—I have never gotten such a laugh. It just went on and on. John Caponera fell apart and I was very proud of myself when I did not even crack a smile. I just sat there and waited and waited. After all these years since Max Liebman had first rolled in the aisles when he heard me say "shit," people still were not expecting me to have a dirty mouth.

We reshot the show in the evening, of course, and I demurely said "Freakin' " but they showed the first version at the wrap party where everybody fell apart all over again. And the writers sent me roses, which has never happened to me before or since.

The Hollywood Party
as an Art Form

In the late 1940s, shortly after I came to Hollywood, William Randolph Hearst decided to give a gala dinner in honor of Louella Parsons. He sent out invitations all over town with a note saying he was charging $25 a ticket.

Most of Hollywood took one look at the invitation, laughed, and threw it in the wastebasket. In the first place, $25 was a lot of money then and although Louella was a dear old soul she was kind of a laughingstock, too. So nobody subscribed to the dinner.

Hearst was furious and sent out the invitations again, but this time they read we "request" your presence at the Coconut Grove to honor Louella Parsons and there was no charge. Now it was a command performance. You *had* to be there.

And just about everybody was, including people who did not ordinarily go to these things. Spencer Tracy, Joan Crawford, Katharine Hepburn, Clark Gable, they all came to honor Louella.

The Coconut Grove was set up with an orchestra on one side and a dais for the speakers on the other. The speeches honoring Louella went on forever, especially when all the studio heads—including the Warner Brothers, Harry Cohn, and Louis B. Mayer—took turns praising Louella. Bob Hope got off the best line of the night when, in the middle of all these paeans, he said, "I love Louella just about as much as she loves me." He was the only one who had the nerve to say anything sassy at all.

But what was really interesting about these speeches is what took place in the middle of them. We could all hear someone at the other end of the room, shouting and cursing and creating a tremendous disturbance.

Larry and I looked at each other and then looked around at everybody else at the table and were amazed that nobody flinched or turned their heads or paid the slightest attention. After a while, the noise kept getting nearer and nearer, but everyone acted as if nothing was happening. People just kept staring straight ahead and listening to the speakers. Finally, the noise was right upon us and we saw two burly guys with a woman in between them. She looked like Gravel Gertie with blonde stringy hair hanging all over her face.

"Thaaattt old Bitch!" she kept screaming and by then she was very close to us and we could see that it was Marion Davies, Hearst's actress-mistress, drunk as a lord.

All the while she was screaming at Louella, these two big guys were dragging her along by the arms out of the room. Nobody looked at her the entire time except Larry and me and we were almost hysterical that this could be happening while everyone pretended not to notice.

About two minutes after they had dragged her off, a man sitting at the table next to me toppled off his chair and just lay there in a drunken stupor. By then, Larry and I had the giggles so bad we couldn't stop. We would just start to calm down a little when one of us would start up again.

Luckily, it was time for the entertainment to begin and I was able to stop giggling with Larry because I had to sing a song. But as soon as I got up on the stage, I saw a lot of stone faces down below because they had cut off the drinks during the speeches and the temper of the audience was grim.

Jimmy McHugh had written a song just for the occasion and I had learned it very studiously. It went:

> *Louella, Louella, Louella,*
> *Everyone loves you.*
> *Louella, Louella, Louella,*
> *And your 900 newspapers, too.*

I thought it was very funny and when I came to the nine hundred newspapers, too, I got down on my hands and knees and did a salaam.

The lyrics of the song were printed in a little card on each table and, when I had finished, I said, "Now, will you all join in." I looked out at the audience and there were people like Spencer Tracy sitting there with a card in their hands going, "Louella, Louella, Louella. . . ." I almost started giggling all over again.

I also sang a song called "That's Good Enough for Me"—about being such a simple soul that all it took to make me happy was a diamond necklace or a mink coat.

The next day, I was called in to the publicity department at MGM. My performance had been all right, they said, but it seemed I had not only made fun of Louella Parsons but all of Hollywood, too. I should be ashamed of myself, they said, for being so disrespectful.

I guess I was a little irreverent in those days. I had not been in town long enough to be intimidated by it. And later, when I did start to learn how nervous people were about so many things in Hollywood, I was lucky enough to be able to get away. Almost every time Larry and I went out of town to do a show, one of us would turn to the other after a couple of days and say with relief, "Hollywood is *not* the most important place in the world, is it?"

Everything seemed directed to make you feel that if you were not successful here, you might as well slit your wrists. It was really insidious so it was good to get away and be reminded there was a whole world outside.

I HAVE A PICTURE of myself with John Huston that somebody snapped while we were talking at a cocktail party. It is so typical of John because he was looking at me as if I were the only person in the world for him at that moment and what I was saying was the most fascinating thing imaginable.

That is the way John was, particularly with women. He just devoured you with his eyes and was so interested in everything you were doing. He was a terribly, terribly charming man. Years before, he invited Larry and me to *the* great Hollywood party of our lives.

The party was at John's ranch in Tarzana and it was to celebrate his anniversary—he was married to Evelyn Keyes at the time—as well as the anniversaries of the Lewis Milestones and the Jean Negulescos. It was a formal evening that just about everybody in Hollywood seemed to be going to and I was still new enough in town to be very excited about it.

Bud and Dottie Bridges were invited, too, but Bud was not making much money then and Dottie said, "I don't think I can go. I don't have anything to wear."

"Dottie, you've got to go," I said. "We'll find something for you to wear."

I had been buying a lot of clothes at a dress shop owned by Frances Bergen, Edgar's wife (and Candace's mother), and when I went to get one for the party I saw two I thought would look good on Dottie.

"Can I take these and let her try them on?" I asked Frances.

"Of course."

"Well, if you see her, don't tell her where they came from."

I told Dottie I had raided the MGM wardrobe department and she picked a beautiful white bouffant dress that looked gorgeous on her and I took the other one back to Frances.

If Hirshfeld had been there that night, the cartoon he might have drawn would have captured half of Hollywood. Danny Kaye entertained while Joan Crawford and Cesar Romero sat on the floor. At one point, some young starlet dove off a balcony outside the living room into a swimming pool with all her clothes on. It was the only party we ever went to where we literally danced all night.

Later in the evening, Rex Harrison, who was rather drunk, danced with Carole Landis and was leaning all over her while Lilli Palmer, whom he was married to, stood in the doorway with her coat on, tapping her foot and waiting for him to finish so they could go home. Carole committed suicide some time later and there were rumors that an affair with Rex had something to do with it.

The whole ranch was simply overrun with horses, which unfortunately Evelyn was allergic to. She took us on a tour of the place and we went into the guest bathroom where there was a pet monkey swinging from the shower rod. Evelyn reached up and the monkey grabbed hold of her and promptly shit all over her arm.

That night we met a young boy John had brought up from Mexico to be their adopted son. It had been a surprise to Evelyn.

"John says he's nine years old," Evelyn said, "but that boy is *not* nine. He's into puberty and he's always looking at my boobs." Evelyn's life with John Huston was a most eventful one, but to this day she speaks of him with great respect and affection.

During the entertainment, we all crowded into one room when Larry motioned to me. "Look," he said.

I looked around and standing against one wall was John Huston while across the room against another wall was his father, Walter. They were casing every woman in the place and signaling to each other with their eyes.

"It's the devil and his son," Larry said. It was a perfect description of those two old rascals.

Dottie and Bud and Larry and I drove home in our two cars along Mulholland Drive as the sun was coming up. We all decided to go to our house for breakfast and when we arrived, Dottie took off her dress and hung it on the door.

"I don't want to get it messed up because you have to take it back to Metro," she said.

"Dottie," I told her, "that dress is yours."

Some time later, I borrowed it back from her when I posed for the cover of *Photoplay* magazine and we've both laughed ever since about the magical night when I gave her a ball gown.

WHEN I WAS making *Take Me Out to the Ballgame*, Esther Williams and I became good friends and she and her husband, Ben Gage, used to double date with Larry and me.

Ben, who was a singer and later became something of an entrepreneur, was a real character and since Esther was a little crazy, too, they were a wonderful couple. Larry and Esther were both a little nearsighted and had a habit of getting in close to you when they talked while Ben and I were far-sighted. We used to spend half the time either leaning close to each other or backing off, which must have looked awfully strange to people who did not know what was going on.

Ben had a habit of drinking a lot, especially early in the evening when he would have so many martinis at dinner parties he would pass out during the soup course. He would fall asleep with his nose an inch from the soup and never fall in. Then he would wake up and be back with us as sober as a judge for the rest of the evening. It was a most unusual phenomenon and typical Ben Gage.

One night, Esther threw a birthday party for Ben and she put up a big drawing of him naked, except what Esther called his *schwanz* was missing. So we all took turns being blindfolded and playing pin the *schwanz* on Ben.

After a night of martinis, Esther woke up the next morning with alarm bells going off in her head. A friend of hers had been taking pictures! Something like that would be laughed off now, but in those days it would have been an incredible scandal. Louis B. Mayer would certainly have had a heart attack. But Esther very coolly called her friend and said, "May I please have that roll of film?" And she destroyed it. I have to hand it to Esther. She's a smart cookie.

In 1973, Norman Lear and Bud Yorkin were chosen to receive awards of achievement by the Hollywood Chapter of the National Television Academy of Arts and Sciences. They made a very generous gesture when they insisted that the people who worked on their shows be honored, too.

The actors, writers, and directors were the ones who made *All in the Family*, *Maude*, and *Sanford and Son* great, Norman and Bud said, and they wanted us all there. The academy liked the idea of having everyone included and arranged a dinner in a beautiful ballroom at a hotel in Beverly Hills.

The tables were set with candelabras and elegant silverware and there were bottles of Scotch, gin, vodka, and brandy in the middle of each one, which was something I had never seen before. No standing in line at the bar at this party. Steve Allen was the emcee, Anthony Newley was the entertainer, Jimmy Lunceford's orchestra played. It was all incredibly elegant.

It had been arranged so Norman and Bud were on stage and as they announced the actors, writers, and directors from the various shows, a spotlight would hit that person. You would stand at your seat, an usher would come over and give you your award and you would take a bow and sit down. This was a nice way of doing it because if we had all gone up to the stage to say thank you, the evening would have been endless.

Vince Gardenia was one of the first actors honored and he set the tone for the evening. All year long, Vince had been getting a little itchy from sitting around and not having much to do in *All in the Family*. So on this night when the usher presented him with his award, he stood up a little drunk and shouted, "Norman, I don't know what I'm doing in the show, but I love you!"

And that opened the gates to what happened next. Aaron Ruben, the producer of *Sanford and Son*, was honored and apparently Redd Foxx, the show's star, didn't like him much. So when they announced his name and he stood up to take his bow, Redd got up from his table and very loudly said, "I'm going to the toilet!"

Steve Allen was so incensed he followed Redd into the men's room and they got into a scuffle. Somebody said later that Steve actually hit him, he was so mad. Apparently, Redd was passing a few things around his table more potent than liquor.

But it was Bill Macy, who played Bea Arthur's husband in *Maude*, who really stole the show. When it was time for Bill to receive his award, he ran up, jumped on the stage and embraced Norman. He started to say thank you, but then he grabbed the microphone, turned to the audience, and shouted, "Cocksuckers of the world, unite!"

The look on everyone's face was complete shock and the room grew silent. But once again Larry and I were hysterical. We were giggling and nudging each other and burying our faces in our napkins.

Norman took the microphone away from Bill and very graciously said, "Now, now, Bill, I know you've had too much to drink. Thank you very much for your brilliant statement. Would you please leave the stage."

And Bill, in a very loud voice, said, "Well, they won't let me talk—so I'll demonstrate." And he made an obscene gesture, which made everything worse. I had never seen so many uncomfortable people in one place.

Poor Steve Allen had to come on after that and announce Tony Newley who sang some songs. And the band broke into swing music, which we were supposed to dance to. But everybody just got up and left. The ballroom was cleared by ten o'clock. It might have been the shortest party we ever went to.

Bill's friends and I will never understand what possessed him to behave in such a bizarre manner. Normally, he is an adorable, soft-spoken man. Of course, he'd had too much to drink, but it may be that his long run in *Oh! Calcutta!*, the first Broadway show to feature frontal nudity, made him equate success and admiration with scatological behavior. He obviously thought he'd get a laugh. Today, what he did would get a great giggle, but at the time it could have been devastating to his career.

As we were leaving, I went into a little room off the main dining room and there was Bea Arthur sitting with Bill, who was holding his head in his hands.

"Oh, God, what have I done?" Bill was saying. "I'll never work again."

"It's all right, Bill," Bea said. "It's all right. It'll be OK. It'll be forgotten tomorrow."

I loved Bea for staying there with him because as Bill began to sober up he was mortified about what he had done.

WHEN I WAS YOUNGER, people used to scold me for my bawdiness. They would say, "Betty, you shouldn't say things like that—it's not becoming," referring to my penchant for putting my foot in it. It went all the way back to boarding school when I piped up at the principal's table in the dining room about the thirteen buttons on sailors' flies.

Later, I would tell some of my raciest stories at Hollywood parties where the atmosphere was more relaxed and nobody really minded if some of them were off-color because shocking people has always been a show business tradition. And now, at my age, I have the freedom to be about as bawdy as I want.

And of course, Larry was like a little kid in so many ways, too, especially when it came to bathroom humor. For some reason, farting was always a very funny thing in our family and the only one who objected was Andy, who could be very stuffy sometimes.

"I was not born into this family," he would say. "I'm adopted."

One of my favorite stories—I've told it at parties when Larry was present so I know he doesn't mind—is about the night we went to a benefit at Gene Autry's huge estate in the Valley. It was held out on a big rolling lawn, with tables and a big platform on the tennis courts for the entertainment. Peggy Lee and Sammy Davis Jr. sang and there was a big swing band, a fabulous buffet, and gorgeous table decorations. At least three or four hundred people were there and it was a great occasion.

The only problem was that there was only one bathroom. They would not allow us to go up into the main house, which was quite a way up on a hill. Instead, we had to use the one bathroom in the poolhouse.

After dinner, just about everybody had to go to the john and the line got longer and longer. Larry got up from our table during the show and said, "I'm sorry. I have *got* to go." And he sneaked out.

A few minutes later, he came back and said, "There's a line a block long," and he sat down again. There were no bushes you could run off and hide behind so he sat there and I could tell he was in agony. I don't know when he took care of his problem—everyone's eyes were glued on Peggy Lee singing "Fever"—but all of a sudden, Larry was very quiet. Then he pointed to a glass on the table and said very solemnly and slowly, "Don't. Drink. That!"

A Death in the Family

One of the few times I ever defied Lou Mandel was when Gordon Davidson asked me to audition for a play at the Mark Taper Forum, then in its inaugural season.

"I know you don't read for parts," said Gordon, who has been the driving force in Los Angeles theater for more than three decades now, "but *Who's Happy Now?* is very special and I would love for you to try it."

Whether it was because I liked the idea of working at the Taper or because the play had been written by Oliver Hailey, something just got into me. So without telling Lou, I went down, read for it, and got the part.

The play was about Oliver's father, who was a butcher and had a very short fuse. Oliver swore that his father chased him around the butcher shop with a cleaver once and the violence of the man became part of the play.

Oliver had encouraged his mother to leave his father because he was so violent, but he always felt it had been a big mistake. He used to tell us how he had taken his mother to see his father when he was sick and even though his father's current mistress was in the hospital room, she just faded as the electricity between his father and his mother became so obvious.

They still adored each other and that is really what the play was about—the fact that love can take all kinds of forms and you can't always judge what love is and what it isn't. It made me think about my mother and father.

The moment I read for the play, I was crazy about it. Oliver was so funny and talented and exuberant and *Who's Happy Now?* was one of his best plays. Warren Oates was the father, Peggy Pope was the girlfriend, and I played Mary Hallen, the long-suffering mother.

The premise of the play was that every night Mary Hallen would bring her six-year-old son to the bar where her husband was drinking with his mistress and they would sit at a table in the corner. "A boy ought to spend some time with his father," she would say, and she would knit and buy the boy Cokes and every once in a while talk to her husband. After a time, she even became friendly with the mistress and they all became part of a family. It was a delicious part.

The play was a great success and when we filmed it for public television in 1975 Albert Salmi played the father and Rue McClanahan was the mistress.

There was a scene where everyone talked about a woman who became so crazy she stripped off all her clothes and ran through the town while the men in the village came out of the bars and started chasing her. Oliver decided that in the movie version somebody could actually do this. The somebody he chose was me.

"Do you mind?" Gordon Davidson asked me. "You'll be running down the street so nobody will see too much. We'll get you a body stocking if you want."

"No, it's not modesty. It's vanity."

So the scene was set up where I took off my dress and slip, came running out of the bar in bra and panties and took off down the street. You saw me from behind as I took the bra off and threw it up in the air and then reached down, pulled my pants off, and threw them, too.

We shot this scene in Yermo, a little desert town, and just by chance there was a wild dust storm that night. The dust was whirling down the street outside this dinky little bar as Albert Salmi accused me of not having any feelings.

"You think I don't feel things!" I shouted at him and I ran out of the bar into the dust storm throwing off my clothes.

The company had hired about thirty townspeople as extras—mostly raunchy-looking men—to chase me and as I ran past they really set out after me. I finished the scene by running into another bar where Rue McClanahan was waiting for me with a robe.

Larry was visiting on the set that night and he said, "I never knew you could run that fast."

We finished the shooting at Malibu Canyon and on the final night, Larry came along. But it was so cold he spent most of the time in my dressing room shivering in his overcoat. It had been about a year since the heart attack he had not told me about and although he seemed all right, he was never in that robust good health I had always associated with him. He was only sixty, but the combination of hepatitis, high blood pressure, and his rheumatic heart was beginning to take its toll. So whenever he seemed ill or uncomfortable the way he did that night I became concerned.

All the following week, we were very busy. We went out to an elegant restaurant with some friends one night and to see Joyce Van Patten in a play the next. Oliver and Betsy Hailey were throwing a wrap party for *Who's Happy Now?* at their home and since we had been out the past two nights, we were not sure whether we really wanted to go.

That day, I went over to Theatre West where we were holding some auditions and when I came back Larry was lying on the couch.

"Do you feel up to going out three nights in a row?" I asked him.

"I feel pretty good. I worked out at the gym and I repotted all the hanging baskets. And Oliver lives right near by. Yeah, sure, let's go."

It was a lovely party and Betsy, a fabulous cook, made a wonderful dessert out of whipped cream and dates. When the Haileys' daughter Brooke passed it around, Larry could not resist teasing her.

"You come back here and leave that dessert or you'll draw back a bloody stump," he said in his best monster voice. Brooke giggled and screamed and brought back the dessert plate. Later, he called her over again and he ended up eating three of those delicious rich desserts.

A little while later Larry said, "I don't feel very well." At first, I was not particularly concerned. Larry often told me to go to parties alone if he didn't feel up to them or to stay after him if I was having a good time and ask someone to drive me home. But something made me ask him if he wanted me to go home with him and he said yes. It was my first indication something really was wrong. And when he wanted me to drive, I knew he didn't feel well at all. Larry always drove when we were together.

"Do you want me to call a doctor?" I asked him after we were home and he was in bed.

"No, no, I'll be all right."

"You get well. I'm tired of you being sick."

"I'm tired of being sick, too."

I tucked him in, said "I love you" and left the room. I was in the den watching television when I heard a terrible crash. I ran into the bathroom and found Larry lying in the shower. He had fallen backwards into the stall with such force he had shattered the shower door.

There was blood and broken glass all over and I did the best I could to wrestle him out of the shower and onto the floor, which was not easy because Larry weighed about two hundred pounds then. I did not know any resuscitation methods so I ran to the phone and called 911.

The paramedics came quickly, but I knew before they arrived that he was gone. It was the same way I had felt when my mother died. He just was not there any more.

The paramedics spent a lot of time with Larry in the bathroom and at one point they would not let me come in. I was in such a complete daze that this did not seem strange to me, nor did the fact that I suddenly found myself talking to a policeman.

He was a lovely man, so concerned, and asked if I had anybody to stay with me. Garry, who was living with us then, would be home soon, I told him.

"Well, I don't want to leave you here alone," he said. "Is there anybody else you can call?"

I mentioned my neighbor, Jo Gorman, who is a very calm, level sort of person, and the policeman suggested I call her. Then his questions began to change.

"Where were you when you heard the crash?"

"In the den."

"What is this medicine?"

"For Larry's high blood pressure."

"And this one?"

"For his heart."

"Was there an argument?"

"An argument? What kind of argument? No, I was in another room and I heard a crash and ran in and found him lying there."

I think if I had realized what was happening, I would have freaked out. But I was in such a daze I didn't think to ask what the police were doing there and why they were asking me all these questions.

Later it hit me. They had seen all the blood and broken glass and thought there had been a violent fight. They thought I had killed him!

Fortunately, they had awakened Larry's doctor who told them he was not at all surprised at Larry's death. He had already had one heart attack and he was due for another.

"I begged Larry to go to the hospital for some tests," the doctor told me later. "His arteries were filled with pure fat. It's a wonder he lived as long as he did."

And I guess the police talked to me enough to understand I had not murdered my husband. I am just grateful they decided this before I realized what they suspected.

Andy, who was living in an apartment in Hollywood, and Garry, who had been out with some buddies, arrived soon to stay with me. They tucked me in bed and put Louise, a little dog we had bought to mate with Snoopy, in my arms. We all sat and talked and hugged each other long into the night.

And we've talked about it many times since. I remember saying once, "If only I could have kept him from eating so much."

"Ma," Garry protested, "Pop didn't die of overeating. He died of disappointment. I've never known a man who had more disappointments that were not his fault. Look at the beautiful Garden of Eden he made on our grounds and the bulldozers came in and destroyed it. Look at the career he worked so hard at, and the 'bulldozers' tore it down, too. He was the best father in the world and his son became a heroin addict."

I had to stop him then. I couldn't let Garry take on that guilt. He had, in the end, made his father very proud. But he was right, in a way. Larry's strength had finally just given out.

The days after Larry's death were a blur of tears, a house full of people, and weepy conversations with friends. It all became even worse somehow when Fredric March died the day after Larry did. I had always adored him and we had felt a connection to him. He and his wife, Florence Eldridge, had the kind of life working together that Larry and I always aspired to and he had won the Oscar for *The Best Years of Our Lives* the year Larry was nominated for *The Jolson Story*.

I remember saying when we got the news of March's death, "If another person I love dies, I'm not going to be able to stand it," but then the *next* day Richard Conte, who had been my friend ever since he was Nicky Conte at the Neighborhood Playhouse, died, too. It was all too much.

About a year earlier, our friend Curt Conway had died and there had been a wonderful memorial service for him at the Mark Taper Forum. We all talked about our days with Curt in New York and

Hollywood and there were a lot of tender memories and a lot of laughs, too. Larry and I had always agreed about how much we hated funerals, but as we were driving home that day he said, "I wouldn't mind having that kind of service when I die."

I agreed and we made a pact. Whoever went first would hold that kind of service for the other. So when Gordon Davidson called and asked if I would like to use the Mark Taper Forum for Larry, I accepted.

Organizing that service was probably the best therapy I could have had. I threw myself into it and it was not long before I realized I was arranging it as if I were directing a show.

I had Sam Locke, who had introduced Larry and me so many years ago, speak first because I knew he would be funny, and I put Lou Mandel on next because I knew he would *not* be funny.

"We had good times and bad times and very bad times," Lou said. "He will not be forgotten as long as there are motion pictures and lawbooks and a history of the United States." He was of course referring to *The Jolson Story*, the landmark lawsuit against Columbia Studios, and his appearance before the House Un-American Activities Committee.

One of the guys from the gym where Larry worked out, which was a whole other life he had, spoke, and John Gorman, our friend and neighbor (and Jo's husband), told about Larry's relationship with the neighborhood children.

Beau Bridges remembered a party at our house and sitting outside with Larry next to a fire he had built. "I will always feel the warmth of Larry's fires," Beau said.

Naomi Caryl spoke about watching *The Jolson Story* over and over again when she was fifteen years old on Great Neck, Long Island, and how Larry had swept her off her feet and made her want to sing. "I never dreamed that one day Larry Parks would become my friend," she said.

Then Bud came up and told funny stories of the days when he and Larry were at Columbia playing "terrible bit parts in lousy pictures." Bud told about Dottie trying to find a wife for Larry and how insulted she was when he found one on his own.

He told about the fights he and Larry had over how to build a barbecue and of our nude grunion hunts on the beach.

"We're going to miss Larry the rest of the trip," Bud said, "and he'll always be a part of the Bridges family."

Andy told about the time his father came to watch him run at track meets. "I wouldn't know if he could make it, but then I'd look up and there was that yellow sweater in the stands. Sometimes, he was the only person, but he was always there."

He also told some funny anecdotes, including one about how Larry had once put on his friends when they came over to play poker.

"Listen," Larry told them privately, "Andy cheats. So you just let me know afterwards and I'll make it good."

"Your father is strange," Andy's friends would say before they realized he had been teasing them.

Garry, when it was his turn, said simply, "My father was the greatest man I've ever known," and I'm sure he was thinking about those nights Larry had held him in his arms as together they tried to shake off his drug addiction.

When it was my turn, I said that Nanette Fabray, a dear friend ever since our days together in *Jackpot*, had called to say I must tell people I was going to be a little "leaky" for a while and they must bear with me.

(Nanette also gave me the best advice, which I've passed on to friends when they've lost someone. Her husband had died the year before and she said, "Don't let people tell you you'll 'get over' Larry. That would mean forgetting him and you don't want ever to forget him. No, you won't get over it, but I promise you will find many things in your life that will bring you happiness and joy." I'm so grateful to her for her loving thoughts.)

I told the people at the memorial service that the things Garry and Andy had said were no more than what they had told Larry when he was alive in their words and their tender regard for him. I said how much I loved Larry for the respect he showed me and my work, and I told about the time his mother and I got together and cut up his ratty old pants so he would not walk around the neighborhood with his behind sticking out.

I also mentioned Larry's obituary in the *New York Times*, which despite everything had made me laugh out loud. The article said he had suffered rheumatic fever when he was a little boy, which left him with a rheumatic heart. That was absolutely true, but then it went on to say the disease had made one of his legs shorter than the other and his millions of fans were never aware of it because he wore a special corrective shoe.

I had no idea where this came from and could only assume that Larry had been putting on some interviewer once and had been taken seriously. Larry not only had great legs, I said, but they were both the same length. As for corrective shoes, his favorites were desert boots and he had been known to wear Bass moccasins with a tuxedo.

I ended the service by reading "The Gardener," the poem I had written about Larry. When I got to the last few lines—"He holds me/ With tenderness and respect and pride/And love that I can feel"—I started to cry, but nobody minded.

Then I think I originated something that I have seen done many times since then. "It's customary to have a couple of minutes of silence for someone who's gone," I said. "But Larry, above all, was an actor and the one thing that an actor fears most at the end of a performance is silence. So before you go, could I ask you to give him a big round of applause." The whole audience—three or four hundred people— stood up and applauded for a solid minute. A standing ovation!

A strange thing happened a couple of months afterwards when I was sitting with Gordon Davidson at a restaurant in New York and I thanked him again for letting us use the Taper.

"I'm glad I could help," he said. "I'm just sorry I missed so much of it."

"What do you mean? You were there. You even spoke and welcomed everybody."

"Nobody ever told you?" he said. "I was out in the lobby arguing with this woman the entire time after that. She tried to stop the service."

"She *what?*"

"She was furious that Larry was being honored at the Taper. She said she thought it was a disgrace."

"My God! Who was she?"

"That's just it," Gordon said. "I never knew. I couldn't even tell whether she was some old Red hunter or some old Red."

Perhaps the sweetest tribute to Larry of all came during a little service we held down by our swimming pool. Milt Slade, a neighbor who lived across the street, had two daughters who were a little older than most of the neighborhood children, but they had loved Larry, too, and wanted to mark his passing.

Milt was a landscape designer for the city and he asked if he could plant a tree for Larry in our yard. I said that was a lovely idea and all the neighborhood kids came to watch him plant a liquid ambar. It was one of Larry's favorite trees and one of the few in California that turns colors in the fall.

One of the children, Jeremy Toback, played a recorder—I'll never forget how Snoopy, our dog, came over and lay down on top of the sheet music Jeremy had spread out on the grass—and one of the girls played the guitar and sang. A couple of the children spoke about Larry, about how he had played with them and showed them his garden and taken such an interest in them.

Two months later, Snoopy, who had always been Larry's shadow, died. I remember sitting on the floor with him in my arms, sobbing, "Oh, Snoopy, don't you go and die on me, too!" I think I cried more then than when my mother died, or even Larry. It was like a total release, the final loss, and only then could I really grieve for everything that had been taken away.

Snoopy was an old dog with a lot of problems, but I would swear he died of a broken heart.

Betty Garrett and Other Songs

In the months after Larry died, I did not feel like doing much of anything. Performing was completely out of the question. It just hurt my heart too much to sing. But I have always considered it a blessing that the theater needed me then because I certainly needed it.

Shortly before Larry's death, I had begun directing a play for the first time, a Theatre West production of Arthur Miller's *The Price*, which I had once done in summer stock with Howard Duff and Don Porter. We had worked up the whole first act, Larry had been to see it, and the fact he honestly seemed to think I had done a good job of directing made me very proud.

After the memorial service, the cast started pestering me to come back immediately even though I was still reeling from all that had happened.

"Come on, you've got to help us," said Guy Raymond, who was in the cast along with Harold Gould, John Carter, and Mary Munday. "We've all worked so hard on the first act, we can't drop it now. Don't leave us in the lurch. Just sit there and watch us and tell us what to do."

I could not say no to that, of course, and in the next few weeks I learned a great lesson. Work is the best healer of them all.

I had seen the original production of *The Price* in New York with Pat Hingle, Arthur Kennedy, Kate Reid, and David Burns and though I loved it there was something that bugged me about it then and about the way we did it later in summer stock, too.

"When you read the play," I said to Pat Hingle, "the curtain goes up on this loft where nobody has been for sixteen years and furniture is all piled up everywhere. But in New York, it took place in a very sensible-looking room with the furniture all neatly arranged. Then you walked in, picked up a bucket with a mop in it, and said, 'Well, the maid did a good job cleaning this up.' Did they put that line in afterwards? I'll bet it wasn't in the original play."

That led Pat to tell me the whole early history of the play, which included the original director being fired and Arthur Miller finally directing it himself.

"It's a wonder the show was a success," Pat said, "because it was just a mess in rehearsals. One day, somebody in the cast said, 'How come everything isn't dusty if nobody has been here for sixteen years?' So they stuck that line in."

"I knew it," I said. "There's no reason for the set to be this way. You've got so much dramatic activity that could be taking place if people walked into a room that hasn't been touched for sixteen years and here is all this old furniture with tons of stuff piled on top of it."

The first twenty-five minutes of *The Price* is the dullest part of the play because it is all so expository and that used to drive me crazy when I did it in summer stock. If the characters were in a messy attic, they could be rummaging through bureaus and trunks and discovering things like old ice skates and toys while they were talking to each other.

So when we did the show at Theatre West, Bob Chambers, my producer, and I went out to antique stores and got them to lend us furniture. Then everybody went home and dug all the old stuff they could find out of their closets and attics. We lined up big packing crates along the stage and piled everything so solid it was hard to find a place to walk. Boxes and furniture were everywhere and we placed a couch with its back to the audience so an actor would sit facing the back of the stage and have to lean back over the couch to talk to someone.

We had sheets all over everything, too, and spread talcum powder and fuller's earth around so when they took off the cloths, little clouds of dust puffed up. It really looked like a room that had been stacked full of furniture sixteen years earlier and not touched since.

There was one barrier of packing boxes lined up across the front of the stage and every time John Carter walked across, he had to step over them. This seemed very realistic to me, especially one day when John tripped over one of the boxes and got so mad he kicked it.

"That's perfect," I said. "Do that every time. It's exactly what the character would do. He's been stepping over these damn boxes and finally he kicks one."

What we were doing was treating the furniture like another character in the play, which it really was. So much of the conflict centers around what they are going to sell, what they are going to keep, can they get a good price for this piece, and so on.

We had one tall chest of drawers upstage and when the two brothers in the play had an argument we put one of them on one side and one on the other as if they were fighting over a piece of furniture. We even found an antique Victrola that played a record of Gallagher and Shean at the beginning and the famous old "Laugh Record" that ends the play.

Another problem I had to deal with was the fact that Arthur Miller had underwritten the woman's part. She just sits and listens to two men argue practically through the whole play. I wondered if sticking the woman right in the middle of the arguments instead of sitting off to the side might not solve this.

"I feel so silly," Mary Munday said. "I don't have anything to say."

"Just listen to everything they say and watch them like a tennis match," I said. "Your life depends on the outcome, on who wins. Make it clear to us that your heart is in your throat that whole time."

Mary thanked me afterwards and said it was an exciting acting experience to be so much a part of the plot without saying much.

I don't suppose any other director ever got the kind of cooperation from actors I did during that production. They were all so tender with me that it did not matter what I told them to do. They just did it. This helped me with the healing process and proved once again that the theater was the best therapy I could have had.

The final blessing came when the show opened. The production was a huge success and the reviews were so stunning I had one of them blown up to five times its normal size. I have hundreds of reviews stuck away in scrapbooks, but that one is still hanging in a hallway. For a while, I even considered putting it on the ceiling of my bedroom so it would be the last thing I would see before I went to sleep and the first thing in the morning!

ABOUT THIS TIME, I found another kind of refuge in the theater, too. I went back to school.

Larry had always raved to me about the classes he had taken at the Group Theater in New York and the work he had done at the Actor's Lab in Los Angeles in the 1940s with Bobby Lewis, who was one of the theater's great teachers. In 1977, Bobby moved out to Los Angeles and rented theater space where he held his workshops.

Andy and I both joined, and one day Bobby asked Andy to be his secretary, a job that included scheduling interviews with prospective students.

Andy tells a wonderful story about sitting in the office as Bobby asked a young woman why she wanted to take his class. "I've done all the studying I want," she said, "but I need to get some stuff ready so I can audition for television shows." Bobby just about hit the ceiling and refused to let her in the class.

The next person who came in was Anne Bancroft, a marvelous actress who was already a big star.

"Why do you want to join the class?" Bobby asked.

"Because I don't know what the hell I'm doing," Anne said. "I need to study and learn."

Bobby loved that because it is just the attitude an actor has to have. You don't know what you're doing, but you keep trying to learn.

Bobby's classes were intense. They lasted twelve weeks and they were some of the most helpful acting experiences I have ever had. It was all so practical.

Bobby insisted that we keep a notebook, which proved to be a tremendous help. One of the worst parts about starting to work on a part is just to *start*. You bring your script home, you look at it, you think about it, you procrastinate. You do everything you can to get out of starting to work.

But in Bobby's notebook method, you would paste a page of the script on one side and leave a blank page for your notes on the other. Once you got into this practical activity, you'd find yourself looking at the play and making notes and the next thing you know you're studying!

The other thing I loved about Bobby's way of teaching— particularly after I directed a few plays—was that right from the beginning he insisted on using your full theatrical voice. If you get to the dress rehearsal and the director says, "I can't hear you," then all of a sudden you're going to have to speak louder and it's going to sound phony to you. Whereas, if you have done it in full voice from the beginning, it feels perfectly natural to you. And if you're going to do an accent, start working on it right away.

"We're in a theater," Bobby would say. "We're not in somebody's kitchen talking softly to one another. We have a responsibility to the audience not only to make them hear us but to make them understand what we're doing up here. Don't get the idea that to be real you have to talk in whispers and not use your body."

What he was fighting was the fallout from the Method school of acting, which was completely misunderstood. When Marlon Brando talked like a truck driver in *A Streetcar Named Desire*, everybody thought it was "acting." It was great, of course, but that was not all Marlon could do. He could put on a British accent and be just as good.

I think it was Lee Strasberg who got actors thinking that if you spoke above a speaking tone or became theatrical, you were a phony. But Bobby said, "Theater is *not* real life. You have to find the *theatrical* reality."

I must have taken at least four of Bobby's twelve-week classes and nobody can say I made easy choices. What I really loved was playing parts in which I would never be cast professionally.

The very first role I played, for instance, was Medea, which is the most impossible part in the world. I also did parts from *Lady's Windemere's Fan* and *Long Day's Journey into Night*. Then, with everybody in the class sitting and watching, I played Maria in *Twelfth Night* for the first time since the Annie Wright Seminary.

"I want you to do it again," Bobby said when I had finished. "Only this time lower your voice at least an octave."

The minute I tried it, I said, "Of course!" It made all the difference in the world. Maria was no longer a light flippant girl as I had played her, but a bawdy lady with a wonderful belting kind of voice. That was the kind of thing Bobby was so good at.

I did a scene from *Phaedra* with another actress, Pamela Printy, and Bobby made us go out to the ocean and do our lines over the sound of the surf, which added another dimension. Then I tried the role of the wife in the first act of *The Bald Soprano*, which was my first attempt at the Theater of the Absurd.

"I don't know how to approach this," I said. "It just makes no sense to me at all."

But with the kind of nerve Bobby instills in you, I decided to use the image of a chicken. When I started moving my head and neck around in a jerky chickenlike way, it developed into a kind of tic that helped me portray the neurotic relationship the woman had with her husband.

"Betty didn't *play* a chicken," Bobby told the class when I was through. "She *was* a chicken."

Coming from Bobby, that was one of the nicest reviews I ever got.

One of the last things I did for Bobby was from *Richard III* with my son Andy. We did that great scene where, even though Richard has killed Elizabeth's sons, he convinces her to give him her daughter for his wife.

> *E: Shall I go win my daughter to thy will?*
> *R: And be a happy mother by the deed.*
> *E: I go. Write to me very shortly,*
> *   And you shall understand from me her mind.*
> *R: Bear her my true love's kiss; and so farewell.*
> [Kissing her. Exit the Queen]
> *Relenting fool, and shallow changing woman!*

Andy was a wonderful Richard and I was a proud queen and mother that day.

IN 1983, Gordon Davidson told me about a play he was producing at the Mark Taper Forum called *Quilters*. It had originally been performed in Denver, where the playwright, Barbara Damashek, had been working. Barbara, who had very strong feminist ideas, felt that pioneer women, particularly those who had traveled across the country, were truly strong and incredible women and she felt that making quilts was the way they had expressed themselves. The quilts were more than just useful, warm, decorative items. They were the history and the art of these women, and very meaningful to their lives.

Barbara based *Quilters* on a book that told the story of how those quilts described each woman's personal experiences. Some were funny and sweet, like the one about the woman who met a big, tall Texan who kept walking by as she was making a quilt with the Lone Star on it, and who later became her husband. And some were tragic, harrowing stories about people freezing to death during the cross-country trek or about losing husbands or children. They all had to do with these women's difficult and dangerous lives.

Barbara linked it all together by having the seven women in the cast play the children, grandchildren, cousins, and nieces of one woman matriarch, which was the role I played at the Taper. We made our quilts and told our stories.

As we talked about traveling west, we picked up hoops and marched forward like a big covered wagon coming across the stage. In another scene, we talked about being baptized in the river as we waved big sheets of silk that looked like water. One of the women played a preacher baptizing someone in these rippling waves of silk.

Barbara had collected music from that period and had written some herself. One of the actresses played the dulcimer, another played the violin, and we had a real country band on stage that allowed us to break into a country dance at one point.

The play was built around true individual experiences, and as each actress told her story she came forward with a block from her quilt, held it up, and explained what the pattern symbolized. Mine was a tree of life.

By the play's end, all our blocks were combined in a huge quilt, which was unrolled and pulled up and up until it covered the entire back of the Taper stage from the ceiling to the floor. It was more than two stories high. All the different blocks we had been working on were there, joined together in this big quilt that represented all of our lives.

The effect was stunning. You could hear the intake of breath from the audience as they saw it unfurl. Some people out in the theater began to cry. At the very end of the show, my character dies and leaves the quilt to her children and grandchildren. It was like a religious experience.

Barbara took the feeling of the play even beyond the stage itself. She wanted us to be instilled with a feeling for each other, to get into the mood where we could understand the strength of these pioneer women, and to become bound by more than just the few hours we spent together playing our parts.

So she asked us to meet every night before the play and share something. Someone would bring in a poem or an anecdote or perhaps a picture she had found that gave us all a sense of the women in *Quilters*. After a while, we began to look forward to this time we spent together almost as much as we did to performing the play itself.

Because I played the matriarch, Barbara made me the mother of the group so these meetings took place in my dressing room. That made me feel even closer to the other actresses, as if I were responsible for them somehow. I began to feel we really were a family and was so happy when I realized this feeling would extend beyond the run of the play.

Quilters has been done in many theaters around the country and Barbara has trusted my friend Teri Ralston, who played the woman who found her husband while quilting that Texas star, to direct other companies of the show. I went to see one of her productions at the Las Palmas Theater in Hollywood and the cast made a fuss over the fact that one of the original grandmas was in the audience. They came out afterwards and we all embraced like sorority sisters. Even today, whenever an actress who has been in the show sees another, she says, "I'm a Quilter" and they hug each other.

The one frustration of our production at the Taper was that the critics were kind of picky and I could not understand why. The review that really made us mad said it was a show for women. Every night during the curtain calls, I would look out at the audience and see so many men with tears streaming down their faces that I wondered what that person could have been thinking.

Later, the show went to Broadway and I was disappointed I could not be a part of it. Lenka Peterson, the actress who had originated the part in Denver, was the logical person to do it and she was probably better in the part than I was.

But the show was not a success in New York, either, and again I could not understand it. New Yorkers must be terribly jaded, I thought, if they don't see the beauty of *Quilters*.

But so many other people did, and even today people will tell me they'll never forget *Quilters*.

"Neither will I," I tell them.

ONE OF THE THINGS I said during the memorial service at the Taper was how glad I had been to be able to speak of my love for

Larry, to sing it from a stage in front of God, and Larry, and everybody in my show. And I promised I would do it again.

Betty Garrett and Other Songs had begun a few years earlier at Theatre West where the members often did performance pieces on Monday nights. Anyone could sign up so you might see a scene from *Born Yesterday*, one from Shakespeare, and an original scene written by a member all on the same night.

I had this idea about doing some songs from my childhood like "What'll I Do?" and "Ballin' the Jack" and telling anecdotes connected with them. I didn't have any intention other than simply getting out of my system an idea that was boiling around in my head and I worked up ten or fifteen minutes with Gerry Dolin and everybody was very encouraging.

"It's so entertaining, do more," they said, so I added a few things. But then I realized if it was going to go any farther, I would need some help.

I went to John Carter, who had directed some of our benefits at Theatre West, because I had always been impressed by the fact that he never seemed to have an axe of his own to grind. He always seemed so intent on just making the actors and the show look good. He did everything so tactfully and affectionately that I nicknamed him Mr. TLC.

"Would you help me with this?" I asked him and that was the beginning of a collaboration that has lasted to this day. John had me start with "A Song for You" that began "I've been so many places in my life and time" and follow that with "My childhood was filled with music," a song I had written about growing up in the music store in Seattle. I sang some modern songs I had never sung before but that meant something to me, like "Cycles," and I tried to connect them all with stories.

I tried a rock song—and quickly abandoned it—and added some songs and stories from my career: "I'm in Love with a Soldier Boy," "Ok'l Baby Dok'l," "Baby, It's Cold Outside," "The Humphrey Bogart Rhumba," and more. It was wonderful to be able to range back through my life, to playing the ukelele and tell about Louis B. Mayer stomping on my feet and being on the bill at the Palladium with Vogelbein's Bears. And somehow it all seemed to fit together.

I had fallen in love with Roberta Flack's song "The First Time Ever I Saw Your Face" and had the idea of doing it to Larry's picture projected on one of the stage walls, but John talked me out of it. "It's just not your type of song," he said, which was a kind way of saying my voice was in no way comparable to Roberta Flack's. But we had been talking about songs that had been cut out of the movies I had been in and he started to say something when I cut him off.

"I know exactly what you're going to say," I said, and that is how the idea of singing "My Funny Valentine" to pictures of Larry projected on the walls of the stage began. They would not let me sing it to Mickey Rooney in *Words And Music*, but they could not stop me from singing it to Larry in *Betty Garrett and Other Songs*.

After a while, I had an entire first act and the people at Theatre West were always saying, "You've got to do more" so the show just grew like Topsy. The next thing I knew, I had two hours of material.

Joyce Van Patten gave me some very good criticism along the way—"Don't do songs that don't mean anything to you," she said— and then a wonderfully feisty little member of the company named Eileen Frank said, "We must put this all together for a show" and she became the producer.

The reviewers were so kind when it was first performed at Theatre West, but the reaction that was most important to me was Larry's. My mother had died a year or so earlier and I had conceived of the show as a tribute to her. But then I realized it was really a tribute to both of them, to the two most important people in my life.

Larry came to the show every night and after he died, Jack Kutcher, a member of Theatre West who often worked as our house manager, told me how he loved to stand at the back of the theater and watch Larry watching the show.

It was not only important to Larry, I realized, but to me, too. It was my life's work in a capsule, and because I created it, it is the thing I am most proud of. Every time I do it, it is like a balm because the applause is not just for my show, it's an affirmation of my life.

The show made Larry so happy that after he died I knew it would be the proper way to return to the stage when I was ready. It would take some time, but it was good to know it would be there when I needed it.

When I did it in London a few years ago, John Carter said, "You know, there's something about this show that has more meaning to the audience as you get older." I thought about that and I realized he was right.

"Cycles," for instance, is a song about getting older and now that I *am* older it means twice as much. Jacques Brel's "You're Not Alone" has come to stand not only for Larry but for a lot of other people I want to say those words to as well.

> *No, love, you're not alone.*
> *It's alright if you cry.*

And then there was another song that meant so much to me from the first moment I heard it:

> *I've stuffed the dailies in my shoes,*
> *Strummed ukeleles, sung the blues,*
> *Seen all my dreams disappear,*
> *But I'm here.*

> *I've slept in shanties,*
> *Guest of the W.P.A.,*
> *But I'm here.*
> *Danced in my scanties,*
> *Three bucks a night was the pay,*
> *But I'm here.*

I opened the second act of the show with "I'm Still Here" and one day the telephone rang.

"Miss Garrett," a voice said. "I am calling on behalf of Stephen Sondheim's agent in New York. We have been informed you have rewritten the lyrics to one of Mr. Sondheim's songs for your one-woman show. We must insist that you cease doing this. Mr. Sondheim's songs must be sung exactly as they were written."

"Rewritten his lyrics!" I said. "I would never rewrite Stephen Sondheim's lyrics. I think the man is a genius and I revere his work. Will you tell him that for me? And tell him something else, too. Tell him I think he's been spying on me. I did every single thing in that song except one. I never stood on a breadline."

275

Been called a pinko Commie tool.
Got through it stinko by my pool.

Later, I bumped into Sondheim backstage at a show in New York and I told him about my conversation with his lawyers. "I would never rewrite your lyrics."

Sondheim gave a little laugh. "Oh, I wouldn't have minded." Nice man.

First you're another box office champ,
Then someone's mother,
Then you're camp.
Then you career from career to career.
I'm almost through my memoirs,
But I'm here.

Of course, no show of mine could be complete without a bawdy number and I loved one I had found on an obscure Dory Previn album called "Mary C. Brown and the Hollywood Sign."

Who-oo do you have to fu-uck to get into this pi-icture?
Who-oo do you have to la-ay to make your way?
Hooray for Hollywood!
Wha-at do you have to do to prove your worth?
Who-oo do you have to know to stay on earth?

I always congratulated the audience for figuring out what I was singing right away.

At first, *Betty Garrett and Other Songs* didn't go much beyond playing in colleges and theaters in California, though I would have liked to have gone further with it. Full stage shows with just one person were not very popular in the early 1970s. People thought audiences felt cheated if they did not see a full cast with scenery and costumes, although since then one-person shows have sprung up like wildflowers to the point where actors are winning Tonys for them.

FINALLY, A YEAR after Larry died, it was time to make good on my promise to do the show again. Gerry Dolin and I practiced like

276

athletes going back into training. For weeks, we did all the songs, all the stories, over and over. We had to get used to them again, get used to how they felt now that everything had changed.

My friends at Theatre West helped me so much—especially at that first emotional run-through—and then, there I was, in my dressing room at the Westwood Playhouse. A real audience was waiting, the first one I had performed before in so many months. I had not been away from a stage so long since I was a teenager.

The stage was dark when I stepped out on it. Then Gerry played a note and a spotlight hit my face. I was not ready for what happened next.

The audience was standing, everyone pounding their hands together, calling out. It was not just for me—I knew that. It was for what had happened in the past year, even the past twenty-five years. It was the kind of applause Judy Garland used to get. You can tell when people are thinking, "Let's give her an extra hand for all the trouble she's been through."

I was very touched, of course, but I felt something else, too, and it threw me. Some of the people out there were old friends who had suddenly disappeared when Larry and I were in trouble. Some of them had been at his memorial service and they had hugged me then just as they were applauding me now. I had gone home from the Taper that night and written a poem:

> *When times were bad*
> *And old friends turned away*
> *I used to dream I saw them smiling*
> *Arms held open to embrace us.*
>
> *Now my dreams are realized.*
> *Old friends come with tearful smiles.*
> *Arms held open to embrace me.*
>
> *And I am sad to feel no joy*
> *For he who felt the hurt the most is gone.*

I stood there unable to get my bearings for a moment that seemed like an eternity. A critic for the *Los Angeles Times* who had loved the show

277

a few years earlier wrote that I seemed intimidated by the larger the-ater, but that was not it at all.

It was the simultaneous feeling of joy and regret I felt that stopped me. It was so good to be back on a stage. It was so bad not to have Larry standing at the back of the theater watching. Every night, though, as I sang "My Funny Valentine," there he was up on the wall of the stage and that meant a very great deal to me.

> *Don't change a hair for me.*
> *Not if you care for me.*
> *Stay little valentine—stay.*
> *Each day is Valentine's Day.*

Stage Struck Me

$\mathcal{A}$ few months after Larry died, I was walking down the street when I saw a couple in front of me with their arms around each other. They were talking happily and stopping every once in a while to give each other a little kiss and as I watched them I thought, "Well, that part of my life is over."

What is strange is that I really felt no sense of regret. I didn't seem to miss male companionship because it just did not interest me. I simply could not imagine being attracted to anyone.

And then, about two years later, Mike appeared at my front door. He is a big man, about six-feet-four and very attractive. He had been a member of Theatre West where we had enjoyed working together.

I had not seen Mike in five or six years because he had been in Italy so it was good to be able to catch up. He told me about his divorce and I told him about Larry and I was very touched when he got tears in his eyes. I mentioned that Andy was in a play at the Company Theatre and Mike said, "I'd like to see it."

"OK, I'll get you a ticket. Will you be bringing anyone?"

"Just you," he said, and before I knew it we were going together.

"I didn't know this was going to happen to me again," I remember thinking. It seemed so strange after being married to someone for thirty years to suddenly have a boyfriend, but it was kind of wonderful to have these feelings again and there were times when I felt like a teenager.

Mike and I went together for about three years and then he went to New York to act in a television soap opera. We still got together whenever we could and sometimes it seemed like the first few years of my marriage to Larry. We were three thousand miles apart and most of our relationship took place by mail.

I had been looking forward to visiting him in New York after a performance of *Betty Garrett and Other Songs* at a theater in La Mirada, just south of Los Angeles. I was getting ready to drive down there the day of the show when I stopped at the mailbox in the driveway. A letter from Mike.

"Don't come to New York," he wrote. "I'm coming back there soon and we have to talk."

"Uh oh," I said, and I could feel my heart break a little as I went off to do the show.

I always thought it was very gentlemanly of Mike not just to write a Dear Betty letter, but to take the trouble to come back and tell me in person. What he told me was he had started going with his leading lady on the soap opera and that was why he did not want me to come to New York.

"The timing of your letter sure was deadly," I told Mike as we sat and talked. "I got it just as I was going down to do a performance of my show."

"And I'll bet you never gave a better performance in your life," he said.

I started to get mad, but then I thought about it.

"You know what? You're right," I said, and I had to laugh. We have remained good friends ever since.

Not long afterwards, I was getting ready to do *Betty Garrett And Other Songs* in San Francisco when a big, tall, gangly man with curly salt-and-pepper hair ambled in to rehearsal. His name was John and he was to be my bass player and later an important part of my life. I've always had a weakness for musicians. I think it's their humor that knocks me out.

After Gerry Dolin died, I took the show to London and played in a club with the unlikely name of Pizza on the Park. It was a basement jazz club with a pizza restaurant on the ground floor. I heard from many of the old acts Larry and I had worked with in variety: Ann White, who had lost her Stan and Mrs. Vogelbein. I found myself constantly in nostalgic tears. I had my own groupie entourage, too. Half a dozen members of Theatre West had decided to come along: Naomi Caryl, Connie Sawyer, Margaret Muse, Marc Grady Adams, Seemah Wilder, Charlie Berliner, and my cousin Carol Smith.

John came along to play the bass and took Gerry's part in "Baby,

It's Cold Outside." He turned out to have a low sexy voice and the twinkle in his eye was perfect for the number.

John has a house and grown children in San Francisco and I go up there every month or so or he comes to Los Angeles. Sometimes, we take a cruise or a trip, but most of the time we just hang out and go to the movies. It is such a comfortable situation that I don't think either of us really contemplates getting married. All that matters is that when we are together we have a lot of fun.

Both Mike and John are considerably younger than I am, but they have made me laugh and enjoy myself and have almost made me feel that I am younger than they are.

"Doesn't it bother you that I'm older than you are?" I asked Mike once.

"Are you kidding? I don't like women who are young. In Europe, the older a woman gets, the more attractive she becomes."

I liked that, and I liked John's reaction when we went to the movies one night shortly after I had turned sixty-five.

"You know what?" I said. "You can buy me a senior citizen's ticket."

John's mouth fell open and then he laughed. "Girl, you just bought yourself a box of popcorn!"

Growing older has also made me feel more and more that women need to bond together apart from men just as men have a need, and a right, to be by themselves sometimes, too. I'll disagree strongly with anyone who doesn't treat women with equality, but I also recognize the difference. I used to feel it was no fun "going out" if you didn't go with a man, but now I find that I enjoy my women friends just as much.

I belong to a group of women who have all been in show business for at least fifty years. We call ourselves the Show Buddies (it used to be "Show Biddies," but we decided we are *not* old biddies). We meet once a month in someone's house where we share potluck, talk, and tell stories and jokes. No one is a prude, believe me. We share experiences, sometimes bring tapes of old or recent performances, give each other moral support in times of trouble, and go see each other when one of us is in a show. It's a great bunch of women, some of them famous names in their times.

Edith Fellows, Gisele Mackenzie, Ceil Cabot Ballantine, Ernestine

Mercer, Jane Kean Hecht, Mary Carver, Barbara Perry, Gloria Leroy, Carol Bruce, Connie Sawyer, Shirley Nash, Pat Carroll, Frances Coslow . . . they are all part of my monthly fix of FUN!

In 1989, Mark Levin, an agent and friend who had started getting TV jobs for me—though to this day we have never signed a contract—called me all excited. They were doing a stage version of *Meet Me in St. Louis* on Broadway, and there was the part of an Irish maid that was perfect for me.

"What a dumb idea," I thought. "Why take one of the greatest movie musicals of all time and try to make a play out of it?"

But Mark kept after me. They were keeping the songs from the movie, he said—including "The Trolley Song," "The Boy Next Door," and "Have Yourself a Merry Little Christmas"—and writing about ten new ones as well. It was going to be a very elaborate production and the part really was a good one.

The more I thought about it, the more sense it began to make. *Meet Me in St. Louis* had not really been a musical; it was more like a play with half a dozen songs. So there was plenty of room for new material. I was still skeptical about the part, though.

"Look, Mark," I said, "it's always been my dream to go back to Broadway. But I don't want to pack up and leave home for a year to play a maid. Get me a starring role, then I'll go back."

But he kept calling. George Hearn, Milo O'Shea, and Charlotte Moore had already signed up for parts similar to mine, he said. The lead roles, the boy and the girl, would be played by newcomers while star billing would go to the parents, the grandfather, and the maid.

I kept tossing it around in my mind, Mark kept bugging me, and I think I said no about ten times. Then one day he called and said some people connected with the show were coming to town. "They want to meet you. Would you just go down and sing for them?"

"That's ridiculous," I said. "After all the musical comedies I've been in, I'm supposed to audition? I will not sing for them. I will not read for them. I just don't want it that much."

"Well, just go *see* them," he said.

So I went down to the Debbie Reynolds dance studio near my house and met Louis Burke, the show's director, and his wife, Joan Brickel, who was the choreographer. We talked for some time and they told me the part was the one Marjorie Main had played in the movie. But they were making her younger, very Irish, and she had to be able to sing and dance.

I was happy to impress them with my Irish accent, but when they played the two songs the maid has in the show to sort of ease me into trying to sing them, I wriggled out of it.

I don't know why I was so stubborn. I was seventy years old, it was a strenuous part, and they had a right to be concerned about how well I could sing and dance and hold up night after night. Maybe it was my doubts about the show or the part. At any rate, I was very laid back about the whole thing. Long ago, I learned that that's when you get things—when you don't really care.

Fortunately, somebody was there that day who remembered a performance I had just given at a big benefit for S.T.A.G.E., which raises money for victims of AIDS. The evening was a tribute to Jerry Herman and I did "That's How Young I Feel" from *Mame*. We had turned it into a pretty wild dance with two young guys and when Joan and Louis saw the tape, they must have thought, "There's life in the old girl yet," because they offered me the part.

I still was not sure, though, especially when I asked Lou Mandel about it and he was noncommittal. That was not like Lou. Although he was well into his eighties, he still had strong feelings about everything.

"You must do this" or "You must do that," Lou would say, but this time his only comment was "You must do whatever *you* want to do, dear. You don't have to do it if you don't want to." It was unlike him to be so cool about it and that made me even more confused.

I went off on a trip to Hawaii with a friend and Mark kept calling me and I kept putting him off. Then one day, Lou called. "You know, Mark is still waiting to hear from you. He really has to have a final answer."

What the hell, I thought. "You know, Lou," I said, "I think I'd like to do it." And at that moment, I could hear him lose twenty years over the telephone.

"Oh, Betty, it will be wonderful. I'll come to New York for opening night and it'll be like the old days." He went on and on, so excited, and I realized he had been dying for me to be back on Broadway and

I could see it would make him feel young again. Doing the show was the best present I could have given him.

Lou did come to New York and, by God, he stayed up until three in the morning at the opening night party. He was his old self—as feisty as he could be and having the time of his life.

FOR SHEER EXTRAVAGANCE, I don't think anything topped *Meet Me in St. Louis* until *Sunset Boulevard* came along.

The scenery and the sets were extraordinary. You would see the front of the house where the family lived and then it would all open up to show the interior with a staircase leading up to the second floor. There was a real skating rink they used during a number called "Ice," a streetcar that rolled across the stage during "The Trolley Song," and when it was time for my scenes in the kitchen the whole room slid onto the middle of the stage on tracks.

It cost a fortune to operate all this—I'm sure that was one of the reasons they could not keep the show running longer than they did—and we almost had accidents a couple of times when the turntables did not spin or somebody's long turn-of-the-century skirt got caught in the tracks. It was all very spectacular, but it might have been too heavy, really. Some of the reviewers said the scenery overpowered the story.

The two songs I sang were not really complicated except for the moment when I had to do a precarious Irish jig on a table top. Somehow, I never fell and I remember telling one interviewer I had only gotten the part because there were not that many old ladies who could sing and dance on top of a small kitchen table.

I had a lot of entrances and exits because I was always baking a cake in the kitchen or serving dinner, and I had most of the zingers in the script. Something would be happening in the dining room and I'd come striding in from the kitchen, say something funny, then, pow!, back through the swinging door I'd go. Shades of the "hi-bye girls" from television. I was glad I had taken the part, though, because it was all so much fun.

The young people in the cast were bright and talented, and then there was the "Irish contingent," as we called ourselves: Milo O'Shea, George Hearn, Charlotte Moore, and me. We hung out in a bar on Twenty-third Street near the rehearsal hall where we would all go at lunchtime and drink Rolling Rock beer except for George, who would have Jameson's Irish whiskey or Glenfiddich, I can't remember which. And since Milo is so Irish and I was playing an Irish maid, before long I had an accent thicker than anyone from Ireland. It got so I talked that way full time.

But the real delight of doing the show was being back in New York. I loved everything about it. The city had changed so much, of course, but to me there was something about it that still had the feel of the 1940s.

I would go up to Central Park and ride the merry-go-round or lie down on the grass near some guy plucking a guitar and fall asleep (with my purse under my head!). I don't know whether I would want to live in New York if I were not in a show, but being there had always been a part of the excitement of performing on Broadway and I had never gotten over it. It's still my home town!

I had a wonderful little security apartment with a doorman on the corner of Sixth Avenue and Fifty-seventh Street and the show was at the Gershwin Theater on Fifty-first Street between Seventh and Eighth Avenue, not far from where my mother and I had lived almost fifty years earlier. I walked to the theater every day and back home at night and I was amazed that I could not make the trip without seeing at least two or three people I knew.

I always took the same route coming home from the theater. I walked up Seventh Avenue to Carnegie Hall, then across Fifty-seventh Street to Sixth Avenue. When I told people about this they were horrified, but I never found it dangerous at all. There were always a lot of people on the streets even late at night and, like Broadway, Seventh Avenue was well lit. After a while, it seemed as if I knew every homeless person in every doorway and I kept my pockets full of dollar bills. There were certain people I always gave money to and I think if anybody had attacked me I would have had an army to protect me.

One night, though, I did a very foolish thing. Down below my apartment, there was a bank with an instant teller in a little enclosed cubicle. You could not get in unless you put your card in the lock, but a lot of street people would follow somebody who had opened it up and spend the night inside. I needed some cash the next morning and I debated whether to get up early and fight the crowd or take it out then. "I'm going to do it now," I decided.

There were four big homeless guys lying down in the cubicle and I just stepped over them and took out $200. One of them was sound asleep but the others were awake. I had given money to a couple of them at times on my way home and they knew me by name.

"It's Mother's Day tomorrow," one of them said. "Happy Mother's Day, Betty."

"Oh, thank you," I said. "I'm kind of blue because I'm a mother and my children are on the West Coast."

And all of a sudden, they became a chorus and said, almost together, "Don't worry. *We* is your children."

I almost fell down laughing and gave each of them a couple of dollars. I finally had to stop telling this story, though, because people always said, "Are you *nuts?*" I guess I was, but I never sensed any danger at all.

MEET ME IN ST. LOUIS ran for ten months, which was surprising because the reviews were not good. They were quite mean, in fact, which surprised me because it was a beautiful and sweet family show.

The most important thing about it as far as the review in the *New York Times* was concerned seemed to be that the backers were from South Africa. They were two dapper little bald-headed twin brothers who looked so much alike I thought I was seeing double when they showed up at rehearsal one day. They made products like Epi-smile, a toothpaste that makes your teeth very white, and a hair remover that I have been told is torture to use because it pulls the hair out by the roots.

Louis and Joan Burke are from South Africa, too, and that just made the connection stronger. Apartheid had not been done away with yet and it became almost a political issue. It seemed as though the show was not being judged on its artistic merit, but on the fact that South Africans were thought to be behind it. It was as if they were saying, "How dare they come here with this tainted money and think they could have a hit on Broadway?"

I was pleased that the reviews I got were nice, and tickled when, forty-five years after his first drawing of me, Hirschfeld did another one for the *Times*. I've been asked why I was not nominated for a Tony for best supporting actress.

The rules, if I understood them, are that if you had billing above the title you could not be considered in a supporting role. Billing, of course, has to do with how well known you are and your salary, not how many lines you have or how many songs you sing, and Louis Burke was just furious I had not been nominated. But my friend Billy Matthews, who was on the Tony committee, was mad at Louis.

"How *dare* they put you in a show like this and not give you another number in the second act?" he said. "Then, you would have been up for an award in a starring role."

It's a moot point whether I would have been nominated anyway, but I did think there was something wrong with the rules when your billing becomes a more important factor than your performance.

I did receive something of far greater value from *Meet Me in St. Louis*, though, and it was entirely unexpected. Garry came to New York to see the opening of the show and of course I was delighted to have him around. The time he had spent stage-managing shows for Larry and me on the road made him perfectly comfortable backstage, and with his trim athlete's body and the dark good looks he inherited from Larry he was always popular with the members of the cast.

"The whole cast is in love with your son, you know," my dresser told me. "The girls *and* the boys."

This time, though, it was Garry who was smitten. "Ma, I'm in love," he said after he had seen the show a few times. "Who's that girl who stands stage right?" He'd been sneaking into the wings and sitting on the trolley side of the stage during one of the numbers.

"You mean Karen Culliver?" I said, mentioning one of the girls in the cast who had a small speaking part.

"That voice knocks me out," Gary said, "and she's the most beautiful girl I've ever seen."

That night, as Karen and I sat on the trolley in the wings waiting for the finale, I said, "My son thinks you're the most beautiful woman in the world."

She giggled and said something that made me think she must already have a serious boyfriend.

But Garry persisted and some time later he found out Karen was playing Christine in *Phantom of the Opera* in Chicago. Very conveniently, there was a racquetball tournament there, which he immediately signed up for.

"Do you think it would be all right if I went backstage?" he asked me when he called that night.

"I'm sure she'd be delighted," I said.

And so he did. They went out for coffee and Garry didn't push anything, but he did find an excuse to go back to Chicago soon afterwards.

When Karen took over the role in *Phantom* in New York, Garry's trips from Los Angeles became longer and more frequent and the next thing I knew they were engaged. And in November 1992, Karen took a vacation from the show and she and Garry were married in our backyard with my friend Naomi Caryl, who is a minister in the Universal Life Church, performing the ceremony.

For the first two years of their marriage, Garry lived in Los Angeles while Karen was in New York. They saw each other as often as possible and all I could think was how weird life could be. It was Larry and me all over again.

FOR A LONG TIME, it had been my dream to take *Betty Garrett and Other Songs* to New York. Lou Mandel tried to make arrangements over the years, but they all fell through for one reason or another so I began to think it might never happen. And then, during the run of *Meet Me in St. Louis*, it all came together. The people who ran a little cabaret called the Ballroom wanted the show and that summer, a few weeks after *Meet Me in St. Louis* closed, we took it there for a short engagement.

John went along to play the bass and Gerry Dolin played the piano as he always did. But as we began to rehearse we could tell something was wrong with Gerry.

For more than forty years, he had been one of the most important people in my professional life. We had written songs together, he had done all the arrangements for the shows Larry and I did together in London, and he had helped me so much with *Betty Garrett and Other Songs* that I came to think of it as his show almost as much as mine.

Whenever I wanted to do it, Gerry was there for me and later he joined Theatre West and became one of our most faithful members. If we needed musical direction, someone to play the piano, almost anything really, Gerry was always available to help.

But Gerry had not been in good health for years. He had emphysema—the fact that he wouldn't stop smoking made it worse—and now he seemed tired and distracted all the time. As we rehearsed, he would play strange things on the piano and it really became a problem.

"Gerry, what do you want me to play here?" John would ask him as we heard these awful chords he was playing. "These are your arrangements, but I can't play against what you're playing on the piano. It doesn't fit."

I took Gerry to my doctor, who said, "This man is very sick," but he couldn't prescribe anything to help. Gerry was simply smoking too much and not eating well and was in bad shape. I didn't know what to do, really. Gerry was a critical part of the show, but I couldn't open with someone who was not playing at all well.

Finally, John Carter, who was directing the show, took Gerry aside and said, "You've got to pull yourself together. The music doesn't sound good and Betty really needs you." And just by sheer will, I think, Gerry did pull himself together and played beautifully the three weeks we performed.

After each performance, John, and Gerry would sit at the bar that served tapas (Spanish hors d'oeuvres) and Gerry would hold forth, telling stories about his long career in show business while I was taking my makeup off. The waiters and bartenders adored him and he started eating again. As soon as I realized what was happening, I began to take longer and longer to get dressed and soon Gerry was eating a full meal every night and taking walks around town during the day. Before long, he had gained seven pounds.

He changed completely and I'm sure the excitement of doing the show had a lot to do with it. It just seemed to rejuvenate him. But when we got home he went right back to his old habits, stopped eating and began smoking too much again.

Gerry died not long after that, but I always felt those weeks we played the Ballroom might have been one of the happiest periods in his life. It was one last good time we had together before he was gone and the tape I have of that engagement of *Betty Garrett and Other Songs* is precious to me.

The show was very well received in New York and I was touched by that. The reviews were wonderful, the papers made a big fuss over me, and business was good even though it was August and I had been warned it was not the best time to open. But having just been on

Broadway, I was ripe to do it then. I wanted to do the show in New York while I could—the show that meant more to me than any other—because who could tell when I might have another chance?

Early in 1994, I was getting ready to go on a long cruise with Dale Gonyea, a terrific young comedian and musician with whom I had worked up an energetic show of our original songs that we called *So There*. It had done well at Theatre West and the Pasadena Playhouse and we had been invited to perform on a cruise that would take us to Tahiti, Bora Bora, and other South Pacific islands and then end up in Australia and New Zealand. I was really looking forward to going, but as the time came I was doing too much as usual and running myself ragged.

One night, when I did not feel very well and should have stayed home, I went to a tap-dancing class and some of us went out afterwards to a restaurant. We were eating and talking when I drank some water and a piece of ice went down the wrong way. I started coughing, which brought on an asthma attack. I tried my inhaler, but that didn't help and my friend Connie Sawyer said, "Should I call 911?"

I nodded my head yes because I couldn't talk and that is the last thing I remember. Two days later, I woke up in the hospital with a tube down my throat, IVs in my arm, and wires from a heart monitor all over me.

In the ambulance on the way to the emergency hospital, the paramedics had put a tube down my throat to help me breathe and it had cut into my esophagus. My throat swelled up like a bullfrog's and thank God there was one doctor on duty, Philip Biderman, who realized what the problem was.

"I think there's an abscess in her throat," he said. "If we don't operate, she's going to go."

There were other doctors who said, "No, no, it's just cosmetic. It'll go down." But Dr. Biderman insisted that I was in grave danger and asked Garry and Andy for permission to operate. And sure enough, a big abscess had already developed that would have killed me within twenty-four hours. Thank God for Dr. Biderman!

I was asked later why I didn't sue the paramedics, but I realized they had stuck the tube down my throat because I had stopped breathing and in my unconscious state I had struggled so they had had great difficulty. All the cortisone I had taken over the years to control my arteritis and my asthma had made the tissues very delicate and that might have been the reason my esophagus had torn.

The abscess had formed immediately and they had to leave a little drain coming out of my neck for about a month. It took a bandage eight layers thick to blot the fluid and even then it would wet my whole nightgown. An IV in my arm had to be changed continually because the veins kept wearing out, so they substituted another tube that ran under the skin from my arm all the way up to my neck. Later on, for nourishment, they had to insert two tubes on my left side, one under my rib cage and one near my belly button. The only tubes I kind of liked were the little ones in my nose for oxygen. They made me feel so clearheaded I think I would like to live on oxygen some time!

I also had patches all over my body that monitored my heart, and at one point the doctors took x-rays that showed my lungs had filled up almost completely. They took care of that, too. Don't ask me how! Along with everything else, I wound up with a foot-long scar down my stomach from the stress ulcer operation that was held together while it healed with big metal clamps connected with thread. (With my history of delicate skin tissue, they were afraid the scar might open up.) I had very little pain, but it was all very uncomfortable.

I was in intensive care for two or three weeks and there were times when I thought I was in a nightmare. Not being able to talk made it an even stranger experience. I couldn't watch television, I couldn't read, I couldn't do anything except just lie there. Your brain goes crazy in circumstances like that. This must be what prisoners in solitary confinement feel like, I thought. People can come in and look at you, but you can't say anything to them.

After a while, Garry and Andy brought me a magic slate so I could write a few words and I also began to talk to myself, to try to think of something nice. "Let go, let go," I would say to myself, and I thought of how to make a three-tiered chiffon skirt or how to get an actress performing in *The Dresser*, (the show I had been directing at Theatre West) to lower her voice to make her character stronger.

I started to think of funny things about being in the hospital, promising myself that if I lived through it I would become a stand-up comic.

(I am just now realizing this promise in a small way.) Thoughts like these were constantly going through my head like a montage.

All the time I was in intensive care, my family—Garry, Karen, and Andy—sat out in the waiting room eighteen hours a day waiting for the five minutes every hour that a few of them were allowed to come in and see me. They wore beepers so they could be summoned at any time. My dear friend Naomi Caryl was *always* there, just as she had been for Larry whenever he was sick.

Naomi notified friends all over the country and set up a hotline with a phone number people could call at any hour to find out how I was. She brought it up to date every day, sometimes giving more information than my friends may have wanted. She would tell them how much mucus I had and that I had tubes coming out of every aperture in my body, but I was feeling better!

My cousin Carol Smith traveled down from San Jose and would come in, kneel by my bed, and say prayers until I had to tell her, "Carol, for God's sake, get up! It looks like you're praying to me!"

One night, I was transferred from intensive care to a private room that had two beds. Andy slept in one and all night long, if I coughed or moved a finger, he would jump up, come over, put his hand on my arm and ask, "Mom, are you OK?" I don't think he got any sleep at all that night, but it sure made me feel better.

When I was in the ICU, Garry would come in for his five-minute visit every hour and run his fingers through my hair, massaging my scalp. "Oh, that feels so good!" I said.

"You used to do that for me when I was a little boy," he answered. What dear sons I have!

Throughout my stay in the hospital, Karen kept a complete log of all my medications and symptoms and doctors to the point that one doctor asked her if she was a nurse.

"No," she said. "I'm just a daughter-in-law."

"I wish I didn't have to put you through this," I said to her one day as she was sitting by my bed.

"Don't you know I love doing this for you?" she said.

When she left, I cried a little and prayed, "Thank you for her, God."

One day, after they took the tube out of my throat, they were wheeling me down the hall to the operating room where they were going to put the two holes in my stomach to insert tubes that would take care of the "ingoing" and "outgoing" food. (I still could not eat or drink because of the drain in my neck.) As they rolled my gurney into the elevator, I looked back and everybody was standing there, looking concerned and waving.

"I'm supposed to be in Bora Bora," I croaked out.

Andy, always ready with a funny, made me laugh out loud when he said, "Mom, just tell the doctors to remember one thing. 'Neatness counts.' "

At one point in my stay at the hospital, I had a terrible asthma attack—almost as bad as the one that started this whole chain of events. I couldn't breathe and I was frightened, but Dr. Pelleg, a dark handsome man who had always seemed very reserved, rushed in and leaned over my bed.

"You've got a lot of congestion in your lungs and we're going to get rid of it," he said. "It's a very simple procedure so don't worry. You're going to feel relief immediately."

"You know," I told him later, "you're a very good doctor. You looked me right in the eye and told me what the problem was and how you were going to solve it, and that I would feel better. I just want to thank you for that."

"Well, I try to be a good doctor," he said, and I thought I saw a tear in his eye. "Nobody has ever told this man what a good doctor he is," I thought. A lot of doctors will talk over your head as though you're not there and use medical terms you can't understand, and it can terrify you. Not Dr. Pelleg.

There was also Dr. Francine Hanberg, a great-looking young woman with a lot of pizzazz, who prescribed the right antibiotics that got me well. And Bill, the therapist who pounded my back to stir up all the congestion in my lungs. I realized that despite all that had happened I was pretty damn lucky.

After about a month, I was able to come home. I still was not allowed to have food or even water pass my lips, although I could suck on a small ice cube once an hour and was given some lemon-flavored swabs to use when the inside of my mouth got dry. That got pretty monotonous after a while.

Garry and Karen and Andy learned how to change the IVs and the food tubes, and even though a home-care nurse named Cynthia Rullo came in the morning they still had a lot of work to do. They would take turns waking up in the middle of the night to come in and change the IV.

At the hospital, the therapists had started walking me in the hallways and giving me exercises. "Don't let yourself just lie there," they warned me when I was about to go home. "Get up and walk around as often as you can."

I tried to do that three or four times a day, just walk back and forth down the hall for five minutes. I was so weak that when I got back in bed I was exhausted, but I would knock on wood and say "Thank you, God" for the fact I could get up at all.

My doctor, Robert Meth, once asked me what my religion or philosophy was. I think he was wondering what gets one through the rather catastrophic illnesses I've had. I didn't know how to answer him and thought about it for months afterwards.

I was raised an Episcopalian and remember being quite religious in my early teens. Somewhere along the line practicality won over and I lost that devotion. I would never be so presumptuous as to say there is no God or afterlife. I just don't know. I wish I was as sure as my friend Shirley MacLaine that I've been here before and I will be here again.

The one thing I *am* sure of is, this is my only chance to be here as this person that I am, Betty Garrett Parks, and it behooves me to make the most of it, to do as much good as I can, and as little harm. And above all, to enjoy every moment of it. That's what I'll say if anyone asks me again.

IT WAS MONTHS before I had regained enough strength to be able to return to Theatre West and though I was still a little shaky I was able to direct *The Dresser*. I got my leading actress, Dianne Turley Travis, to lower her voice (she was wonderful in the part) and I could feel myself getting stronger every day.

Not long afterwards at the theater, I was crawling around in a little hole under the spotlight booth where we had stored some seats. I was bent over double and lifting all this heavy stuff out of the way when I thought, "Isn't it wonderful that I'm this limber and strong when just a year ago I could barely walk up and down the hallway? And isn't it wonderful I have the theater to come back to?" Work is a great healer!

The one lasting effect from all the problems started by that ice cube was to my singing voice. I used to be able to hit B-flat and sing falsetto up to soprano ranges, but now I can't get above G any more. This means I have to choose the songs I sing in public very carefully. It also means I don't know if I can ever perform *Betty Garrett and Other Songs* again.

There are other things I can do in my life, though. I still dream of going back to Africa. I've been there twice and as soon as my friend and travel agent, Bobbie Philips, puts together another safari, I'll be there with the elephants and zebras and lions—

And there's always the theater. I can act and I can direct, and recently I resurrected an evening of show business anecdotes and stories from my career that John Carter and I had worked up a few years ago called *No Dogs or Actors Allowed*.

Every year, I perform in a S.T.A.G.E. benefit for AIDS organizations. An amazing genius, David Galligan, puts these shows together honoring great songwriters. A few years ago, I sang the Harold Arlen song, "It's a Woman's Prerogative to Change Her Mind," starting off in a Bo Peep costume and stripping down to a dominatrix outfit: a leather leotard with chains, high boots, and a bullwhip! Yes, the body is still in good shape. It just needs a pressing.

In 1997, we honored Cole Porter and I sang "I'm in Love with a Soldier Boy." Little did Cole Porter dream I'd be singing his hillbilly-boogie-woogie song when I was seventy-seven years old.

I still take tap-dancing lessons every week from Lou Wills, who was an acrobatic teenage tap dancer in *Something For The Boys* and *Laffing Room Only* with me so many years ago. And as I write this, I have just finished acting in a play at Theatre West called *Tom Tom on a Rooftop*, written by another member of the theater, Daniel Keough.

There is still something about walking out on a stage in front of an audience that gives me the biggest thrill. I feel more at home there than anywhere else and I can't imagine there will ever be a day when I won't want to perform.

It reminds me of a song I came across from a show called *The Good Companions* that was all about British variety artists. I had to laugh when I learned it had been written by those two venerable "British" songwriters André Previn and Johnny Mercer!

They did their homework, though, because they really captured the character of all those wonderful performers Larry and I had worked with who had polished their acts until they were like gems. More and more these days, I find myself thinking about that song. This is how it ends:

> *When in heaven I wake up*
> *I bet I wake up in makeup*
> *Emotions high for the scene*
> *Doing my tap routine.*

> *And when the angels play Lohengrin*
> *If it is in my key*
> *Stand aside, though I'm starry-eyed*
> *And petrified as can be.*
> *Hey, St. Peter, it's me!*
> *It's stage . . . struck . . . me.*

Coda

1997

Early in 1996, at the age of seventy-seven, I became a grandmother for the first time. I know Garry and Karen will be the best parents in the world and Andy the best uncle. And I, lying on the floor next to Maddy Claire and looking in her eyes, will try to be the best grandmother. I can't wait to start giving her tap-dancing lessons.

And so it all begins again.

> *Life is like the seasons,*
> *After winter comes the spring*
> *So I think I'll stick around a while*
> *And see what tomorrow brings.*

Index

About the Authors

Betty Garrett made her Broadway debut at the age of 19 in the Orson Welles production of *Danton's Death* ("I was an understudy to an off-stage voice") and went on to win a Donaldson Award, the forerunner of the Tony, in *Call Me Mister*. In Hollywood, she starred in such classic movie musicals as *On the Town*, *Take Me Out to the Ballgame*, *Words and Music*, and *My Sister Eileen*. She had featured television roles as Irene Lorenzo, Archie Bunker's friend and nemesis, on *All in the Family*, and as Edna Babish-De Fazio, the landlady who married Laverne's father, on *Laverne and Shirley*.

Ron Rapoport is a writer, an editor for the Chicago *Sun-Times*, and sports commentator for National Public Radio's "Weekend Edition with Scott Simon."